Molecular Gastronomy

SCIENTIFIC CUISINE DEMYSTIFIED

JOSE SANCHEZ, CEC, CHE

Photography by Koji Hanabuchi

Foreword by Ferran Adrià

WILEY

DEDICATION

To my inspirations,

DAIGO SANCHEZ —my son

MARISOL SANCHEZ —my twin sister

Library of Congress Cataloging-in-Publication Data

Sanchez, Jose (Food scientist)

  Molecular gastronomy : scientific cuisine demystified / Jose Sanchez ; photography by Koji Hanabuchi.

    pages cm

  Includes bibliographical references and index.

  ISBN 978-1-118-07386-5 (hardback : acid-free paper) 1. Molecular gastronomy--Popular works. 2. Food--Experiments--Popular works. I. Title.

  TX652.95.S26 2013

  641.01'3--dc23

                                    2013034131

Printed in the United States of America

SKY10059248_110323

CONTENTS

My first encounter with Jose Sanchez occurred during his tenure as a culinary instructor at The Culinary Institute of America. I can recall our fervent conversations on what was happening in the world of modern cuisine and the evolution of culinary techniques. Of course, this topic is my specialty and I was more than happy to impart my passion with someone who shared this interest.

Jose is able to create a platform for teachers, students, and cooks, ranging from amateur to professionals alike, to use this book as a master reference to manipulate emulsifiers, cutting edge equipment, and progressive techniques in today's kitchens. For culinary researchers such as myself, we strive to discover new approaches and this book is an outlet to share this knowledge to create unique culinary possibilities.

Molecular Gastronomy: Scientific Cuisine Demystified is a beautiful culmination of art, cuisine, and education, where Jose's passion shines page after page. Through the dialog of science and cooking, his approach enlightens the reader with the ingredients and techniques that are often misunderstood, in such an easy-to-follow format.

I invite you, as a curious reader, to experience Jose's journey through deciphering a much debated topic between professional chefs. Regardless of whichever term is used to describe the evolution of cuisine, we are constantly evolving food and how our perception translates into how food can be presented in an unimaginable manner.

All you need to do is to open the book and be inspired!

Ferran Adrià

Molecular Gastronomy: Scientific Cuisine Demystified provides students, instructors, and chefs with an essential handbook on this ever-evolving field of culinary arts. Written by a chef who has spent years cultivating his craft through trials and failures in the kitchen, this is a book from a cook's point of view, presented in a very practical manner. Anyone with interests in modern cooking will benefit from the instructions here.

Maintaining relevance within the culinary community requires continual development and fluency of techniques. To bring out the most delicate flavors or to create phenomenal textures, sometimes only the most modern techniques will do. Here, you will find dedicated chapters on the modern techniques that will help you become familiar with innovative applications to develop a distinctive culinary approach.

MODERNITY IN THE KITCHEN

Molecular Gastronomy: Scientific Cuisine Demystified aims to clarify and explain the fascinating world of molecular gastronomy. It offers the reader crucial knowledge of key ingredients and provides fundamental step-by-step techniques for application. Professionals within the culinary industry cannot ignore the influence that molecular cooking has had on today's kitchens. Applying science to cooking is not a new approach, however. Controlling the reactions of ingredients (such as an acid and an alkali) or the formation of molecules, changing temperatures to manipulate textures, and creating a more complex final product without diminishing nutritional content are simple "scientific" undertakings regularly used in cooking.

Cakes leavened with baking soda, sauces thickened with cornstarch, and breads baked with commercial yeast are all examples of a result being altered through chemical reactions. For this reason, *Molecular Gastronomy: Scientific Cuisine Demystified* explains the basics of this style of cooking by introducing the primary functions of gums, stabilizers, thickeners, and gels—otherwise referred to as "food hydrocolloids." In addition to the basics of food hydrocolloids, this book features recipes utilizing the sous vide method, liquid nitrogen, and other modern techniques used in today's competitive kitchens.

This book has three primary objectives:

1. To create a standard for chefs, students, instructors, and food-curious individuals alike when venturing into the study and application of food hydrocolloids

2. To empower the reader to take the articulated techniques and mold them into something personal and unforgettable

3. To eliminate ignorance surrounding this subject by defining food hydrocolloids and teaching daily culinary applications

Chefs must be aware of the customers' constant search for new experiences and delicious surprises. With the abundance of easily accessible information, an increasing number of progressive customers are becoming familiar with the modern culinary movement of molecular gastronomy. Some chefs may have difficulty keeping up with this information due to lack of time to conduct research, the inability to test recipes, or simply the difficulty of finding adequate and correct information. *Molecular Gastronomy: Scientific Cuisine Demystified* not only helps the reader enrich the understanding of modern cooking ingredients, but it also offers hands-on techniques ready to be used immediately. To maximize efficiency, only the essential and latest information directly related to the current trends in the culinary world have been incorporated. This book is a great resource for current and future chefs to build their foundation of molecular gastronomy while fueling the creation of new creations.

STARTING WITH THE BASICS

No matter how kitchen trends may change, the basics are what create a solid foundation. There are many resources available for modern cooking; however, this all-inclusive book is unique in its approach to breaking down and consolidating the extensive and expanding subject of molecular gastronomy and modern cuisine into an easy and understandable approach. The flood of information currently available can be difficult to fully understand and digest, as it often can be very academic or scientifically advanced for those who are not familiar with this topic. This book focuses on the fundamentals in a simple and refined manner that will help the reader comprehend the essential information needed to apply these new techniques confidently.

CONTENTS AND ORGANIZATION

CHAPTER 1—Modern Cooking Evolution and Its Pioneers and Practitioners. Captures the evolution of molecular gastronomy and profiles famous chefs who have contributed to this movement. A better understanding of the origins of the movement can help broaden one's knowledge and awareness of the subject matter.

CHAPTER 2—Sanitation and Safety. Includes standard sanitation and safety procedures necessary to conduct the recipes in this book. Beyond basic sanitation and safety concerns, specific precautions are necessary when handling certain ingredients or equipment to avoid accidents and potential harm.

CHAPTER 3—Equipment and Tool Identification. Covers representative techniques commonly used in molecular gastronomy and the necessary equipment or tools needed to implement those techniques. Also discussed are precautions that will ensure a safe cooking environment.

CHAPTER 4—Introduction to Hydrocolloids: New Frontier. Introduces an overview of food hydrocolloid functions in nontechnical language to better describe the overall categories and their applications. This chapter also provides useful functionality table of each food hydrocolloid. The table is formatted with the food hydrocolloids contained in one row so each one can be known by its source, function, characteristics, or application. This straightforward reference helps establish the needed ingredients while also comparing one food hydrocolloid to another in a consolidated manner.

CHAPTER 5—Food Hydrocolloids: Thickeners, Gelling Agents, Emulsifiers, and Stabilizers and **CHAPTER 6—Sweeteners, Antioxidants, and Others.** Include detailed descriptions of each food hydrocolloid, sweetener, and other additives often used in molecular gastronomy. Basic information is outlined in an easy-to-follow format:

- **Definition:** explains the basic information about the ingredient or subject, including its properties and basic functions.

- **History:** provides a brief background to educate the reader with regard to origins, extractions, and how a product was discovered/is produced.

- **Culinary Use:** explains how a product is typically used in the kitchen and discusses how the product can be used or incorporated in other applications.

- **Notes:** provides additional information and general tips, as well as advanced applications of molecular gastronomy not typically described. These can be very beneficial for practical uses of food hydrocolloids.

CHAPTER 7—Overview of Techniques. Delivers an overview of common modern cooking techniques and applications. The purpose of each technique is given, as well as tips and alternative approaches. In addition, various tables are included for easy reference and to enhance reader comprehension.

CHAPTER 8—Small Treats, Hot and Cold, CHAPTER 9—Surprises, CHAPTER 10—Composed Dishes, and **CHAPTER 11—Sweets.** Contain recipes that utilize the ingredients and techniques from the preceding chapters. Practical applications, including alternatives for methods or equipment, are listed so that the reader may venture deeper into modern cooking techniques with fewer limitations.

STARTING AT ANY LEVEL

Although all the chapters provide an abundance of information, it is the reader's choice to determine the optimal starting point. *It is highly recommended that you become familiar with all safe handling and sanitation procedures as described in Chapter 2 as a necessary precaution before venturing further with modern cooking applications.* A broad comprehension can be achieved by progressing through all the chapters within the book in their given sequence to build upon the provided information and apply the learned material. Both beginners and professionals will find relevant information that will fit personal needs with ease of applicability.

RECIPES, PHOTOS, AND DEMONSTRATIONS

Molecular Gastronomy: Scientific Cuisine Demystified's recipes are dramatically illustrated and thoroughly explained. The book highlights food hydrocolloids' potential by demonstrating the ability to recognize their basic applications, while also laying the groundwork for infinite other possibilities. The recipes emphasize the function of the food hydrocolloid (whether to thicken, gel, or stabilize), and also demonstrate other inherent features of an extraordinary mix of ingredients.

Each recipe is illustrated with stunning photography to provide an example of how to present the dish as it would be in a sophisticated, restaurant-type atmosphere. The recipes also include numerous practical step-by-step photographs to fully visualize the recipe procedures in an actual kitchen environment. These features distinguish *Molecular Gastronomy: Scientific Cuisine Demystified* from other recipe books because the goal is not simply to re-create signature restaurant dishes. Rather, the main purpose is for the reader to master basic techniques so they can be applied to create new conceptions of culinary creations.

PROVIDING LEARNING TOOLS FOR EACH READER

Students and seasoned professionals can use *Molecular Gastronomy: Scientific Cuisine Demystified* as the basis to understand innovative cooking and food preparation methods. Different and exciting approaches to conventional cooking and eating provide the ability to experiment with various food hydrocolloids.

Instructors will find the theoretical and applicable components of the book to be a great curricula source for lectures on molecular gastronomy and modern cuisine. Each chapter summary allows instructors to build lessons plans around the key topics needed to obtain basic comprehension, which can be easily tested at the end of each chapter. Safety and potential hazard concerns that are ever-present in the kitchen are addressed, in addition to important product information and safe handling guidelines. Each chapter can be taught separately; however, a comprehensive approach is recommended to obtain a well-balanced understanding of the topic.

Current and future chefs will appreciate the simple approach taken to explain a very detailed subject. Multiple styles of learning are taken into consideration, with the inclusion of easy-to-follow recipes, abundant technique photographs and eye-catching food photography, and a nontechnical vocabulary that anyone can easily follow. Beginners to advanced learners have the potential to gain invaluable knowledge from the information in this book. Recipes were developed for real kitchen applications and professional environments. Mastering the skills in this book will deepen one's ability to confidently expand in this competitive field.

Serious home chefs can use this book to eliminate the mysticism and fear of these common food hydrocolloids. Many of the recipes can be performed at home with common kitchen equipment. The techniques can be used to create a surprise at a gathering or simply bring a little excitement to the dinner table. The book is intended to encourage you to try something new by exploring a bit deeper and questioning the infinite possibilities of the kitchen.

SUPPLEMENTAL OFFERINGS

A comprehensive online *Instructor's Manual* with *Test Bank* accompanies this book and is available to instructors to help them effectively manage their time and to enhance student learning opportunities.

The *Test Bank* has been specifically formatted for *Respondus*, an easy-to-use software program for creating and managing exams, which can be printed to paper or published directly to E-Learning Course Managment systems. Instructors who adopt this book can download the *Test Bank* for free.

A password-protected Wiley Instructor Book Companion Web site devoted entirely to this book **(www. wiley.com/college/sanchez)** provides access to the online *Instructor's Manual* and the text-specific resources. The *Respondus Test Bank,* as well as *PowerPoint* lecture slides and an *Image Gallery,* are also available on the Web site for download.

ACKNOWLEDGMENTS

This book would not have been possible without the participation, vast knowledge and continuous devotion from the team of professionals who assisted me during this incredible journey. Their tireless efforts during every stage of the production of this book and the keen insight on logistics, research, product development, proofreading, recipe analysis, and kitchen testing trials was invaluable. Thank you, it was truly a delight to share this experience with all of you (pictured above from left to right, and I am fourth from the left):

Shinichiro Imoto, executive sous chef at Conrad Tokyo Hotel, training in culinary arts at Narashino Cooking School, Japan.

Seungmin Bae, chef at Conrad Tokyo Hotel, training in culinary arts at The Culinary Institute of America, Hyde Park, NY.

Kensuke Yano, chef at Conrad Tokyo Hotel, training in culinary arts and English studies in Toronto, Canada.

Gregory E. Ferris, corporate executive chef at Cezars Kitchen Tokyo, training in culinary arts at Le Cordon Bleu, Austin, Texas.

Megumi Kozuma, guest relations at Conrad Tokyo Hotel, undergraduate from Florida State University and master's degree in intercultural communications from Tokai University in Tokyo, Japan.

Masako Kato, merchandise manager, LVMH Watch & Jewelry Japan, K.K. CHAUMET Tokyo, diploma G.G.,G.J.,A.JP., (GIA) San Diego, CA, bachelor of arts in Spanish language and cultural studies at Tokyo University of Foreign Studies, Japan.

Ryunosuke Nakazono, investment advisor, ProExport Colombia in Tokyo, bachelor of arts, humanities and liberal arts major, School of Letters, Arts and Sciences, Waseda University, Japan

Ai Kawazoe, chef at Conrad Tokyo Hotel, training in culinary arts at Le Cordon Bleu Tokyo, major in English at Tokyo Women's University, Japan.

Sayaka Kodama (not pictured), Spanish – Japanese translator, bachelor of arts in Spanish language and cultural studies at Tokyo University of Foreign Studies, Japan.

Special thanks to the entire executive, management, and culinary departments at Conrad Tokyo Hotel, and to Mori Trust Co., Ltd.

I'm in deep gratitude to all of the companies that supported us during the development of this project, providing chinaware, glassware, equipment, and ingredients for testing recipes. Bernadaud, Glass Studio, Verre-Moriyama Glassware Co., CP Kelco, GPI Inc., Le Santuare, LLC, Ingredion Incorporate, Ajinomoto North America, EYELA (Tokyo Rikakikai), FMI Corporation, Genevac, Guzman Gastronomia-Division Solegraells, Hi-Tec Vacuum, ICC–International Cooking Concepts, Julabo Japan, Fusionchef GmbH&Co., JB Prince, 100%Chef, Kotobuki Sangyo, Kubota Co., NTG (Nippon Tansan Gas Co.,LTD), Pacojet AG, PolyScience, and Vitamix Co.

My deepest appreciation and thanks for the incredible work —"the Magic" to photographer Koji Hanabuchi and to Ema Koeda for introducing me to him.

I would like to say a special thanks to Mary Cassells, senior acquisitions editor, at Wiley. I owe thanks to Wayne Gisslen for introducing me to her and to both of them for believing in me and my project. I would also like to express my gratitude to Julie Kerr, senior developmental editor, for guiding me throughout the process of this book and to editorial assistants Jenni Lee, Helen Seachrist, and Jessica Kinsella, for all of their help and assistance. I am also grateful to Michael Olivo, Production Manager, Anna Melhorn, Production Editor, and Marketing Manager Suzanne Bochet. Finally, I want to express my thanks to the sales groups at Wiley.

In addition, I would like to thank all of the instructors who contributed to the review of this book with their expertise, constructive feedback, and guidance:

James Bodanis
Humber College, Canada

Rudolf Fischbacher
Humber College, Canada

Jill Golden
Orange Coast Community College, California

John Placko
Humber College, Canada

Mario Ramsay
Algonquin College, Canada

Ryan Schroeder
Fox Valley Technical College, Wisconsin

Peter Storm
Niagara College, Canada

Klaus Tenbergen
California State University–Fresno

Grace Yek
University of Cincinnati, Ohio

Finally, I am glad to have the opportunity to thank and acknowledge everyone who helped and inspired me to become a better person and professional throughout the years:

Gregor Andreewitch
Rosendo Chavéz
Stephane Coste
Ron DeSantis
Joel Guillon
George Halpern
Jean Claude Lair
Caroline Larrouilh

Jacques Manuera
Adam Mathis
Kiyomi Mikuni
André Pachon
Arno Schimidt
Antonio Silva
Toyomi Ueda
René Verdon

My students:

Emmanuel Arrambide
Tom Carfrey
Andrew Hermann
James Hughes

Franny Krushinsky
Renee Neco
Joel Stocks
Noriko Yokota

My closest friends:

Yoko Akimoto
Rafael Bautista
Barbara Billac
Marc Bonard
Jeff Bowron
Saeko Ikeda
Isabel Jeanneret
Nathalie Kocherhans
German Maldonado
Vincent Menager
Benedit Meneust
Jorge Najera

Damian Olivares
Keiko Onodera
Oscar Ortega
Leonel Polanco
Agustin Ramirez
Nathalie Robert
Norma Salgado
Elizabeth Spiess
Alexandra Steinkellner
Khaled Tabet
Jorge Tellez
Angel Tienda

My family:

Jose Ramon Aguilar
Arturo Martinez
Jacob Matilla
Javier Matilla
Jorge Matilla
Josefina Matilla

Estela Rodriguez
Juan A. Sanchez
Miriam Sanchez
Pablo Sanchez
Arnulfo Soto

My in-laws:

Takako Okuyama

Tetsuo Okuyama

Thank you to my mom, Lucina Barrios; my father, Jose Sanchez Pino; and last, but not least, my lovely wife, Asako Sanchez, for her great support, understanding, and constant advice.

Modern Cooking Evolution and Its Pioneers and Practitioners

1

After studying this chapter you should be able to:

- Name the key people, events, and dates leading up to the first workshop on molecular gastronomy

- Explain the study of molecular gastronomy as a science

- Identify pioneer chefs and practitioners, and their contributions to modern cooking applications

Molecular gastronomy is defined as the application of science to culinary practice. It includes using new tools, ingredients, and methods, and many consider it a gastronomical phenomenon. This style of cooking is also known as avant-garde cuisine, deconstructed cuisine, experimental cuisine, techno cuisine, modern cuisine, progressive cuisine, and molecular cuisine; however, *molecular gastronomy* is the term most commonly used by chefs and professionals.

MODERN HISTORY OF MOLECULAR GASTRONOMY

The term *molecular gastronomy* originally referred to the scientific investigation of cooking; however, the term was adopted by a number of people who applied it to cooking, and now it describes a particular style of cuisine. In 1969, Nicholas Kurti, a Hungarian-born physicist who presented "The Physicist in the Kitchen" to the Royal Society in Oxford, England, first contributed to the establishment of this field. Subsequently, Hervé This, a French chemist affiliated with the Institute National de la Recherche Agronomique (INRA), joined Kurti's study and named their research "Molecular and Physical Gastronomy," which eventually became known as "Molecular Gastronomy" after Kurti's death in 1998. In the late 1990s and early 2000s, the term "molecular gastronomy" began to be used to describe a new style of cooking.

In 1992, Kurti organized the International Workshop on Molecular and Physical Gastronomy (previously known as Science and Gastronomy) at the Ettore Majorana Foundation and Centre for Scientific Culture in Erice, Italy, and invited chefs and scientists from around the world to participate. Yet, according to science writer Harold McGee's blog "Curious Cook," he states that this workshop has another version of its start and its origin is credited to Elizabeth Cawdry Thomas, who ran a cooking school in Berkeley, California. Thomas and Professor Ugo Valdrè of the University of Bologna agreed that the science of cooking was an unrecognized subject and decided to organize a workshop in the late 1980s. Thomas and Valdrè approached Nicholas Kurti to be the director of the workshop, with Hervé This and Harold McGee as coorganizers. Regardless of who initiated the movement, this workshop was a significant step for molecular gastronomy by opening doors for chefs to become more aware of the science behind cooking.

Hervé This continued the research and began focusing on the culinary transformations and sensory phenomena associations of molecular gastronomy. A select number of chefs began to explore new possibilities in the kitchen by embracing science; research; technological advances in equipment (including the use of sous vide, centrifuge, rotary evaporators, etc.); and various cooking methods to enhance flavor, texture, aroma, and appearance of food.

The success of this molecular gastronomy workshop has continued; between 1992 and 2004 six additional workshops took place. Participants, primarily scientists and renowned chefs, examined the science behind the practices carried out in the kitchen, including discussing the role of emulsions and the effects of cooking methods on food quality and food flavor. Harold McGee, who stepped down after the initial workshop, subsequently became involved again and wrote detailed accounts about the "Erice" workshops and the types of people who attended. According to McGee's records, of the 30 to 40 individuals who participated in each workshop, the majority of them were scientists and only 1 out of 5 were professional cooks.

Defining Molecular Gastronomy

Beyond the act of cooking, the application of scientific knowledge has become identified as molecular gastronomy

But it is also important not to confuse molecular gastronomy with cooking. Although cooking is considered a craft by some, it is the ideas and thoughts that transform and elevate basic cooking or food to an art form.

The culinary arts are defined as the skill of preparing and/or cooking foods. Knowledge of the science behind foods and an understanding of diet and nutrition are also truly beneficial in becoming a successful chef.

Cooking is simply the process of preparing food by applying heat in some instances. This is done using a wide range of tools, methods, and techniques (many of which have been known and used for hundreds of years). Cooking methods include baking, roasting, sautéing, stewing, frying, grilling, barbecuing, smoking, boiling, steaming, braising, and microwaving. During the process of cooking, the flavors, textures, appearances, and chemical properties of the ingredients are greatly altered.

Molecular gastronomy focuses on these physical and chemical changes that occur while cooking (e.g., the effect when creating an emulsion for a mayonnaise or the effects of searing the surface of a steak, thereby causing a Maillard reaction). Furthermore, it incorporates the transformations of food ingredients and the sensory phenomena associated with eating. This includes how new cooking methods may produce improved results in texture and flavor.

Molecular gastronomy is considered a new science and a subdiscipline of the food sciences. The ultimate goal of this study is to combine scientific understandings and knowledge of physical properties in the exploration of cooking. Food science is generally categorized as one of the life sciences; it is the study of all science-related aspects of food (This includes the cooking process and the consumption of the food item. While these two disciplines may overlap somewhat, they are considered to be separate areas of food science.)

One of the important principles of molecular gastronomy is to respect the ingredients and to present the food in its purest form, while finding ample grounds to modify classic recipes and apply different techniques. Among these explorations is the utilization of various gums (food hydrocolloids) to replace fats and oils, resulting in particular textures. One goal is to use various new food hydrocolloids to enhance the product's richness and preserve its nutritional value by exploring the physical and chemical reactions that occur during cooking.

It is often incorrectly believed that the term "gastronomy" refers exclusively to the art of cooking; in actuality it studies the relationship between the senses and the food. In other words, it views and treats enjoyment at the table as a specific form of science. This area of study was further verified as a significant area of science when in 2004, the founders of the Slow Food movement established the University of Gastronomic Sciences in Bra, Italy, devoted to the principles of gastronomy.

The work of the pioneers of this movement has evolved over the last two decades; chefs of the new generation are advancing molecular gastronomy by establishing their own styles while influencing each other. The prominence of molecular gastronomy is increasing; it has established its position in the contemporary culinary world. Yet those in molecular gastronomy aim not to replace the conventional way of cooking but rather to elevate it to a higher level. Molecular gastronomy simply is a progressive and evolutionary journey of cuisine. Like the imagination, its possibilities and potentials are infinite.

PIONEERS AND PRACTITIONERS

1962 to Present: Ferran Adrià

Often called the Salvador Dalí or the Pablo Picasso of cuisine, Ferran Adrià changed the face of gastronomy through innovations such as deconstruction. Adrià is best known for extraordinary techniques such as spherifications, which are flavored liquids captured in small spheres (e.g., melon caviar), and culinary foams, now used by chefs around the world. His restaurant, El Bulli (which closed in July of 2011), was only open for a limited number of months during the year because Adrià and his chefs experimented with foods and techniques for the rest of the year. In 1997, El Bulli received its third Michelin star, and it was named Best Restaurant in the World by *Restaurant Magazine* for a record four consecutive years from 2006 to 2009. Adrià shocked the world of high cuisine by closing El Bulli. He then announced the creation of a research foundation called the elBulli Foundation that will serve for further exploration in food techniques. The foundation is tentatively set to open in 2015 in Roses, Spain.

Ferran Adrià
Courtesy of El Bulli

Adrià had the same humble beginnings as most dedicated chefs. He started his career as a dishwasher in a French restaurant in Castelldefels, Spain, where he picked up classic cooking skills from the head chef. These skills carried him through various jobs in other small restaurants, as well as his service in the military.

Adrià's career was never the same after attending a conference in Nice in 1987 during which Chef Jacques Maximin defined creativity as "not to copy." Those three words ignited his passion for change, and for more than 20 years Adrià has spent countless hours manipulating ingredients and experimenting with new techniques and unconventional cooking styles. His creations are designed to surprise and enchant his guests, but taste is always the ultimate goal. This marked the beginning of a collaboration of chef and scientist; Adrià spends six months of the year with scientists and designers perfecting recipes in his Barcelona workshop El Taller.

Both Adrià and his restaurant are recognized for their research in the realm of molecular gastronomy—a term that Adrià has renounced. He believes there is nothing molecular about his practice and prefers to use the term "techno-emotional" cuisine, which includes his studies on the microproperties of specific foods, spices, and ingredients that have led to the development of unique recipes. Harvard's School of Engineering and Applied Sciences agreed to provide El Bulli with scientific and technical knowledge about the configuration of foods, textures, and structures. Adrià was also the first chef to be invited to participate in the 2008 German contemporary art exhibition *Documenta*, which is comparable to the Olympic games of the art world as only the most talented and world renowned artists can exhibit there.

He has been traveling across the world, and took part in the G9 World Summit of Gastronomy in Tokyo in 2009 and 2012. Adrià remains an inventor of eccentric and description-defying food that has influenced chefs and has changed dining experiences and the way many eat and think about food.

1966 to Present: Heston Marc Blumenthal

Heston Marc Blumenthal
Photo by Alisa Connan

Chef Heston Marc Blumenthal has been described as a culinary practitioner for his innovative style of cooking. Blumenthal's style marries French haute cuisine with experimentations born of boundless curiosity about gastronomic techniques. His combinations are legendary—dishes such as bacon-and-egg ice cream, snail porridge, and triple-cooked chips. His world-renowned, three-Michelin-star restaurant, The Fat Duck, in Berkshire, England, was ranked first in 2005 by *Restaurant Magazine* and ranked second in 2006 through 2009; and in 2007 through 2009 it was named "the best restaurant in the UK." In December 2010, Blumenthal's latest restaurant, Dinner by Heston Blumenthal, opened in the Mandarin Oriental in Hyde Park, London; it earned one Michelin star in 2012 and was named the ninth best restaurant by *Restaurant Magazine*'s World's 50 Best Restaurants in the same year. Blumenthal continues to win accolades and Dinner by Heston Blumenthal was ranked seventh in *Restaurant Magazine's* World's 50 Best Restuarants in 2013, with the Fat Duck ranking number 33.

Blumenthal's beginnings were unconventional. Books such as *On Food and Cooking* (1984) by Harold McGee revolutionized the way he thought about cooking and encouraged him to think about how to apply science in the research of his recipes. This self-taught chef opened his own research and development kitchen in early 2004. His fame is also based upon molecular gastronomy, a term that he (similar to Ferran Adrià) dislikes. Blumenthal is a proponent of low-temperature, ultra-slow cooking (a technique that does not melt fat or release many juices); other signature techniques include the use of a vacuum jar and sous vide–style cooking.

Blumenthal has collaborated with many scientists, such as Peter Barham, author of *The Science of Cooking* (2001); Charles Spence, an experimental psychologist at Oxford; and Tony Blake, vice president of research at Firmenech, among others, to expand upon a complete sensory experience with food. Working with these scientists has resulted in, for example, the concept of using headphones during eating to enhance the interaction of sound and taste—completing the eating experience through all five physical senses by playing sounds of the seaside when serving his signature dish "Sound of the Sea" during a seafood course. Blumenthal has published and collaborated on numerous books, including *Kitchen Chemistry* (2005), which is intended to be an educational tool for students in chemistry.

Blumenthal has become deeply interested in the history of British gastronomy and has begun to incorporate his signature touches, the results of his exploration and reinterpretation of traditional British dishes, at his restaurant The Fat Duck.

1974 to Present: Grant Achatz

Grant Achatz has received worldwide attention for dynamically yet delicately prepared hyper-modern dishes, such as the All-American Peanut Butter and Jelly Sandwich, served with bread wrapped around a grape on a specially made service piece.

Achatz won awards for Rising Star Chef of the Year in 2003 and for Outstanding Chef in 2008, both from the James Beard Foundation, in addition to winning various other awards from major culinary organizations. As a teenager working at his parents' restaurant in Michigan, Achatz acquired basic cooking skills and developed enthusiasm for the culinary world. He decided to pursue his skill further and enroll at the Culinary Institute of America. After graduation, Achatz gained experience at several prestigious restaurants, including Thomas Keller's French Laundry in the Napa Valley. In 2001, Achatz returned to the Midwest and became the executive chef at Trio in Evanston, Illinois, which had a four-star rating from the *Mobile Travel Guide.* Achatz's talent continued to flourish, and with him at the helm, Trio received four stars from the *Chicago Tribune* and *Chicago Magazine* and garnered five stars from *Mobile Travel Guide* in 2004.

In 2005, Achatz opened his own restaurant, Alinea, in Chicago; that has been awarded three Michelin stars since 2010 and is now recognized as the cutting edge of progressive cuisine. By 2009, Alinea was rated one of the top 10 of the 50 best restaurants worldwide by *Restaurant Magazine,* reaching number 6 in 2011, number 7 in 2012, and number 15 in 2013, in addition to being named the Chef's Choice Restaurant in the same year. Achatz opened Next, his second restaurant, in 2011.

Grant Achatz
Courtesy of Grant Achatz

1976 to Present: Homaro Cantu

Among the most eye-popping creations of Chef Homaro Cantu is edible paper—a soybean and potato starch paper printed using a fruit and vegetable ink—which was chosen as one of the best ideas of 2005 by *The New York Times.*

Cantu enjoyed science and experiments as a young boy; he organized his kitchen as his laboratory and generated numerous inventions. After graduating from Le Cordon Bleu in his hometown of Portland, Oregon, he worked on the West Coast for several years and traveled to Chicago to take a position as sous chef at Charlie Trotter's. Cantu opened his own restaurant, Moto, which features postmodern cuisine (i.e., molecular gastronomy), including his polymer box oven (which cooks tableside in front of the guests) and unique aromatic utensil, just a few of his worldwide-recognized creations.

Cantu utilizes everything from liquid nitrogen to helium to ion particle guns in his kitchen to create his edible specialties such as Caramel Apple and Sweet Bacon or CO2 Fruit.

Selections of Cantu's patented inventions are on display at the Smithsonian Cooper-Hewitt, National Design Museum, New York, and at The Museum of Science and Industry, Chicago.

Homaro Cantu
Courtesy of Homaro Cantu

1970 to Present: Wylie Dufresne

Wylie Dufresne
Courtesy of Wylie Dufresne

Wylie Dufresne is chef and owner of wd~50 and Alder restaurants in New York City. He added his own modern flair of molecular cooking to the fundamental culinary techniques that he believes are very significant. He took Ferran Adrià's innovative use of warm gelatin and applied it further with the use of gellan, thus creating the possibility to serve gelatin not only warm but deep-fried. This technique was utilized when a beef tongue sandwich Dufresne once served at Dufresne's restaurant wd~50 was deconstructed and its shape transformed into his famous Pickled Beef Tongue with Fried Mayonnaise.

Born in Providence, Rhode Island, Dufresne completed a bachelor's degree in philosophy at Colby College, Maine, in 1992 and enrolled in the French Culinary Institute in New York City. From 1994 to 1999 he worked for Jean-Georges Vongerichten's restaurants, at JoJo and Jean-Georges in New York, and at Prime in Las Vegas. In 1999, he returned to New York to become the first chef at 71 Clinton Fresh Food on Manhattan's Lower East Side; and in 2003, he opened wd~50 with his business partners, Jean-Georges Vongerichten and Phil Suarez.

Dufresne and wd~50 have garnered countless accolades, including one Michelin star from 2006 to 2013 and Best Chef, New York City, from 2007 to 2010, from the James Beard Foundation. In May of 2007, Wylie received an honorary Doctorate of Culinary Arts from Johnson & Wales University, Rhode Island.

1950 to Present: Pierre Gagnaire

Pierre Gagnaire
Courtesy of Pierre Gagnaire

Pierre Gagnaire is a three-Michelin-star chef, famous for his highly personalized cooking combining exceptional creativity and a mastery of techniques. One of the most contemporary chefs in the last century, he has been dubbed the "maestro of French traditional cooking." He gained interest in the field of molecular gastronomy when working to expose French culinary art from around the world. In 2001, Gagnaire contacted Hervé This and proposed they work as a team developing his menu. Since then, Gagnaire and This have come a long way, composing a 10-course tasting dinner—the Science and Cuisine menu—showcasing their work. Their recent study concerns the use of seaweed products, such as nori and agar-agar, which often appear on Gagnaire's menus. These are prime examples of modern-day molecular gastronomy.

Gagnaire started his career in Lyons, France, when he took apprenticeships to acquire fundamentals of traditional French cooking. In 1974, he moved to Paris and worked at Lucas Carton, where Gagnaire was influenced to begin constructing his own vision of new cuisine as an art form.

He soon returned to his family's restaurant, Le Clos Fleury, near Saint-Étienne; and in 1977, Gagnaire earned his first Michelin star. Since opening his first restaurant in 1981 in Saint-Étienne, Gagnaire has continued to add Michelin stars to his empire; he now has total of seven stars in 10 of his restaurants around the world and has been on *Restaurant Magazine*'s World's 50 Best list for 10 years. His latest addition to his empire is the Michelin-starred restaurant Les Solist at the Waldorf Astoria in Berlin, 2013.

Gagnaire is iconic not only for his highly praised restaurants but also for his contributions to fusion cuisine by introducing new ideas for combining global ingredients to achieve new flavors and textures. In 2000, Gagnaire presented a "science and cooking" menu at the Academy of Sciences Conference during his lecture on molecular gastronomy; the movement quickly spread among scientists and professional chefs. In 2006, he was presented the Chevalier de la Légion d'Honneur.

1969 to Present: José Andrés

Chef Andrés is credited for introducing the United States to innovative avant-garde Spanish cuisine that embraces science and technology, as well as traditional Spanish small- plates dining known as "tapas." Andrés states "the connection of your brain, eyes, taste buds, and palate" are interrelated, and it is his avant-garde approach to cooking that has put him at the top of his field. Some of his signature dishes include Cotton Candy–wrapped Foie Gras, Deconstructed Clam Chowder, a Hot and Cold Cocktail, and Dragon Popcorn.

José Andrés
Photo by Jason Varney

Born in the northern region of Asturias and raised outside of Barcelona, Andrés first learned the art of cooking from his family, and at the age of 16 he enrolled in the prestigious Escola de Restauració i Hostalatge de Barcelona. Soon after, he worked alongside his friend and mentor, world-renowned chef Ferran Adrià, at El Bulli.

In 1990, Andrés made his way to New York City to work for the Barcelona-based restaurant El Dorado Petit. Two years later, he moved to Washington, DC, and became chef of Jaleo. Andrés then went on to transform Café Atlántico into a celebrated restaurant and to open some other celebrated dining concepts in Washington, DC, including minibar by José Andrés; Zaytinya; Oyamel Cocina Mexicana; and, most recently, America Eats Tavern, a collaboration with the National Archives.

Having expanded his reach, Andrés also has dining destinations in Los Angeles and Las Vegas with The Bazaar by José Andrés at the SLS Hotel at Beverly Hills and China Poblano and é by José Andrés at The Cosmopolitan of Las Vegas. He also extended The Bazaar by José Andrés at the SLS Hotel South Beach Miami — and his first concept outside of the United States: Mi Casa at the Ritz Carlton Reserve at Dorado Beach, Puerto Rico.

Often referred to as Spain's unofficial ambassador to the United States, Andrés has played an important role in popularizing Spanish food culture. He is the executive producer and host of the Public Broadcasting Service (PBS) series *Made in Spain,* the first television series to promote Spanish wine and food in the United States. He has published several cookbooks on Spanish cooking, and in 2010, the government of Spain awarded him the prestigious Order of Arts and Letters medallion for his achievements in promoting Spanish culture worldwide. Since arriving in the United States, Andrés has also received the praise of the press, his peers, and the public. In 2011, he received the Outstanding Chef award from the James Beard Foundation. Andrés also teaches science and cooking at Harvard University in Cambridge, Massachusetts.

1964 to Present: Joan Roca

Joan Roca
Courtesy of El Celler
de Can Roca

Chef Joan Roca has become well known for his work with aroma, flavor, and avant-garde experiments to fuse the two. He respects tradition but is not bound to it in his cooking, nor does he hesitate to embrace modern techniques. Roca utilizes sous vide to create some of his dishes, such as Iberian Suckling Pig and a unique twist on surf and turf that involves distilling soil and using it to create a gel that is applied to an oyster dish.

Roca is co-owner and head chef of El Celler de Can Roca, along with his younger brothers Josep, the sommelier, and Jordi, the pâtissier. The restaurant is located in Girona, Catalonia, Spain, and in 2009, was voted fifth best in the world by *Restaurant Magazine,* in addition to being awarded three Michelin stars. In 2010, El Celler was voted fourth best, and in 2011 and 2012, it was voted second best. El Celler de Joan Roca won the top award in *Restaurant Magazine*'s World's 50 Best Restaurants in 2013, retaining its third Michelin star.

Roca's first contact with the profession was at the family restaurant. He began helping out in the kitchen when he was 11 years old and learned traditional Catalan cuisine from his mother and grandmother. He studied at Girona Catering School (*Escola d'Hostaleria de Girona),* along with his two brothers, and eventually became a teacher. In August 1986, the three brothers opened El Celler de Can Roca, where they presented modern cooking style utilizing the most advanced techniques.

In 2003, the brothers opened their second restaurant, Moo, in Hotel Omm, Barcelona, which earned one Michelin star from 2006 to 2013.

Roca has also published several books. *La cocina al vacio* (*Sous Vide Cooking*; 2003) introduces the substantial advantages and the results that the sous vide technique bring forth through recipes from El Celler de Can Roca. In the fall of 2010, Roca gave a lecture on molecular gastronomy at Harvard University and presented amazing dishes, such as cigar smoke ice cream, mushroom ice cream accompanied by a caramel balloon filled with oak smoke, and prawns cooked in sherry wine vapor.

1975 to Present: Dani García

Dani García is best known as one of the pioneers of using liquid nitrogen (LN2) in the kitchen. Some of his creations, such as Frozen Raff Tomato Popcorn with Raw Motril Baby Shrimp and Cold Olive Oil Semolina with Ham and Croutons, are excellent examples of his innovative technique.

Born in 1975, in Marbella, Andalucía, Spain, García studied at La Consula School of Hostelry in Málaga. In 1996, he completed an apprenticeship in the restaurant of Martín Berasategui in Lasarte, País Vasco. At the age of 24, he started working at the famous Tragabuches Restaurant in Ronda, where he became known for his innovative cooking. In 2005, García opened Calima Restaurant, situated in the Grand Hotel Meliá Don Pepe in Marbella, which earned two Michelin stars.

Dani García
Courtesy of Dani Garcia

At Calima, García developed the culinary use of liquid nitrogen in collaboration with Raimundo García del Moral, a professor of pathological anatomy at the University of Granada. As a result of his research, he went on to promote Andalusian cuisine, and he worked alongside the Ministry of Tourism to introduce Spanish cuisine worldwide. He combines traditional Andalusian ingredients with modern techniques of cooking. As one of the most recognized chefs in Spain, García was awarded the Best Chef Award in 2008 by Spain's Royal Academy of Gastronomy, particularly for his contribution to the promotion of Spanish cuisine.

In early 2008, García took charge of the Meliá hotel bars and restaurants, renaming them UNO by Dani García. Later in the same year, Calima was reopened after extensive structural alterations to expand both the kitchen and dining areas. García also announced his personal culinary concept, called *cocina contradición*, which brings together conventional flavors and contemporary preparations. Since July 2008, his cuisine has been available at the Calima Palacio de Isora, within the Hotel Gran Meliá Palacio de Isora on the Canary Island of Tenerife. In 2012, García opened Manzanilla, a 6,600-square-foot Spanish restaurant in New York City.

A new genre of cooking that emphasizes the science behind flavors and textures is developing throughout the culinary world. The chefs listed within this textbook are a fraction of the people who have helped pioneer this new phase and, undoubtedly, more chefs are to come.

Among other chef/practitioners of this movement are:

- Andoni Luis Aduriz: Mugaritz (San Sebastian, Spain)
- Dave Arnold: Museum of Food and Drink (MOFAD) (New York, USA)
- Juan Mari Arzak: Arzak (San Sebastian, Spain)
- Oriol Balager: Oriol Balager (Madrid, Spain)
- Peter Barham: professor at the University of Bristol (UK)
- Martin Berasategui: Martin Berasategui (Lasarte-Oria, Spain)
- Jacob Jan Boerma: De Leest (Vaassen, Netherlands)
- Massimo Bottura: Osteria La Franzescana (Italy)
- Davide Cassi: professor of theoretical physics (University of Parma, Italy)
- André Chiang: André (Singapore)
- Alberto Chicote: NO-DO (Madrid, Spain)
- Jonantan Gómez-Luna Torres: Le Chique (Cancun, Mexico)
- Peter Goossens: Hof Van Cleve (Belgium)
- Mitsuo Hazama: Terakoya (Tokyo, Japan)
- Daniel Humm: Eleven Madison Park (New York, USA)
- Rasmus Kofoed: Geranium (Copenhagen, Denmark)
- Alvin Leung Jr.: Bo Innovation (Hong Kong, China)
- Thierry Marx: Mandarin Oriental (Paris, France)
- Harold McGee: science writer, author of *On Food and Cooking: The Science and Lore of the Kitchen*
- Adam Melonas: Sunbar (Brisbane, Australia)
- Nathan Myhrvold: cofounder of Intellectual Ventures (Washington State, USA)
- Yoshihiro Narizawa: Les Creations de Narizawa (Tokyo, Japan)
- Enrique Olvera: Pujol-Cosme (Mexico, New York, USA)
- Daniel Patterson: Coi (San Francisco, USA)
- René Redzepi: Noma (Copenhagen, Denmark)
- Cristiano Rienzner: Maremoto (Germany)
- Paco Roncero: La Terraza del Casino (Madrid, Spain)
- Jorge Ruiz: associate professor (University of Extremadura, Spain)
- Koji Shimomura: Edition (Tokyo, Japan)
- Yoshiaki Takazawa: Takazawa (Tokyo, Japan)
- Hervé This: INRA (Paris, France)
- Paco Torreblanca: Paco Torreblanca (Alicante, Spain)
- Chikara Yamada: Yamada Chikara (Tokyo, Japan)
- Seiji Yamamoto: Nihonyuri Ryu Gin (Tokyo, Japan)

As the most influential movement in modern cooking, molecular gastronomy is similar to any artistic field; it contains controversies ultimately debated by the leading figures of this movement. How these leaders apply science to modern cuisine, whether to stimulate new exotic flavor combinations or to invoke properties not normally seen in food, remains the creative difference between the two perspectives. As individuals, these chefs have taken it upon themselves to push the limits beyond what is expected or common within the culinary boundaries of the dining experience.

In Chapters 8–11 of this book, techniques used with modern cooking applications are detailed by recipe; through personal experience you can learn which style (e.g., spherification or the use of liquid nitrogen) best enables you to personalize a recipe. Evolving and polishing skill sets to utilize modern techniques will create essential background knowledge, and an awareness of the work of the movement's founders and current trendsetters will enable young chefs to develop new and greater creations. The question is: What will be created tomorrow?

Sanitation and Safety

After studying this chapter you should be able to:

- Identify the three major causes of food hazards

- Describe how to prevent foodborne illness and cross-contamination

- Identify the "danger zone" and explain how to avoid it

- Explain and follow the seven principles of the HACCP (Hazard Analysis Critical Control Point) system

- Take appropriate actions to create and maintain a safe and sanitary working environment

- Understand and discuss safety issues related to modern cooking applications and techniques

This chapter is not meant to be a complete discussion of sanitation in food service; however, it covers the basic guidelines for maintaining a clean and safe workplace, preventing foodborne illnesses and contaminations, and implementing safety measures when using certain ingredients common to modern cooking applications. The approach to using innovative techniques and nonstandard ingredients typical of modern cooking and applying it to conventional cooking should not change the basic rules and procedures of maintaining proper food safety and sanitation in the kitchen.

FOOD HAZARDS

Harmful bacteria can cause diseases or infections within the human body. Anything found in the kitchen, including food, can be contaminated as well as become a cause of contamination and danger if not handled properly.

There are three main hazards that one must consider when cooking:

- **Biological hazards:** These include natural toxins such as poisonous plants, or pathogens such as parasites, fungi, viruses, and bacteria. Taken together these are considered the major cause of most foodborne illness.

- **Chemical hazards:** These include harmful chemical residues such as those in pesticides or cleansers.

- **Physical hazards:** These include fragmented glass, metal, or any other nonedible materials.

How to Prevent Foodborne Illness and Cross-Contamination

There are several key points for preventing illness and cross-contamination when working in the kitchen. All should be fully understood and practiced on a daily basis.

Personal Hygiene

Personal hygiene is one of the most basic and effective precautions in cooking. Person-to-food or person-to-utensil/equipment contact can be one of the major causes of foodborne illnesses if one's hands or used equipment are unsanitary. Keep fingernails short and clean and wash hands regularly after contact with any possible source of contaminant. Wear a clean work uniform at all times, including a hat (if required), and tie back long hair.

Sanitation of Food Contact Surfaces

Any surface or tools that have direct contact with foods must be kept sanitized. Countertops, cutting boards, utensils, pots, pans, and dishes must be properly cleaned and sterile before and after use. Boiling water or hot water (at temperatures of 171°F/77°C or above) or disinfectant solutions can be used to eliminate bacterial substances and minimize the risk of contamination.

Food Storage

Food must be stored carefully to avoid contact with probable causes of contamination. Raw material and cooked material must be stored separately. After receiving food from the suppliers, inspect all the goods to ensure that they are in perfect sanitary condition, and move them into storage at once. Keep food properly sealed and store under the appropriate conditions.

Washing

Dirt, harmful microorganisms, and residual chemical and pesticides on fresh produce such as fruits and vegetables must be removed by washing the produce with cold water. Fresh produce should be washed right before use because the excess moisture can easily spoil it. A hard-bristled brush is useful for removing dirt from root vegetables, while fresh leaf vegetables should be washed under running water.

Pest Control

Kitchens can be a place for pests such as roaches, flies, and rodents to look for food. They may hide in the corners or in equipment to nest and breed. They can be carriers of harmful bacteria from garbage or the outside world. Garbage should be kept in sealed containers and disposed of regularly. Seal any cracks, holes, or gaps around pipes leading into walls.

Temperature Control

Temperature is the most important factor in safety control. Bacteria grows the most in temperatures ranging from 40°F/4°C to 140°F/60°C, called the "danger zone." After the cooking process, food must not be kept in this range of temperature.

Contamination can be avoided by keeping hot food's internal temperature at 140°F/60°C or above and keeping cold food at 40°F/4°C or below. In order to kill any bacteria present, foods must be cooked to a minimum internal temperature and sustained at that temperature for at least 15 seconds.

Refrigerators must be adjusted to a temperature at or below 40°F/4°C to minimize bacterial growth. Frozen foods can be kept safely because bacteria do not grow when the temperature is at or below 0°F/-17.78°C. However, freezer burn can develop if foods are frozen for too long, resulting in deterioration in quality.

Cooling and Reheating

Cooling is important, as it is one of the causes of foodborne illness. After being cooked, foods must be cooled down below 41°F/5°C as quickly as possible if they need to be stored for later use. The cooling must be done below 70°F/21°C within 2 hours, and to below 41°F/5°C within an additional 4 hours. In the same manner, one must reheat the cooked product as quickly as possible to avoid the "danger zone." Any previously cooled and stored foods must be heated to 165°F/74°C or above for at least 15 seconds, and/or kept at 140°F/60°C until it is served.

HACCP System

The HACCP (Hazard Analysis Critical Control Point) System is an effective procedure that is widely adopted in the foodservice industry. It is used to identify elements in the preparation process with potential food safety hazards in order for immediate key steps to be taken to prevent, reduce, or eliminate risks. Although it is not obligatory to establish a HACCP system, food manufacturers, restaurants, and governmental agencies such as the U.S. Food and Drug Administration (FDA) and U.S. Department of Agriculture (USDA) have adopted it as an effective technique to prevent sanitation hazards.

There are seven HACCP principles to control and monitor a safe environment:

Principle 1. Conduct a Hazard Analysis: Identify hazards associated with food products. Any biological, chemical, or physical property that may cause a food to be unsafe for human consumption must be analyzed.

Principle 2. Identify Critical Control Points: Identification of critical control points (CCPs) is the central feature of HACCP analysis. A CCP is a step or procedure in the food chain where control can be applied and a food safety hazard can be prevented, eliminated, or reduced to acceptable levels.

Principle 3. Establish Critical Limits for Each CCP: A critical limit is defined as a criterion that must be met for each preventive measure associated with a CCP. Each CCP will have one or more preventive measures for which critical limits must be established and controlled for prevention, elimination, or reduction of hazards to an acceptable limit.

Principle 4. Establish Procedures to Monitor Each CCP: This is the development of procedures to monitor CCPs and use results to adjust and control processes. Monitoring consists mainly of observations and the measurements taken to determine if a CCP is properly controlled.

Principle 5. Establish Corrective Actions: These are actions to be taken when monitoring indicates a change from an established critical limit. The final rule requires an HACCP plan to identify the corrective actions to be taken if a critical limit is not met. Corrective actions are intended to ensure that no product is injurious to health or otherwise becomes contaminated as a result of the deviation entering a given market.

Principle 6. Establish Recordkeeping Procedures: Effective recordkeeping systems are used to document the HACCP system. The National Advisory Committee on Microbiological Criteria for Food (NACMCF) in accordance with the FDA states that the installment of an HACCP plan and its associated records must be maintained on file at the establishment.

Principle 7. Establish Procedures for Verifying the HACCP System Is Working as Intended: These procedures verify that the HACCP system is in compliance with the predetermined plan and indicate whether the plan needs modification or revalidation.

SAFETY

Allergen Caution

Food allergies are a great concern in the food industry. Some food allergies can result in death. Symptoms of food allergies include breathing difficulties or anaphylactic shock. Proper disclosure of ingredients used in recipes is necessary, especially common allergens such as nuts, dairy, shellfish, etc.

Injury

The kitchen is a dangerous place, filled with sharp metal objects, flames, oils, breakables, and piled-up boxes. It is necessary that workers follow established safety procedures to prevent accidents.

Tools and Appliances

Basic kitchen safety guidelines should always be applied when handling equipment such as electrical appliances, blade-operated mixers, and blenders. Proper caution and awareness are important for avoiding bodily harm and other kitchen accidents. Such safeguards include ensuring that pot and pan handles do not block the aisles and that countertop electrical appliances are not near water.

Avoiding Burns

The use of open flames, hot oils, and boiling liquids creates an environment where a kitchen employee is especially susceptible to burns. To avoid both severe and minor burns, the following preventative measures should be followed:

- Use dry towels to handle hot pots or pans.
- Ask for assistance when lifting hot and/or heavy items.
- Keep liquids away from the frying areas.
- Wear proper protective clothing (i.e., long sleeves, close-toed leather shoes, and gloves) when handling hot foods and liquids.
- Be cautious when opening steam table lids, oven doors, and other cooking units that may emit hot air or steam when opened.
- Assess kitchen ventilation before using gases such as propane, carbon dioxide, or nitrogen.

Fire Prevention and Awareness

Professional kitchens should be outfitted with fire extinguishers and proper guidelines on how to use the four classifications of extinguishers accordingly. Those four classes are as follows:

Class A: For combustibles such as wood, paper, and cloth.

Class B: For flammable liquids such as grease, oil, gasoline, and solvents.

Class C: For mechanical equipment such as motors, appliances, and other devices.

Class K: For cooking appliances using combustible cooking ingredients (i.e., vegetable or animal fat).

Always check fire alarm systems regularly and turn off gas lines and electrical equipment if an alarm does sound.

Proper cleaning regimens should be followed in areas where grease buildup could occur and create a fire hazard.

In case of a fire emergency, proper planning and exit identification are necessary for both customers and employees.

Working Habits

Common-sense work habits should be practiced. These include cleaning up spills, asking for help when it's needed, watching your back, and alerting people when passing behind them—especially when carrying hot or dangerous items.

SAFETY MEASURES FOR MODERN COOKING APPLICATIONS AND TECHNIQUES

Just as in the world of conventional cooking, proper training and precautions are required when handling or applying new ingredients and equipment. Below are basic guidelines that will prepare any chef for working safely and avoiding potential hazards.

Basic Safety with Liquid Nitrogen (LN2)

Acquiring LN2 can be difficult, but it can be purchased from local suppliers at inexpensive prices. Before purchasing LN2, however, a special thermos known as a Dewar flask is needed for storing LN2 in small quantities. The Dewar flask is designed to keep the chemical in stable condition and dispense it safely through a fitted nozzle. These flasks are available in different sizes at laboratory supply stores.

Due to its extremely low temperatures (–321°F/–196°C), careless handling of LN2 could result in very serious injuries such as cold burns or suffocation. Even an experienced person should exercise caution when handling LN2. The following are the essential rules of safety:

1. Use cryogenic gloves and eye protection at all times.

2. Wear long sleeves and protective shoes at all times.

3. Ensure that there is adequate ventilation since LN2 will reduce the oxygen concentration in the air.

4. Use double walled metal containers, or insulated containers such as those made of Styrofoam.

5. Avoid using glass, plastic, or wooden utensils because they will freeze, which can lead to breakage.

6. Small stainless-steel tools with rubber handles are recommended to work with LN2.

7. Do not store LN2 in closed containers that do not have pressure valves or hermetic lids.

8. Do not fill a Dewar flask directly from the storage tank in order to avoid possible accidents. Use a discharge tube or a funnel and slowly pour the LN2 without overfilling the flask.

9. Never drink or consume LN2 directly from the flask or in its liquid state. If dizziness or lightheadedness occurs, move to a well-ventilated area, keep the individual warm or administer oxygen until medical personal arrives. If any direct contact results in tissue damage, warm the area with lukewarm water (107°F/42°C). Do not warm with temperatures over 115°F/45°C or further damage may result.

Keep in mind that LN2 is considered a hazardous material. There are some restrictions for its purchase, sale, transportation, storage, and usage. Please contact the local health department or fire department for more details. In order to handle LN2 properly, first review the Material Safety Data Sheet (MSDS) provided by the supplier.

Basic Safety with Food Hydrocolloids

Using new ingredients can be controversial. Yet the majority of the new ingredients known as "food hydrocolloids" have undergone processing just like traditional ingredients such as flour and granulated sugar, which have been milled or bleached before distribution to consumers. Food hydrocolloids mainly derive from natural origins or have been harvested from good bacteria, as described in the Chapters 4 and 5 (see definitions of food hydrocolloids). Many of the food hydrocolloids introduced in this book are considered to be food additives, but are categorized as Generally Recognized As Safe (GRAS) by the FDA.

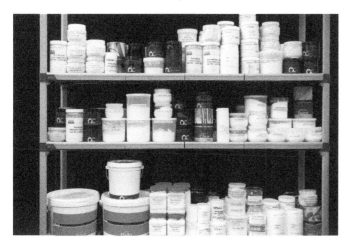

Working with Food Hydrocolloids

Food hydrocolloids are hydroscopic; the cells have a tendency to attract and retain water. When materials containing food hydrocolloids are spilled, they will become gel-like in consistency, which might cause slippage when combined with a liquid. This characteristic of food hydrocolloids could create respiratory difficulties. If inhaled, the nasal airway will become blocked as the ingredients begin to gel. For similar reasons, direct consumption of powdered food hydrocolloids must be avoided. When working with food hydrocolloids, it is recommended that any contact with the eyes, mouth, and nose should be avoided to prevent any irritation. Food hydrocolloids should be stored in a sealed container to keep out humidity and prevent any possible gelling from occurring.

Material Safety Data Sheet (MSDS)

A Material Safety Data Sheet (MSDS) is a widely used list of information on chemicals. MSDS information can include instructions for safe use of potentially hazardous materials associated with a substance or product. It is mainly used to create a safe work environment by providing workers and the person in charge of emergencies with safety procedures for handling or working with the given material(s). The data sheet contains basic information on each substance, such as physical data, storage, disposal, protective equipment, and spill-handling procedures. MSDS formats vary from country to country due to differences in national requirements. They can contain exposure limits or warnings regulated by OSHA (U.S. Occupational Safety and Health Administration), although in many cases a specific limit is forthcoming.

Table 2.1 (pages 34–35) lists a few examples of information one can gather from the data sheet.

Modern Cooking Equipment

For the modern kitchen equipment mentioned in this book, the proper guidelines and manufacturer's instructions are always recommended when using such equipment, in addition to becoming familiar with these tools with the help of an instructor or a trained professional. As one must become accustomed to using a knife or a conventional oven, one must achieve a level of familiarity with modern kitchen equipment. For example, misusing extremely high-powered machines that operate at a high velocity (such as a centrifuge or a rotary distiller) can be fatal or result in severe bodily harm. Regular professional maintenance may be needed to ensure safe operation. For more detailed information on equipment, refer to Chapter 3: Equipment and Tool Identification.

Basic Safety of Sous Vide

Sous vide cooking requires extra attention to temperature control. It can be difficult to determine the temperature based on the appearance of the food cooked in this style. It usually does not have the same appearance as foods cooked with traditional techniques. A thermometer will help control the temperature and maintain proper food safety procedures.

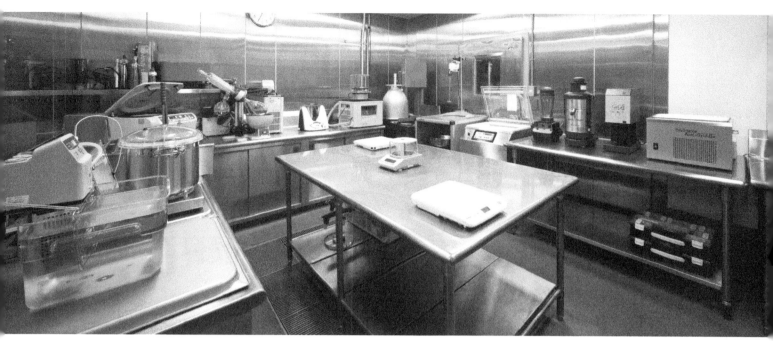

Unfortunately, an oxygen-free environment does not inhibit the growth of some bacteria, such as *Clostridium botulinum*, *botulism*, and *listeria monocytogenes.* If sous vide products are kept in unsafe conditions, these pathogens can grow to dangerous levels without displaying the simultaneous spoilage that would normally signal bacterial presence. This is the reason why it is extremely important to have a well-managed food safety system to minimize the danger of bacteria and pathogens in sous vide cooking. Restaurants that utilize the sous vide method must implement an HACCP plan devised with the department of health to maintain proper sanitation procedures. Consistent and stable cooking temperatures, in addition to precisely controlled cooking times, are necessary to achieve safe sous vide cooking. After cooking, food items must undergo appropriate cooling and reheating measures as mentioned in the discussion under "Temperature Control" on page 27.

Another main concern of sous vide is cooking food in plastic. Many scientists and chefs believe that cooking food in plastic at these low temperatures does not pose any risks, but sous vide is a relatively new technique and it is important to understand that potential health risks or benefits have not yet been identified. Nonetheless, the use of vacuum sealing is widespread and the technique of sous vide can expand one's ability to create specific textures and results. It is relatively a simple and accessible approach to low-temperature cooking.

Name	Usage	Appearance in Color	State	Odor
Agar	Stabilizer, binding agent	White to tan	Powder	None
Arabic gum	Gelling agent, thickener	White to orange-brown	Solid	None
Carrageenan	Stabilizer, binding agent	White to tan	Powder	None
Gelatin	Gelling agent	White to amber	Powder or solid	None
Gellan gum	Stabilizer, gelling agent, binding agent	White to tan	Powder	None
Guar gum	Gelling agent, thickener	Yellowish white	Powder	None
Konjac	Stabilizer	White to tan	Powder	None
Lecithin	Emulsifier	Golden to light tan	Granular solid	None
Locust bean gum	Gelling agent, thickener	Cream to light tan	Powder	None
Methylcellulose	Stabilizer, thickener	White to tan	Powder	None
Pectin	Gelling agent, thickener	Cream to light tan	Powder	None
Sodium alginate	Stabilizer, gelling agent, binding agent	White to tan	Powder	None
Starch	Gelling agent, thickener	White	Powdered solid	Slight
Tara gum	Gelling agent, thickener	Off-white to yellowish	Powder	None
Xanthan gum	Stabilizer, thickener	White to tan	Powder	None

Potential Hazards	OSHA Warning
Slip hazard when spilled material comes in contact with fluid or liquid sources.	Accumulation of settled overhead dust may form explosive concentrations in the air when particles are disturbed and dispersed.
Hydroscopic properties of gum can form a paste or gel in the respiratory airways.	
Direct particle contact with the eyes may cause irritation.	
Slightly hazardous in case of contact with the skin (irritant), when ingested, or inhaled.	Not yet established
Slip hazard when spilled material comes in contact with fluid or liquid sources.	Accumulation of settled overhead dust may form explosive concentrations in the air when particles are disturbed and dispersed.
Hydroscopic properties of gum can form a paste or gel in the respiratory airways.	
Inhalation of dust may cause irritation in the respiratory tracts.	
Direct particle contact with the eyes may cause irritation.	
Slightly hazardous in case of contact with the skin (irritant), when ingested, or inhaled.	Not yet established
Slip hazard when spilled material comes in contact with fluid or liquid sources.	Accumulation of settled overhead dust may form explosive concentrations in the air when particles are disturbed and dispersed.
Hydroscopic properties of gum can form a paste or gel in the respiratory airways.	
Inhalation of dust may cause irritation in the respiratory tracts.	
Slightly hazardous in case of contact with the skin (irritant)	
Direct particle contact with the eyes may cause irritation.	
Repeated inhalation of dust can cause sensitization to susceptible individuals.	Not yet established
May cause allergic skin reactions.	
May cause eye, skin, and respiratory tract irritations.	
The toxicological properties of this material have not yet been fully investigated.	
Slip hazard when spilled material comes in contact with fluid or liquid sources.	Accumulation of settled overhead dust may form explosive concentrations in the air when particles are disturbed and dispersed.
Hydroscopic properties of gum can form a paste or gel in the respiratory airways.	
Direct particle contact with the eyes may cause irritation.	
Slightly hazardous in case of contact with the skin (irritant), when ingested, or inhaled.	Not yet established
Slip hazard when spilled material comes in contact with fluid or liquid sources.	Can be a combustible dust. Avoid ignition sources in dusty environments.
Hydroscopic properties of gum can form a paste or gel in the respiratory airways.	
Direct particle contact with the eyes may cause irritation.	
May form a flammable dust–air mixture	Can be a combustible dust. Avoid ignition sources in dusty environments
Slip hazard when spilled material comes in contact with fluid or liquid sources.	
Prolonged contact with dry powders may cause drying or chapping of the skin.	
Hydroscopic properties of gum can form a paste or gel in the respiratory airways.	
Inhalation of dust may cause a respiratory tract irritation.	
Direct particle contact with the eyes may cause irritation.	
Slip hazard when spilled material comes in contact with fluid or liquid sources.	Not yet established
Hydroscopic properties of gum can form a paste or gel in the respiratory airways.	
Direct particle contact with the eyes may cause irritation.	
Slip hazard when spilled material comes in contact with fluid or liquid sources.	Accumulation of settled overhead dust may form explosive concentrations in the air when particles are disturbed and dispersed.
Hydroscopic properties of gum can form a paste or gel in the respiratory airways.	
Inhalation of dust may cause a respiratory tract irritation.	
Direct particle contact with the eyes may cause irritation.	
Slightly hazardous in case of contact with the skin (irritant), when ingested, or inhaled.	Not yet established
Slip hazard when spilled material comes in contact with fluid or liquid sources.	Not yet established
Hydroscopic properties of gum can form a paste or gel in the respiratory airways.	
Direct particle contact with the eyes may cause irritation.	
Slip hazard when spilled material comes in contact with fluid or liquid sources.	Accumulation of settled overhead dust may form explosive concentrations in the air when particles are disturbed and dispersed.
Ingestion may cause irritation to the mucous membrane.	
Hydroscopic properties of gum can form a paste or gel in the respiratory airways.	
Direct particle contact with the eyes may cause irritation.	
May cause a slight skin irritation on contact.	

Equipment and Tool Identification

After studying this chapter you should be able to:

- Understand the basic safety and sanitation concerns when handling specific equipment

- Identify modern equipment and their alternatives

- Understand basic equipment needed for sous vide cooking

- Differentiate between the various types of available blenders (immersion, bottom-up, ultrasonic, and specialty)

- List tools used for measuring ingredients

- Identify tools needed for handling liquid nitrogen (LN2)

- List tools needed for spherification

- Differentiate between the primary types of siphon systems (cartridge and tank-based) and recognize the different results when using NO2 and CO2 gases

- Have a basic knowledge of available specialty tools and their purposes

A growing number of professional chefs have come to realize that a memorable dish is created with more than the best ingredients available. The equipment used during preparation can also greatly enhance the outcome. Although it may seem odd to modern-day culinarians to think that anything beyond the basic sauté pan, knife, or whisk is necessary, in reality all these tools are evolving products based on trial, error, and preference. A sauté pan exchanged for a wok results in a larger heated surface area, which then marks the ability to cook greater amounts of food quickly. A mandolin slicer instead of a knife will produce more uniform and thinner cuts, while an immersion blender instead of a whisk will not only create smoother consistencies but also will cut down on the time needed to do the same job.

When using modern tools and equipment, the ultimate goal is to produce the best result for a desired effect.

SAFE HANDLING AND SANITATION CONCERNS

Within any kitchen environment, a level of awareness should be maintained to ensure proper and safe handling. For heavy machinery, confirm that the unit is balanced and correctly installed to avoid tipping or undesired movement during operation. The outlet connections should be inspected for voltage usage, proper connectivity, and dangerous situations such as frayed cords or wet conditions. Before using any equipment for the first time, refer to the manufacturer's manual to ensure that all specification requirements have been met.

Proper sanitation regimens should be established for before and after using specific equipment. Avoid incidents such as cross-contamination of raw and cooked products by using thermometers to measure internal temperatures of cooked proteins, and follow the Hazard Analysis Critical Control Point (HAACP) guidelines when heating, cooling, or holding foods for service. Clearly label items with the date the product was made and/or opened and with the intended use of the product. Follow all basic sanitation and safety guidelines described in Chapter 2, and for further safety concerns please consult the local health department.

PRODUCT IDENTIFICATION

Heavy Equipment

Kitchens around the world are being outfitted with equipment that appears to be more like what would be found in a scientific laboratory than a traditional kitchen. While it may be difficult to find an opportunity to experience every advanced apparatus during a developing culinary career, it is important to have awareness of the unique qualities of these machines, and of the variety of possibilities that these machines can contribute to a given recipe.

Centrifuge

Centrifuges, often considered as laboratory equipment, recently appeared in progressive kitchens. Maintenance and proper handling are critically important for these powerful machines.

In the kitchen, a centrifuge is used to separate the sediments from a liquid, clarifying and concentrating the flavors. A centrifuge simply spins canisters or tubes of equal weight around a central axis at high rates of speed called rpm (rotations per minute), causing the heavier elements in the liquid to hit the walls of the tubes and fall down while the lighter (mostly clear) particles remain separated at the top. Establishing a balanced weight/volume distribution of the canisters is vital for a stable rotation; otherwise a potentially dangerous situation could damage the machine and result in possible injury from a large piece of the machine operating in a volatile manner (i.e., machine moving spastically).

Centrifuge
Courtesy of Kubota Corporation

Combination Centrifuge

A combination centrifuge/distiller effectively unites the functions of a centrifuge, dryer, and rotary evaporator in one machine. For the kitchen, these machines eliminate the need for other costly equipment that can occupy a significant amount of counter space. The automated setting is practical for the kitchen environment; and although the machine is designed to handle larger volumes of liquids, it also can quickly concentrate or dry liquids.

Cold Griddles

Using cold griddles allows chefs to create frozen items for immediate service. Currently there are two types of cold griddles available:

**Rocket 4D
(Combination Centrifuge)**
Courtesy of Genevac

- **Refrigerant-Cooled Griddles:** Features a flat griddle that is cooled down to −30°F/−34°C. Note that proper prechilling of the griddles is necessary for desired cooling temperatures to be achieved.

- **Liquid Nitrogen (LN2)–Chilled Griddles:** LN2 is poured inside a polystyrene container, chilling a griddle that is placed on top of the polystyrene. Cold cooking applications can then be applied to the griddle due to LN2's extremely low temperatures of −321°F/−196°C. Also, the LN2-filled polystyrene container can be used to cryo-fry and cryo-blanch items (see the discussion of liquid nitrogen in Chapter 7 for further information).

**Anti-Griddle
(Refrigerant-Cooled Griddle)**
Courtesy of PolyScience

Dryers

Drying food can have several beneficial effects, such as the concentration of flavors, prolonged shelf life, and texture alteration. It also can be used for powdered food production. Variables can be manipulated, which makes this a difficult technique to master. For instance, higher temperatures can cause color change or result in bitter flavors, while the thickness of the item being dried can affect its overall ability to be completely dried.

In progressive kitchens, these advanced and readily available machines take drying to a level of precision that traditional drying methods such as a low-temperature oven and sun-drying cannot achieve.

**Teppan Nitro Salva-G
(LN2-Chilled Griddle)**
Courtesy of 100%Chef

Freeze Dryer
Equipment courtesy of
Eyela; photography by
Koji Hanabuchi

Freeze Dryer

There are three types of freeze-drying machines: rotary, manifold, and sheet (or tray) freeze dryers.

- Rotary types typically handle liquid products.

- Manifold types are geared for large-scale production of sizeable batches and for immediate use after drying. Manifold types will not completely dehydrate the item being freeze-dried in the first stage; a secondary drying method with a higher temperature than the first stage is required to completely dehydrate the product. Therefore, a manifold type will require a two-step dehydration process (refer to Table 7.1: Freezing temperature).

- Sheet or tray freeze-dryers can handle larger-scale production and are typically used in the manufacturing of freeze-dried noodles, fruits, and vegetables. A more complete drying state is achieved and sustained, which allows for an almost indefinite shelf life, independent of refrigeration.

Sheet Dryer
Courtesy of 100%Chef

Sheet Dryer/Dehydrator

Sheet dryers/dehydrators utilize a thermostat and enclosed layered racks. Sheet dryers are conventional for the prolonged drying of anything from beet chips to citrus zest.

Spray Dryer

A spray dryer combines a misting, shower-like device and a warmed or heated tube to disperse vapor-size droplets of a soluble liquid into a chamber tube. The tiny particles trickle down from the head of the drying device, quickly dry, and then are collected in a compartment connected to the main chamber tube.

Spray Dryer
Courtesy of Eyela

Vacuum Dryer

Vacuum dryers work by applying low pressure in a vacuum tube in which the boiling point is reduced, allowing water to vaporize at a lower temperature. It also does not cook or degrade the product being dried, making it ideal for products that would be damaged at higher temperatures.

Circulating Water Bath and Immersion Circulator

Immersion circulators have an electric heating element that circulates water at a desired temperature, either until a food temperature is reached, or for a designated amount of time in order to maintain a food temperature. This method is normally referred to as sous vide cooking, which is discussed in Chapter 7.

Vacuum Dryer
Equipment courtesy of Eyela;
photography by Koji Hanabuchi

Circulating Water Bath

Circulating water baths are stationary heating units with thermostat controls that can vary in size depending on the model. Similar to the jets of a Jacuzzi, the water keeps circulating to maintain an even temperature level. The benefit of a circulating water bath is its fitted lid, which is usually included. This lid reduces the amount of evaporation during the sous vide cooking process and contributes to maintaining a consistent and even temperature.

Immersion Circulator

Portable immersion circulators can be attached to almost any pot for creating a circulating water bath with temperature control.

Other varieties of immersion circulators have compact insulated bath tanks that range in water capacity, allowing for sous vide cooking or for making normal water-bath temperature control more convenient for kitchens with limited counter space.

Immersion circulators can adjust water temperatures accurately (to about +0.01°C, depending on the model). Units are often equipped with internal thermometer probes; others offer amenities that will link your computer and the circulators with a touch panel via USB cable or wireless connection, creating data charts to track results on different trial recipes.

Immersion Circulator
Courtesy of PolyScience

**Diamond XL
Insulated Bath Tank**
Courtesy of fusionchef
by Julabo

Basic Equipment Used for Sous Vide

A wide range of sous vide equipment is available on the market; however, essential equipment includes:

1. Core Temperature Sensor (e.g., cooking thermometer)
2. Adhesive Sealing Tape (e.g., Foam Patch)
3. Separation Grid for Water Bath
4. Vacuum Sous Vide Pouches (Polyethylene bags are deemed safe.)

Core Temperature Sensor
Courtesy of fusionchef by Julabo

**Adhesive
Sealing Tape**
Courtesy of
fusionchef by Julabo

Separation Grid
Courtesy of fusionchef by
Julabo

**Vacuum Sous Vide
Pouches**
Courtesy of 100%Chef

Oil/Water Poaching Hot Plate with a Magnetic Stirrer

Oil/water poaching hot plates include an integrated magnetic stirrer. The dual controls allow separate adjustment of the hot-plate heating surface temperature and the stirring speed.

The hot-plate heating surface temperature is adjustable and can reach its maximum temperature within a few minutes. Depending on the model, the magnetic stirrer is adjustable from 0 to about 1,400 rpm and can withstand various volumes of poaching liquid.

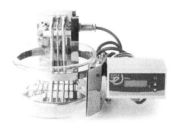

**Oil/Water Poaching
Hot Plate with a
Magnetic Stirrer**
Equipment courtesy of Eyela;
photography by Koji Hanabuchi

Pressure Cooker/Gastrovac

Gastrovac
Courtesy of ICC —International
Cooking Concepts

Pressure cookers and Gastrovacs are dedicated machines that are having a greater influence on food preparation in modern cooking. These two machines utilize the effects of high and low pressures, respectively. Pressure cookers are used to speed up the cooking time of items compared to conventional cooking (i.e., braising or boiling) times. Steam is trapped inside the pot, raising the pressure within, which then allows the boiling point of liquid to be much higher than normal and thus allows higher temperatures to be reached.

The Gastrovac applies pressure by vacuuming out the air and lowering the pressure, which then lowers the boiling point of liquids and the frying temperatures. It enables food to be cooked at very low temperatures. As a result, the color and nutrients in the food are maintained. Additionally, when pressure is restored in the Gastrovac, the items within absorb the surrounding liquid and are infused with flavor.

Rotary Evaporator

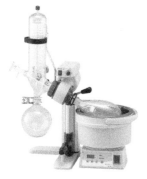

Rotary Evaporator
Courtesy of Eyela

Also known as distillers, rotary evaporators are used in kitchens because of the machine's ability to concentrate flavor and create immaculate clarity. Essentially, one flask is filled with the ingredients to be distilled while another flask is connected on the other side. This second flask is designed to collect the vapors that are emitted from the ingredients that are being carefully pressurized, rotated, and heated simultaneously. The speed of the rotating flask is controlled by a motor that increases the surface area of the liquid being distilled by moving the liquid within the flask as it increases in speed. A separate gauge is used to control heat and pressure in order for the vaporized liquid contents to be more readily dried. This process can be indefinitely fine-tuned to accommodate desired effects. For example, the machine can be adjusted to a very low heat and high pressure or to a high heat and no pressure. These settings create very different flavor profiles and require trial tests to understand the desired results.

Vacuum Sealer

A vacuum sealer is a machine that removes the air from a specialized bag (referred to as a vacuum bag or pouch) and seals the food item under pressure. Removing the oxygen extends the shelf life of the food item and reduces the growth of fungal matter. In this sealed state, the food item can then be cooked in a controlled-temperature water bath known as the sous vide method. Vacuum sealing also marinates, brines, infuses, and cures food items more efficiently than other methods. Vacuum sealers have been optimized for large factory output or small personal kitchen use in the past, but due to a growing market demand restaurant kitchens are now equipped with vacuum sealers, which are continuingly rising in popularity.

Chamber Sealer (Vacuum Sealer)

Chamber Sealer
Courtesy of Hi-Tech
Vacuum Inc.

Available in an array of setups, chamber sealers enclose and vacuum air out of vacuum-pack pouches placed within an almost atmosphere-free environment. Most chamber sealers have optional settings and allow adjustments to the amount of pressure to which a given

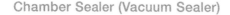

item will be exposed during the sealing process. Unless mounted on a movable island or equipped with wheels at the base, chamber sealers typically are heavy, stationary pieces of equipment.

Depending on the model, chamber sealers have either one or two sealing strips on either end of the chamber interior. A vacuum bag is placed inside, with the open end placed neatly on top of the sealing strip. The vacuuming process begins when the chamber lid is closed. After the sealing process is complete, the lid on most models opens automatically, which allows for easy retrieval of the sealed item.

External Sealer

External sealers, as the name implies, enclose the vacuum bags on the outside. The device is first clamped along the open sides of the bag, and then it begins to vacuum- and heat-seal the plastic opening. The initial cost of external sealers is more affordable compared with chamber sealers, but the bags used for these devices typically cost more per sheet compared to chamber and other sealer bags. In addition, because the length of the item being vacuumed is determined by the length of the purchased bag rather than the chamber size, external sealers are ideal for packing longer items such as sides of fish or whole loins. The compact size of the external sealer machine and its low weight also add to its versatility in a smaller kitchen where space is limited. However, external sealers have a tendency to overheat quickly and cannot be used for prolonged periods of time. And when vacuuming an item in which the shape has to be maintained, external sealers will squeeze and crush items during the process as external atmospheric pressure causes moisture to be pulled out of specific proteins.

External Sealer

Mixers, Blenders, and Homogenizers

Aside from the knife, perhaps the most overworked tools in the kitchen are mixers and blenders. These appliances are the go-to tools for getting the job done quickly, and for tasks such as smoothing out sauces, stabilizing emulsions, or even kneading dough. The evolution of these machines almost coincides with the evolution of cuisine, in which the demands of the chefs are met with innovative and upgraded machines The more advanced and efficient mixers and blenders become, the more these machines allow chefs to concoct recipes that hone in on perfection.

Blade Type, Hand Blender/Immersion Blender

Hand blenders/immersion blenders deploy a handheld, top-down mechanical shearing blade to mix food items. Hand blenders vary in size and motor strength, and usage varies from food hydrocolloid dispersion to creating purées and foams.

Immersion Blender
Courtesy of J.B. Prince

Blender (Bottom-up)

Bottom-up blenders, which house a mechanically spinning blade at the internal base of the blender, have been raised to a professional level. Companies can now offer commercial

**Vitaprep
(Bottom-up Blender)**
Courtesy of Vitamix

kitchens blenders with a variety of options ranging from normal blending to hard-spice grinding. The latest improvements include higher-horsepower blender motors, increased volume capacity, and preprogrammed operational runs.

Specialty Blenders

Pacojet (Specialty Blender)
Courtesy of PacoJet

The Pacojet is specifically designed to create fresh, micro purée with an ultra-smooth texture from frozen foods without thawing beforehand. Smooth ice creams, sorbets, and granité as well as savory sauces and purée preparations can be created. To use, a storage vessel is filled with a mixture that is then frozen by means of LN2, a freezer, or a blast chiller. The frozen vessel is inserted into the machine, where, according to desired specifications, the item is pulverized by a blade that spins at a high rpm, shaving ultrathin layers from top to bottom and then from bottom to top of the vessel. After completion, the food item can be stored in the vessel, which is kept in the freezer for later use, and it can be churned again before use.

Vorwerk Thermomix (Specialty Blender)

The Thermomix is an all-in-one specialty appliance that includes measuring, cutting, mixing, kneading, heating, and emulsifying functions in a blender-style design. The Thermomix has become an object of desire for many chefs due to its versatility in food preparation. For example, the Thermomix can boil and purée a potato in the same liquid without having to use any other devices. The Themomix is also capable of steaming food in a basket attachment connected to the top of the pitcher; it can be set at a desirable cooking temperature; and also can hold foods such as tempered chocolate at a consistent temperature. Cold food items such as sorbets and shakes can be created, and coffee beans or nuts can be ground. The appliance includes a digital scale that can weigh all the ingredients placed inside the pitcher before preparation to ensure recipe consistency.

Rotor Stator Homogenizer (Colloid Mill)

Rotor Stator Homogenizer
Courtesy of Eyela

Rotor stator homogenizers, also referred to as colloid mills, are efficient at dispersing food hydrocolloids and creating emulsification. Controlled by rpm, variables to consider include the blade either being made of steel or rubber and the power capacity based on specific application needs.

Ultrasonic Homogenizer

Ultrasonic Homogenizer
Courtesy of PolyScience

Ultrasonic homogenizers thoroughly disperse and emulsify foods by causing sonic pressure waves to disrupt the cells walls of the item that is being homogenized. Model sizes and power vary. Larger models will produce more heat, which is a factor for food items that are affected by higher temperatures.

Tools for Handling Liquid Nitrogen (LN2)

As discussed in Chapter 2: Sanitation and Safety, it is important to maintain proper procedures when handling this extremely cold elemental substance. The tools necessary when working with LN2 in a safe and creative manner are described below.

Cryo Gloves

Cryo gloves are needed to protect the hands when working with LN2 because the extreme cold temperatures could cause frostbite and skin damage. The multilayered structure of cryo gloves is designed for those who might have direct contact with LN2.

Cryo Sprayer

Cryo sprayers disperse LN2 and freeze the outer layer or the exterior of the food item instantaneously. The cryo sprayer's can contains LN2 and is comparable to small Dewar flasks, which makes them safe to carry LN2. Caution should be taken to avoid cold burns and spillage when filling the cryo sprayer container. Using cryo gloves and goggles and wearing long-sleeved chef jackets can help to avoid serious injuries.

Dewar Flask

Dewar flasks are used to store and refill LN2. The design of the specialized flask is created to efficiently insulate a substance by keeping hot liquids hot and cold liquids cold for extended periods of time. LN2 should only be stored in a Dewar after purchase to maintain appropriate temperature while also keeping the substance from evaporating too quickly. Dewars are insulated so that the LN2 at room temperatures does not evaporate as quickly as if just left in a unsealed container.

Protective Eyewear

Goggles, face shields, or protective glasses are recommended to avoid splashing LN2 into the eyes. Materials for eyewear should be resistant to the low temperatures of LN2; typically polycarbonate is used in the production of face shields and goggles. The eyewear should wrap completely around the eyes and the side of the eyes to avoid accidental contact that can cause serious injury to the eye area.

Nitro Bowl

Nitro bowls are double-layered bowls that are capable of withstanding the low temperatures of LN2. The LN2 is poured into the hollow interior between the layers of the bowl, while the item that is to be frozen is placed into the exterior layer of the bowl and mixed without the risk of breaking the bowl. Materials deemed unsafe to use with LN2 are items such as plastic, wood, and glass. These should not be used when using the Nitro Bowl. The most ideal type of utensils recommended to use with LN2 are ones made with stainless steel that have rubber-reinforced handles.

Tools for Measurement

Food hydrocolloids are ingredients that require precise measurement when being applied to a recipe. In order to reproduce consistent results, correct measurements must always be taken when applying them to any recipe. Described below are the tools that will control irregularities in the final result and help you to better understand the use of the ingredients.

Measuring Cups/Spoons
Courtesy of J.B. Prince

Measuring Cups and Spoons

Measuring cups and spoons are available for a variety of volumes, including cups, liters, and ¼ teaspoon to 1 tablespoon. These types of measuring devices are suitable for any kitchen to help maintain consistency of ingredients within recipes. The various materials used to make these tools range from glass, silicone, and Pyrex to plastic and metal.

pH Meter

pH Meter
Courtesy of 100%Chef

pH meters are probe-like thermometer devices that measure acidity and basicity levels of a liquid solution within a range of 0 pH to 14 pH. Typically, readings lower than 7 pH are classified as acidic and readings above 7 pH are classified as basic. The presence of high or low acidity can cause irregular outcomes in a recipe due to under- or over-reactivity when using certain food hydrocolloids. A pH meter is crucial for consistent results with food hydrocolloid recipes.

Refractor

Refractor
Courtesy of J.B. Prince

Among other readings, refractors measure the amount of sucrose within a solution. The scale used by refractors for sugar is expressed in units of Brix where 1 gram of sucrose in 100 grams of solution equals one degree Brix. Winemakers, fruit juice companies, and those in the honey industry use refractors to gauge sugar content within their products. Refractors are commonly available as monocular devices or small scales that digitally analyze the sucrose level. To analyze the sucrose content, a small amount of the solution is smeared across the glass surface of the refractor. Then by looking through the lens, the readout of the sucrose level displayed in Brix units is gauged. The area within the lens where the two different colors on the scale meet is the measured Brix level of the solution.

Rheometer/Viscometer

Rheometer
Courtesy of J.B. Prince

Rheometers and viscometers are used to measure the rate of flow or the viscosity of a liquid. Handheld and simple versions that resemble a ruler are used for thicker liquids to gauge the drip rate. More complex versions have a mechanical plunger that is pressed into the liquid; the force needed to enter the liquid is measured to obtain viscosity.

Scale

A scale that is accurate and reliable is required to obtain consistent results. Digital scales with a reading starting at 1 gram are efficient for normal product measurement; however, high-precision analytical laboratory scales with a minimum reading of 0.01 grams are necessary when working with food hydrocolloid powders (analytical scales with a reading of 0.1 gram to 0.1 milligram are not typically used in the kitchen). These very sensitive scales are often equipped with an enclosed case that sits around the scale's weighing area to maintain readings by blocking the slightest detection of air fluctuations while measuring a given item. One will have to slide open the panel of this enclosure case to insert the item being measured and close it to create a stable environment and to take the appropriate measurement. (The weight of the cover does not affect the measurement of the item being weighed.)

Digital Scale
Courtesy of 100%Chef

Thermometer

Thermometers are used to gauge temperature and are available in several styles: mercury or alcohol in glass, dial readouts, digital readouts, and infrared. Spring-based atmospheric pressure thermometers are also available. The range of temperature in which the thermometer can be used should be considered when purchasing a model for food preparation. For example, a thermometer for candy making or frying will need to withstand higher temperatures not typically registered by normal thermometers.

Analytical Scale
Courtesy of 100%Chef

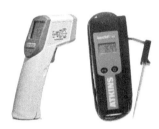

Thermometers
Courtesy of J.B. Prince

Tools for Spherification

Spherification has become a popular technique in the kitchen due to its ability to translate flavors into unordinary rounds of creativity. This technique highlights the chef's ability to manipulate flavor and the gelling properties of food hydrocolloids in order to create a unique experience. While the technique for making any flavored spheres may vary, the tools necessary for this process are typically the same.

Caviar Dropper

Caviar droppers are used to achieve perfect pearl shapes and are convenient for simultaneously forming multiple uniform-shaped spheres. The dropper box is fitted with a small tube that is connected to a syringe. The dropper box is held in the flavored liquid while the plunger of the syringe is pulled to fill the dropper box with the liquid. The syringe plunger is then slowly drawn over a bath (pretreated for the desired type of spherification: regular or reverse). Droplets are forced out of the box, forming perfect caviar-shaped pearls that will begin to cook or harden in the liquid. The caviar pearls are removed from the solution and rinsed in water before being served.

Caviar Dropper
Courtesy of J.B. Prince

Slotted Spoon

A slotted spoon is used to remove excess water and gel from the pearls or spheres when retrieving them from the solution and the water baths.

Slotted Spoon
Courtesy of 100%Chef

Syringe

Syringes with needles are used to inject flavors or gels into the center of existing spheres in order to expand their flavor profile. Syringes without needles are used to form spheres directly in a setting bath.

Syringe
Courtesy of J.B. Prince

Siphons and Accessories

Siphons are the main device behind airy concoctions such as foams, airs, espumas, and bubbles. Siphons are canisters with a screw top that have a nozzle attachment to disperse the solution. The solution is poured into the canister, then the lid is screwed tightly and a gas is introduced to the solution by two different delivery methods in order to charge the canisters and solutions with gas.

The two methods for charging siphons are as follows:

Cartridge-Charged Siphon

Cartridge-charged siphons or canisters are used to create foam, cream, airs, or bubbles. The number of charged NO2 cartridges necessary varies accordingly. It is sometimes recommended to shake the canister to spread the gas within an area; however, excessive shaking of the siphon should be avoided when preparing creams; otherwise a product that is too stiff or overwhipped will be dispersed from the canister.

Siphons
Courtesy of ICC - International
Cooking Concepts

Another application for these siphons is to use carbon dioxide (CO_2) rather than NO2 cartridges to give the food item a carbonated effect. Similar to an NO2 cartridge, a CO_2 cartridge is inserted into the chamber, and then screwed into the siphon canister, piercing the cartridge and releasing the gas into the canister. Multiple charges can be used to enhance or revive the carbonated effect. After use, it is important to release all of the CO_2 gas from the siphon by pressing the lever before unscrewing the canister. The siphon can be then be safely opened without concern that the siphon contents might be unintentionally expelled.

Cartridge
Courtesy of J.B. Prince

Charging Station Siphon

Charging station–type siphons contain NO2 (nitrogen dioxide). The canisters are filled at a charging station after the ingredients have been inserted. These stations are large tanks containing NO2 that can be recharged after depletion. Always follow the recommended fill-line recommendations; fill with NO2 until the hissing sound of the gas stops.

A variety of tips are available for use with the siphons to disperse foams, creams, and airs in specific shapes. Canister holders and clips are available as optional accessories.

**(Charging Station Siphon)
Espuma Advance**
Courtesy of NTG (Nippon Tansan
Gas Co.,LTD)

Specialty Tools

Aerator

Aerators are battery-operated foaming devices used for sauces, drinks, and foams. Aerators typically have a stainless-steel shaft with an attached whisk.

Aerator
Courtesy of J.B. Prince

Butane Torch

The butane torch, often referred to as a brûlée or blow torch/gun, is a butane-powered torch that can be used to char the outer skin of fatty tuna or to caramelize sugar on a brûlée among other brief high-heat source applications.

Butane Torch without Fuel
Courtesy of J.B. Prince

Confectionary Rulers

These often metallic rulers are available in various widths and dimensions and allow for easy separation of batters and mixtures during cooling or baking into exact shapes or angles. Four rulers are placed on a tray connecting at each other's edges to create a square. The batter is then poured into the designed trays. At this point, the batter with the positioned rulers is baked and the pan can be easily separated from the rulers, leaving behind a perfectly shaped product. In other words, these rulers can act to section off batter by creating temporary partitions in straight lines or exact angles due to their variable thickness and available lengths.

Confectionary Rulers
Courtesy of J.B. Prince

Confi Kit

Confi kits are used for coating food items. The apparatus is available as a KitchenAid mixer attachment. The mixer motor rotates the barrel coating pan so that food items such as nuts or candies are evenly glazed or sugar coated.

Confi Kit
Courtesy of 100%Chef

Cotton Candy Machine

Cotton candy machines melt sugar in a central dispenser and then spin the melted sugar until it has the appearance of woven silk, which is then spun onto a stick or tube. The raw sucrose can be infused with flavors such as vanilla or tinted with powder food coloring beforehand.

Cotton Candy Machine
Courtesy of 100%Chef

Edible Film Sealer

Edible film sealers are similar to external vacuum sealers in appearance and operation, but do not seal by creating a vacuum. These sealers are particularly useful with edible papers and films to encase items such as jellies, sauces, and compotes.

Edible Film Sealers
Courtesy of 100%Chef

Edible Paper and Ink

Fish Tank Bubbler

Forceps Tweezers
Courtesy of J.B. Prince

Induction Cooktop or Burner
Courtesy of J.B. Prince

Pipette
Courtesy of J.B. Prince

Test Cups

Macarron Kit
Courtesy of 100%Chef

Microplane
Courtesy of J.B. Prince

Edible Paper Printer

An edible paper printer is a specialized printer that uses food coloring as ink to print onto specialized edible paper typically made from rice. Edible decorations or menus can be created using this printer. It is important to use edible ink and to also dedicate a printer for this purpose to avoid contaminating the edible ink with previously used ink cartridges not meant for consumption. Only inkjet and bubble jet printer setups can be used with this technique; laser printers are not yet compatible with this operation.

Fish Tank Bubbler

Fish tank bubblers are used to create air bubbles in fish tanks, but can also be applied to create foams from foaming food hydrocolloids in liquids. These create semistable bubbles that can sustain the liquid flavors and colors, which can then be applied à la minute to a finished dish.

Forceps Tweezers

Forceps tweezers, typically made of stainless steel, are used to handle fragile and small items during plating, allowing one to work with a delicate touch to add finer details.

Induction Cooktop or Burner

Induction burners are portable electric stovetops that use ferromagnetic metals to create friction when vibrating to provide immediate direct heat. These burners interact with a pot or pan made from a ferromagnetic metal and can supply direct heat into the cooking vessel in a prompt manner while also maintaining a cool surface area.

Pipette

Pipettes vary in size and materials. Those commonly used in the kitchen are small plastic tube droppers used to deliver controlled amounts of liquid droplets.

Plastic Test Cup

Plastic test cups are suitable for measuring dry powders or small amounts of liquids in convenient reusable cups.

Macarron Kit

A macarron kit can create different tubes and cylinders of flavored gelatins. It is used by inserting the chilled rods into a liquid gelatin base that then hardens around the rods, leaving hollow tubes that can be cut to size (similar in shape to macaroni pasta).

Microplane

Microplanes come in varying sizes, with blades designed for grating, zesting, or shaving food items.

Silicone/Plastic Molds

Molds are commonly used to create flawless shapes, and the silicone or plastic coating in these molds provides a nonstick surface. A variety of shapes, sizes, and counts per tray are available for customizing specific operational needs.

Silicone Molds
Courtesy of J.B. Prince

Smoke Gun and Accessories

Smoke guns create smoke to enhance dishes and provide a certain atmospheric effect. The smoke gun does not smoke a food item from start to finish, but it can accentuate the taste of a previously smoked item by re-exposing the item to smoke. The smoke gun is portable and flavor chips of various types are available commercially.

Specially made optional glass covers can be used in conjunction with the smoke gun to allow the smoke to fill the glass compartment through a tube fitted at the nozzle of the gun and attached to the glass cover piece.

Smoke Gun
Courtesy of PolyScience

Spaghetto Kit

Spaghetto kits are long, clear tubes in which liquid gels are filled and then set into thin, elongated shapes. The set gels in the tubes are pressured out using a siphon with a specialized tip; the result is a long spaghetti-like gel.

Spaghetto Kit
Courtesy of 100%Chef

Spatula

Spatulas are available in a variety of sizes and shapes. Uses vary from simply lifting food objects to folding in creams to spreading tuile bases. Materials for spatulas include stainless steel, heat-resistant silicone rubber, plastic, and wood.

Spatulas
Courtesy of J.B. Prince

Spice Grinder

Spice grinders are used to pulverize dried items into powder, or can be used as an alternative wet grinder for small amounts of liquids for items such as pesto or vinaigrette. Electric grinders are usually high powered and can quickly process small amounts of dry or wet items.

It should be noted that spice grinders should not be used for extended periods, as a risk of overheating may occur.

Spice Grinder
Courtesy of J.B. Prince

Superbag

Superbags are ultrafine mesh strainers used as an alternative to a muslin or cheesecloth. Superbags ensure that any unwanted particles or textures are removed from the final sauce, purée, or juice. Superbags are available in a range of sizes and fineness: 1.3-liter and 8-liter sizes at four filtering levels of 100, 250, 400, and 800 microns.

Superbag
Courtesy of J.B. Prince

Turning Kit

Turning kits are used to create perfect coils for items such as pulled sugar. The device is a rounded tube that is coated with a nonstick material with a drill bit connection. The drill device is set in order to spin the device mechanically.

Turning Kit
Courtesy of 100%Chef

Introduction to Hydrocolloids: New Frontier

4

After studying this chapter you should be able to:

- Define hydrocolloids and describe their relationship with food rheology

- Identify the main functionality and behavior of food hydrocolloids

- Explain the terminology used to describe gelling and thickening

- Identify the terms used to describe the properties of food hydrocolloids

- Explain two major factors to consider when properly incorporating food hydrocolloid into a recipe

- Identify the basic formulations to create recipes

- Correctly apply food hydrocolloids

INTRODUCTION TO FOOD HYDROCOLLOIDS

The use of hydrocolloids, or gelling and thickening agents, in food production typically generates immediate debate. The reality of hydrocolloids is that their use and practicality applies further back in history than most people realize. Water-based paints, glues used for mummification, and wood-binding pastes were all applications for hydrocolloids used by the ancient Egyptians. These techniques were possibly due to the ancient Egyptians' basic understandings of the vegetation within their region; they successfully utilized the specific properties of these plants (in particular, the *acanthus* genus). Beyond practical applications, hydrocolloids have been implemented in foods throughout different regions and various periods of time. The Mediterranean cultures utilized the sweetening properties of the seeds from a carob tree, commonly known as locust bean gum or St. John's bread. Meanwhile, Asian culture took advantage of the coagulating effects of seaweed and Western cultures isolated pectin in fruit. In general, the use of modern food hydrocolloids is not a completely new concept but rather a new approach to achieve a specific result of texture modifications in culinary applications.

DESCRIPTION OF FOOD HYDROCOLLOIDS

A colloid substance that is spread evenly throughout some medium, such as a solid, gas, or liquid, and a colloid particle dispersed in water are both called a hydrocolloid.

When a hydrocolloid particle is introduced to a water-based food solution, the particle attaches to a sugar molecule in order to form a stable suspension. The result is perceived as a gelling or thickening effect.

The hydrocolloids used in foods and beverages are often called food hydrocolloids, but they are also referred to as emulsifiers, stabilizers, thickeners, and gelling agents. Food hydrocolloids originate from several sources, including animal, terrestrial plant, aquatic plant, microbial, and synthetically produced derivatives. A prime example of food hydrocolloids from animal origin is *gelatin*, which is widely used as a gelling agent. On the other hand, *xanthan gum* and *gellan gum* are produced by microbial fermentation activity, while *pectin* and seed gums such as *arabic gum*, *guar gum*, *locust bean gum*, *tara bean gum*, and *starch* have their origins in terrestrial plants. Aquatic plants are also sources of food hydrocolloids, which include *carrageenan*, *agar*, and *alginate*. *Cellulose gums* such as *methylcellulose* are produced from natural resources such as wood and cotton, but are still considered chemically modified hydrocolloids. No matter the source, once added to aqueous foodstuffs, hydrocolloids mainly affect the viscosity or the thickening and gelling properties of the food. While working with food hydrocolloids, many factors can affect their ability to gel, thicken, emulsify, and stabilize. Considerations such as temperature, pH, ionic level, volume of water to hydrocolloid ratio, and which food hydrocolloid is being applied are necessary to successfully use them within a given recipe.

Emulsions are a type of colloidal suspension, such as the mixture of two insoluble liquids like fat or oil and water.

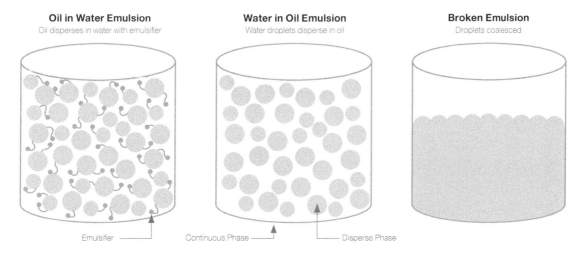

Oil in Water Emulsion
Oil disperses in water with emulsifier

Water in Oil Emulsion
Water droplets disperse in oil

Broken Emulsion
Droplets coalesced

Emulsifier ———

Continuous Phase ———

——— Disperse Phase

Emulsion Type of Colloidal Suspension

Food Rheology

Rheology is the study of fluid flow transformations, such as the effects of food hydrocolloids on water-based foods. The ability to control the gelling and thickening flow properties is the key to quality and consistency in food textures. Having a greater understanding of the rheology can result in an enhanced application of the food hydrocolloid. Film formation in spherifications, foam stabilization of airs or espumas, flocculation or lump formation in improperly dispersed food hydrocolloids, and adhesion and suspension in thickened sauces and gels are all properties that can be controlled. Viscosity control (the degree of thickening) is possibly the most utilized function of food hydrocolloids in cooking. In rheology, one can examine the changes in viscosity when a hydrocolloid is applied to aqueous foods by using a viscometer or a rheometer to acquire a numerical value of viscosity.

Hydrocolloid Composition and Behavior

To understand whether food hydrocolloids will gel, thicken, emulsify, or stabilize, one must take a basic look at the molecular structures. The majority of food hydrocolloids are polysaccharides (poly = "many" and saccharide = "sugar"), which are a combination of individual sugar molecules. An exception is *gelatin*, which is not a polysaccharide but rather a digestible protein. Polysaccharides are categorized into two types of chemical structures: linear and branched configurations. As the name entails, linear hydrocolloids are chains of sugar molecules with small sugar molecule appendages protruding out of the original chain. Branched-type hydrocolloids have many sugar units extending in several directions. When comparing hydrocolloids with more linear features to those with branched ones, the linearly structured hydrocolloids (i.e., *xanthan gum*) allow higher viscosity at lower concentrations, while the branched hydrocolloids (i.e., *arabic gum*) demonstrate a lower viscosity at the same concentration. Beyond technical factors that can alter food hydrocolloid composition (such as the source, extraction method, and processing), food hydrocolloids from all origins have similar molecular structures, but their individual characteristics are defined by how they evolve from their original sugar molecular structure.

Polysaccharides: String of Monosaccharides Bound Together

Gelling and Thickening

Each hydrocolloid will react differently when introduced to water-based foods, resulting in gelling or thickening. Applying the correct food hydrocolloid in the correct amounts is essential for the desired results to be achieved. Sensory factors that are considered for both gelling and thickening are taste, bite, flavor release, and mouthfeel.

Gelling

A "gel" is characterized as a solid, jelly-like form with weak fluidity that can maintain solidity with some flexibility, yet there is a wide range of gel types, including those with more or less fluidity. A "gelation" is the process of a fluid becoming a gel when fibers are formed (similar to a web). When using food hydrocolloids, the created fibers trap the food hydrocolloids and water inside the solution to create a resistance, hence the gel. The type of food hydrocolloid used for gelling can result in hot or cold gels that will not lose their shape when added to hot or cold liquids. Attributes of physical characteristics of gels are commonly described as brittle, elastic, soft, or hard.

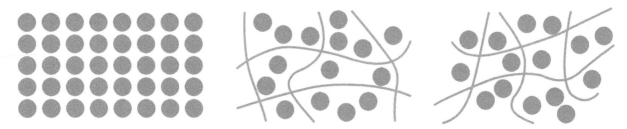

Process of Fibers Trapping Food Hydrocolloids and Water into a Gel Structure

Thickening

When thickening a liquid, the result is viscosity and not solidity. It can be said that a thickened solution is in between a liquid and a gel; however, a thickened solution does not form web-like fibers inside (as a liquid does in gelling). The flow is relatively free and can lose its viscosity when additional liquid is added to the thickened product. Physical factors in these observations are referred to as texture, flow, water content, stability, stickiness, cohesiveness, resilience, transparency, springiness, extensibility, brightness, processing time, and process tolerance.

Temperature Behavior

Temperature plays an important factor in the appropriate handling of food hydrocolloids. Certain food hydrocolloids will gel immediately, while others require cooling, shearing, or even higher temperatures for thickening or gelling to occur. A prime example of the unconformity within food hydrocolloids is methylcellulose, which sets when heated and melts when cooled. Yet there is a possibility that an overheated food hydrocolloid (e.g., *guar gum* and gelatin) can degrade, or that with the use of a carrageenan, the combination of high heat and over-acidic mediums can cause the gel to break down. The goal is to fully dissolve the food hydrocolloid within the aqueous solution while not jeopardizing the viscosity when applying heat or shear force.

pH Tolerance

To avoid recipe malfunction, the balancing of food hydrocolloid mediums and other ingredients is crucial since acidity and alkalinity greatly affect gelling abilities and strength. pH is a relative measure of acidity and alkalinity on a scale of 0 to 14, with the neutral solution having a pH of 7 (see Table 4.1). Each food hydrocolloid has an ideal pH range where it will be most effective. For example, high-methyl pectin will gel with the existence of an acid, but not in an alkali environment. Understanding the intended result with the products used (in conjunction with monitoring the pH levels), will help eliminate errors. Not only will observing pH control consistency, it can also enhance natural flavors while limiting the chance for any microbial contamination to occur. In order to boost the natural acidity, citric or tartaric acid is used, while sodium citrate can be applied if less tartness is desired.

TABLE 4.1: PH SCALE

pH Scale			
Acid	0		
	1	Gastric fluid (1.5–2)	
	2	Lemon (2.5)	Vinegar (2.5)
	3	Apple (3–4)	Wine (3–3.7)
	4	Beer (4–4.5)	Soda water (4.6)
	5		
	6	Milk (6.5)	
Neutral	7	Tap water (5.8–8)	Neutral zone
	8	Baking soda (8.5)	Sea water (8–8.5)
	9	Soap water (9–10)	
	10	Cement (10)	
	11		
	12	Ammonia (11–12)	
	13	Lye	
Alkali	14		

Chelating Agent

Chelating agents (or sequestrants) are calcium, potassium, and magnesium ions, which have a positive charge in solutions and combine with the negatively charged ions of food hydrocolloids to form gels. Errors such as pregelatinization, instant gelling, and overfirm or brittle gelling can occur from high concentrations of calcium (e.g., calcium in tap water causing pregelation). In order to balance the ionic charges, the use of chelating agents (or sequestrants) is helpful. *Sodium citrate*, *sodium phosphate*, and *sodium hexametaphosphate (SHMP)* are often used as sequestrants to control the calcium concentration because they bind the calcium ions. While they do not completely remove the controlled substance, sequestrants do reduce the effects that calcium can have on a gel if left unattached. Using sodium citrate requires a pH system of at least 4 on the pH scale, while SHMP can be applied to a wider range at 0.1 percent concentration. These sequestrants act as an additive by improving stability and overall quality with consistency.

TABLE 4.2: BASIC OUTLINE OF FOOD HYDROCOLLOIDS THAT DO NOT NEED, REQUIRE, OR BENEFIT FROM THE USE OF A CHELATING (OR SEQUESTRANT) AGENT

Often Does Not Require a Chelating Agent	Benefits From Chelating Agents at Times	Requires Chelating Agent
Agar	Carrageenan	Iota carrageenan
Guar gum	Gellan gum	Kappa carrageenan
Locust bean gum	Pectin	Gellan gum
Xanthan gum	Konjac	LM pectin
	Sodium alginate	Sodium alginate
	Sodium carboxymethyl cellulose	Sodium chloride

Synergy

Synergy is the process of combining two or more food hydrocolloids, which can alter their original rheological properties to create, modify, or enhance inherent traits of each food hydrocolloid. A synergic technique can provide several benefits, including cost, consistency, and quality effectiveness. Cost is affected by reducing the amount of food hydrocolloids needed to create the same effect. For example, xanthan gum can be a costly food hydrocolloid, but konjac can be added to the xanthan gum as a bulk ingredient to create the same effect. Also with synergy, the traits of the food hydrocolloids can be positively affected, as with the synergy between *carrageenan* and *locust bean gum*. Locust bean gum does not gel, but when added to kappa carrageenan it produces a strong yet less brittle gel than when only kappa carrageenan is applied. Another type of synergy is observed when a food hydrocolloid acts uniquely with a nonhydrocolloid food product. A common example is when carrageenan and milk protein combine to form a gel. Furthermore, food hydrocolloids can also interact with naturally occurring proteins in ingredients to have positive and negative reactions. Ultimately, synergy is utilized to apply the best aspects of one food hydrocolloid to another in order to create a balance of texture, flavor, and structure without degrading the quality of the ingredients or the outcome.

Properties of Food Hydrocolloids

Following are some of the terms used to describe the impact that food hydrocolloids have on gels and thickening properties.

Appearance and Clarity

Some food hydrocolloids are used as clarifying agents. They are most often employed in the brewing of beer, but the same food hydrocolloids can be applied to basic gel formation to enhance the clarity. *Gelatin* is typically used for clarification as it attracts the negatively charged contaminants or haze particles in beer. Some hydrocolloids contain insoluble (or nondissolving) particles that will cause opaqueness; if this is an undesirable result, the reduction of fat content in the recipe may reduce this problem. Food hydrocolloids can also offer a transparent quality. Sodium alginate, xanthan gum, and carrageenan have had their insoluble components extracted during processing, allowing a clear gel or thickened product to form. The proper dissolving of these hydrocolloids is required to gain the best possible result (see the discussions of dispersion and hydration in Applying Hydrocolloid, pages 62–63).

Texture and Flow

When working with food hydrocolloids, the immediate reaction that can be perceived is the change of texture and viscosity. The key is to control the texture and viscosity in order to create a new perception of dining. For example, the question to ask when making a sauce thickened by different food hydrocolloids is how each would affect the final taste. The food hydrocolloids may taste similar, but in reality each ingredient performs very differently. One observation is the differences in flow of the food hydrocolloid—whether it runs on a plate and how it clings on the food. Another factor is mouthfeel (whether it is smooth, coarse, light, or sticky) sensed by the mouth and the tongue, followed by its lingering taste or lack of taste after the food has been swallowed. Understanding how each food hydrocolloid impacts the final result can help control the final outcome. For gels, the texture varies from the brittle and hard gels of agar to the very springy and elastic gel of gelatin. Gel texture control is very important to bring the best out of the foodstuff and to create completely new flavors.

Flavor Release and Suppression

Some gels melt or break in different conditions. This texture property helps to release or hold the flavors in the mouth and enhance palatability. Choosing the correct food hydrocolloid to bring out the intended flavors is crucial. Gelatin, for instance, melts at 95°F/35°C, which is closely equivalent to the temperature of the human body; so it will immediately melt in the mouth and release greater flavor.

Suppression of flavor is commonly due to the overaddition of certain hydrocolloids such as sodium alginate or *cornstarch*. If suppression is desired, adding starch is the most effective manner to achieve this result. One reason that suppressions in taste occur is the dilution of strong natural flavors, such as acidity or sweetness. For example, the acidity or sweetness of wine used in braises and stews is less profound when a roux or cornstarch is used as a thickening agent.

Shear Stability

The term "shear" is often used when working with food hydrocolloids. Shearing is basically the act of stirring or blending, but as a technical term it describes creating thin parallel layers in internal surfaces that are moving away from each other when force is applied (e.g., the motion when cutting with scissors). Simply put, whisking is a form of shear force because the tines of a whisk can cut through the product being whisked. For food hydrocolloids, shear force can affect the consistency by creating a stabilized gel state while having the properties of a pourable liquid. If the viscosity decreases when the food hydrocolloid is agitated, this is called shear thinning (food hydrocolloids such as xanthum gum, gellan gum, and locust bean gum share this effect). On the other hand, shear reversibility refers to a gel that has lost its viscosity but re-forms a gel after the shear force is removed. Other than *low methyl pectin*, there very few hydrocolloids that demonstrate shear reversibility.

Thermo-Reversible/Thermo-Irreversible

Gels that melt when heated have thermo-reversible effects, while those that do not melt or liquefy after gelling are considered to be thermo-irreversible. For instance, when heating gelatin-based gel at above melting point (95°F/35°C), it melts into a liquid form, but once cooled, it re-gels again; hence, gelatin is thermo-reversible. On the other hand, when applying heat to an egg white, it hardens but it does not return to liquid form once it sets because the egg white proteins link into a network and stay connected even when heat is applied. This is a prime example of a thermo-irreversible state.

Hysteresis

Some thermo-reversible food hydrocolloids (such as *agar* and *gellan gum*) have different gelling and melting temperatures and create a unique phenomenon called temperature hysteresis. For example, once agar is melted at 185°F/85°C, it is tempered to remain a liquid between the temperatures of 104°F/40°C and 185°F/85°C. If agar is not melted, the mixture will remain a solid gel up to 185°F/85°C.

Syneresis

What appears to be condensation from a gelled item is a result of a phenomenon called syneresis. The gelatin undergoes a dehydration process and squeezes out the water from the inside. This is common in certain food hydrocolloids that gel into a hard texture, but it may also occur after a gelled item has been frozen and thawed. As a *gelatin* ages, the water has a tendency to suppurate from the gel. Meanwhile, gels created from *citrus pectin* are not inclined to undergo syneresis, even at pH levels of 2.0 and lower. Exceeding the amount of food hydrocolloids that can be contained in a liquid solution can also be a cause of syneresis.

Freeze–Thaw Stability

Generally speaking, freezing predisposes the gel to weaken the cell structure and leads to unwanted textural and structural changes or the loss of water from the gel. The ability to freeze and thaw gel repeatedly is called freeze–thaw stability. For example, *iota carrageenan* is a stable food hydrocolloid, whereas gelatin and konjac have poor stability. By choosing the appropriate food hydrocolloids with high freeze–thaw stability and utilizing the synergy between them, one can easily minimize the damages caused by freezing and thawing.

Applying Hydrocolloids

In order to use food hydrocolloids, the identification of proper ways to incorporate them into a recipe is necessary. While each food hydrocolloid can be used with different techniques of thickening, gelling, or emulsification, these tips can help incorporate food hydrocolloids thoroughly and limit errors.

Dispersion

The separation of individual dry gum particles into a liquid is called dispersion (e.g., preparing a beurre manié).

Most food hydrocolloids disperse evenly in cold liquids. Depending on which food hydrocolloid is used, evenly mixing a food hydrocolloid with an ingredient such as sugar, a spice, or a natural starch is applicable. Salt is not recommended because sodium ions in a dispersant can interfere with the hydration. With dry ingredients, a mixture of 10 parts dispersant and 1 part food hydrocolloid is ideal, while for some food hydrocolloids, liquids such as vegetable oil, glycerol, or alcohol can be used as dispersant. Dispersion as the first step ensures that the food hydrocolloid will spread and activate properly by using more than one thickener, or combining all before dispersing them into the liquid. Since they are used in smaller quantities, stabilizers and emulsifiers require thorough dispersion to ensure proper results. The most common ways to disperse the food hydrocolloids in dispersants are:

1. Dry dispersion: Simply mix the food hydrocolloid with a dry dispersant (i.e., sugar, spices, or natural starch).

2. Liquid dispersion: Sprinkle the mixture of dry food hydrocolloid into the liquid dispersant (i.e., vegetable oil, glycerol, or alcohol).

3. Mechanical dispersion: If none of the above is applicable, create a high-speed mixture (i.e., with an electrical blender) to disperse the food hydrocolloid evenly. Be careful not to overmix or incorporate air, which can undermine the performance of the food hydrocolloid.

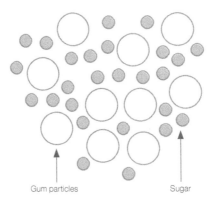

Gum particles   Sugar

Dispersion Diagram

Hydration is the process during which gum particles disappear when each individual molecule attaches to water, causing the molecule to swell and slough away to form a uniform solution (e.g., adding cooked roux to a simmering liquid).

Food hydrocolloids are dependent on water or some other type of aqueous solution for the properties to be effective. The goal when hydrating a food hydrocolloid is to surround the dispersed particles with liquid in order to inflate the particles to full size, thus allowing dissolving within the solution to occur. After proper dispersion, combining the food hydrocolloid with a liquid under shear force or through some other type of electrical blending device or immersion blender is essential. This step will ensure that lumps or "fish eyes" (flocculation) do not occur, and will leave a uniformly gelled or thickened product. Without hydration, a food hydrocolloid will not be able to expand properly; one must work quickly, as the expanding and dissolution processes occur simultaneously.

Some food hydrocolloids, such as carrageenan, gellan gum, and pectin, must be heated in order to fully hydrate. Also, some hydrocolloids, such as sodium alginate, will not hydrate if the acidity level is too high. Acidity and sodium levels can be controlled with the addition of citric acid, sodium citrate, tartaric acid, or potassium citrate after hydration of the food hydrocolloid is complete. It is important to identify the temperatures and conditions with which a food hydrocolloid can be properly hydrated. The basic steps for hydration are as follows:

1. Bring the liquid food solution (e.g., stock, sauce, milk, etc.) to be thickened, gelled, stabilized, or emulsified with the hydrocolloid to its proper hydration temperature.

2. Monitor the temperature with a thermometer. A temperature that is too high or too low can be problematic, leading to improper gelling results.

3. Add the already dispersed food hydrocolloid to the liquid solution and apply shear force with an immersion blender, stirrer, or homogenizer.

4. Maintain the shearing and allow the food hydrocolloid to fully dissolve at the proper temperature for at least 1 minute. Adding too much shear force can yield improper gelling results.

5. If applicable, the liquid food solution should set or rest. Check to confirm if the food hydrocolloid was properly integrated.

6. Check for desired consistency after each application at appropriate setting or resting periods (i.e., gelled, thickened, stabilized, or emulsified results).

The most conventional method for properly hydrating food hydrocolloids involves using a simple saucepan over heat with a thermometer and using an immersion blender or whisk to add shear force to the solution. Another method utilizes the convenience of the Thermomix blender, which enables the heating, mixing, and blending of a solution in an all-in-one blender-type apparatus while also being able to set a timer. An alternative method to properly hydrate food hydrocolloid is to vacuum pack the liquid and hydrocolloid mixture and maintain accurate temperature by using a thermo circulator and a water bath.

Factors to consider when dispersing and hydrating:

- Degree of fineness or coarseness of the hydrocolloid and the dry ingredients: If a powder is too fine, dispersion is difficult, but the hydration rate will increase.

- Usage of other ingredients: Salts, pH, and acidity levels can accelerate or degrade the final thickened or gelled product.

- Temperature: Some hydrocolloids are temperature-sensitive. *Gellan gum* requires temperatures of above 167°F/75°C for it to fully hydrate properly.

- Do not combine the food hydrocolloid powder with a liquid too quickly or too slowly.

- Do not incorporate air.

FORMULATING AND MEASURING FOOD HYDROCOLLOIDS IN RECIPES

In order to acquire the same consistent results, one must measure and formulate food hydrocolloids within a recipe in the same manner and method. This aspect is where one of the "scientific" aspects of modern cooking is applied. Measurements and calculations must be exact in order for desired results to be achieved. This is especially essential when working with a delicate food hydrocolloid that can quickly compromise its properties when too little or too much of any factor is applied. It is important to scale up accuracy to the value of 0.01 (equivalent to 0.0004 oz.) when measuring food hydrocolloids. Normally, food hydrocolloids are identified in percentage by weight using the following formula:

Percentage of food hydrocolloid solution (%) = Amount of food hydrocolloid (g) ÷ Amount of total solution (g) × 100

Below is an example of formulating and measuring the percentage of solution calculation:

To produce 1,000 grams (35 oz) of 2.5 percent of agar solution, one will need 25 grams (0.8 oz) of agar and 975 grams (34g) of water.

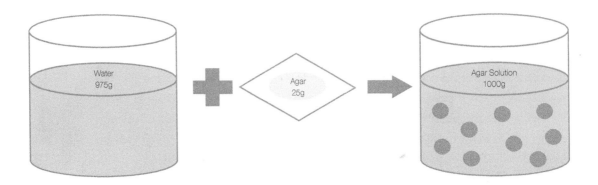

Formula

2.5% = X (g) ÷ 1000 (g) × 100

X = 25 (g)

Water needed = 1000 (g) − 25 (g) = 975 (g)

The following example is a typical mistake chefs make but often use as an approximate formula of measurement:

1,000 grams (35 oz) of water and 25 (0.8 oz) grams of agar to produce 2.44 percent of agar solution as a result.

Y = 25 g ÷ (25 g + 1000 g) × 100 = 2.44%

Although this calculation is incorrect, it is commonly used in the kitchen as a practical way to calculate food hydrocolloids in order to determine the approximate amount needed to obtain the desired result. To be exact, 25.64 grams (0.9 oz) of agar is necessary to make 2.5 percent of solution that must be added to 1,000 grams (35 oz) of water. Although there is variability within the recipe used and the type of food hydrocolloid being utilized, even the smallest difference can be crucial. It is ideal to work with accurate and exact calculations.

FOOD HYDROCOLLOID FUNCTIONALITY REFERENCE

Table 4.3 (pages 66–71) offers a practical overview of correctly choosing the appropriate hydrocolloid(s) for testing during product development. Each food hydrocolloid is described in further detail in Chapters 5 and 6; however, their physical properties are listed in the table. Important criteria to consider when choosing the best hydrocolloids are the texture properties required for the finished product, and the outcome that a particular food hydrocolloid should accomplish.

- Look at sensory factors as well as texture properties.
- Is a thickened- or a more gelled-structure outcome required?
- If the final product is a multiphase system (i.e., foam, suspension, emulsion), the hydrocolloid should also deliver some stabilizing properties.

This comprehensive table offers a quick reference for all food hydrocolloid properties in order to create and formulate new recipes.

TABLE 4.3: HYDROCOLLOIDS FUNCTIONALITY REFERENCE

Name	Synergy	Source	pH Stability	Solubility		Hydration/ Dissolution		Usage	Effect of Ion or Salt
				Cold (68°F/20°C)	Hot (185°F/85°C)	°F	°C		
Agar	Only gelidium agar with 10% LBG, more elastic, cohesive gel Tara gum	Variety of seaweed	2.5–10 pH	No	Yes	194	Lower than 90	0.5%–2.0%	Not affected
Arabic gum		Tree sap from acacia tree	2–10 pH	Yes	Yes	Hot and cold water		5%–50%	Not affected
Carrageenan, Iota	Starch, kappa	Red seaweed	4–10 pH	Sodium form: yes	Yes	>158	>70	0.75%–1% in water 0.35%–0.5% in milk	Gels in the presence of calcium or potassium but is most sensitive to calcium
Carrageenan, Kappa	With LBG, konjac, iota, pectin, xanthan gum. Strong reaction with milk		4–10 pH	Sodium form: yes	Yes	>158	>70	0.75%–1% in water 0.35%–0.5% in milk	Requires potassium salts to form gel
Carrageenan, Lambda			4–10 pH	Yes	Yes	68	20	0.1%–0.8%	Requires potassium salts to form gel
Gelatin		Collagen from animal skin, bone, and hide	4.5–10 pH	Swells	Yes	140	60	1%–1.5%	Not affected

Gel Character (gel strength shown in star ratings of 1 to 5 stars [★])	Appearance	Functions	Applications	Shear Stability	Temperature to Form Gel	Freeze–Thaw Stability	Alcohol Tolerance
Hard and brittle (★ ★ ★ ★ ★) Thermo-reversible	Clear to translucent	Gelling agent Stabilizer Thickener Suspension Emulsifier	Jellies, jams, puddings, custards, artificial caviar, fermented dairy products, candies, wine clarification, cakes, icings, noodles	Resistant	Depends on the type of agar In general 90°F/ 32°C to 113°F/45°C Thermo-reversible at 185°F/85°C to 203°F/95°CF	No	0%–20%
Soft (★)	Clear	Thickener Emulsifier Film-forming Stabilizer Suspension	Beverages, wine stabilization, confectionaries, bakery, emulsions	No effect	Nongelling	Yes	0%–60%
Soft, elastic, and cohesive (★) Thermo-reversible	Hazy on its own; clear if sugar is added	Thickener Gelling agent Emulsifier Stabilizer Suspension	Foams, jellies, crème caramel, dairy products, ice creams	Gel re-forms after shear (shear-reversible) and forms fluid gel (shear-thinning)	104°F/40°C to 158°F/70°C Increases with ion concentration	Yes	0%–15%
Firm, strong, and brittle (★ ★ ★ ★) Thermo-reversible	Hazy on its own; clear if sugar is added	Gelling agent Stabilizer Thickener Emulsifier Suspension	High-sugar chocolate syrups, frozen doughs, protein stabilizer, fat substitute, dairy products, meat products	Normally breaks gel with shear (shear-irreversible)	86°F/30°C to 140°F/60°C Increases with ion concentration	No	0%–15%
Does not form gel on its own	Hazy on its own; clear if sugar is added	Thickener Stabilizer Emulsifier Gelling agent Suspension	Beverages, sauces, dressing, dairy products, ice cream, jams, marmalades	Normally breaks gel with shear (shear-irreversible)	Below 104°F/40°C With ion concentration	Yes	0%–15%
Elastic Low bloom <125 = soft (★) Medium bloom 150–200 = medium (★ ★ ★ ★) High bloom >220 = hard (★ ★ ★ ★ ★) Thermo-reversible	Clear and bright	Gelling agent Thickener Emulsifier Stabilizer Texturizer	Gelatinous desserts, confectionaries, dairy products, Film forming	Sensitive	39°F/4°C to 95°F/35°C to gel and reverse	No	0%–20%

(continued)

Name	Synergy	Source	pH Stability	Solubility		Hydration/ Dissolution		Usage	Effect of Ion or Salt
				Cold (68°F/20°C)	Hot (185°F/85°C)	°F	°C		
Gellan, high acyl		Product of bacterial fermentation	3–10 pH	Swells	Yes	>185	>85	0.04%–1%	Calcium and potassium increase gel temperature and strength but are not needed for setting
Gellan, low acyl		Product of bacterial fermentation	3–10 pH	Possible with sequestrants	Yes	167–203	75–95	0.04%–1%	Gels in the presence of calcium or potassium but is most sensitive to calcium
Guar gum	Xanthan gum, LBG	Guar pods	4–10 pH	Yes	Yes	Cold and hot water		0.05%–1%	Not affected
Konjac gum	Kappa, LBG, xanthan gum	Konjac root	4–10 pH	Swells	Yes	Cold water		0.5%–1.2%	Not affected
Locus bean gum (LBG; carob gum)	Agar, methylcellulose, kappa, konjac, xanthan	Carob seeds	4–10 pH	Swells	Yes	>194	>90	0.5%–1%	Not affected
Methylcellulose	Viscosity increase with LBG	Cellulose from wood and cotton sources	3–10 pH	Yes	No	Cold water		0.5%–5%	Not affected

Gel Character (gel strength shown in star ratings of 1 to 5 stars [★])	Appearance	Functions	Applications	Shear Stability	Temperature to Form Gel	Freeze–Thaw Stability	Alcohol Tolerance
Elastic, springy, cohesive (★ ★ ★) Thermo-reversible Milk gels are more easily melted.	Hazy	Thickener Gelling agent Emulsifier Stabilizer Suspension	Confectionary, dairy desserts, bakery fillings	Normally breaks gel with shear (shear-irreversible) and forms fluid gel (shear-thinning)	158°F/70°C to 176°F/80°C	Yes	0%–50%
Firm and brittle (★ ★ ★ ★) Thermo-irreversible Heat stable	Clear	Thickener Gelling agent Emulsifier Stabilizer Suspension	Fruit water–based gels, confectionary, beverages	Normally breaks gel with shear (shear-irreversible) and forms fluid gel (shear-thinning)	86°F/30°C to 122°F/50°C	No	0%–50%
Does not form gel on its own	Clear	Thickener Stabilizer Emulsifier Film-forming Suspension Antifreeze Gelling agent (in synergy)	Bakery fillings, preserves, jellies, jams, ice creams, cheeses, sauces	Decreases viscosity under shear and re-forms after shear (shear-thinning)	Nongelling	Yes	0%–20%
Firm and elastic (★★★★) Thermo-reversible Thermo-irreversible at high (ph 9–10)	Milky white to light brown, plus a small amount of impurities	Thickener Gelling agent Stabilizer Film-forming Binding agent Suspension	Fruit jellies, candies, pastas, fat substitutes	Shear stable (shear-thinning)	Higher than 104°F/40°C Thermo-stable	No	0%–20%
Does not form gel on its own Produces soft gel/firm elastic in synergy with other hydrocolloids (★ to ★★★★) Thermo-irreversible	Clear to hazy	Thickener Stabilizer Film-forming Suspension Gelling agent (in synergy)	Bakery fillings, beverages, puddings, jams, jellies, cheeses, ice cream, sauces, soups	Decreases viscosity under shear and re-forms after shear (shear-thinning)	Nongelling	Yes	0%–20%
Soft to hard brittle and elastic gel (★ to ★★★★★) Thermo-reversible	Hazy when gelling; clear when cooling	Thickener Gelling agent Emulsifier Stabilizer Film-forming Suspension	Sauces, baked-stable fillings, salad dressing, ice cream	Pseudoplastic Decreases viscosity under shear thinning	118°F/48°C to 154°F/68°C Thermo-reversible when cooled to >41°F/5°C	Yes	

(continued)

Name	Synergy	Source	pH Stability	Solubility		Hydration/ Dissolution		Usage	Effect of Ion or Salt
				Cold (68°F/20°C)	Hot (185°F/85°C)	°F	°C		
Pectin, HM	.	Citrus peel, apple pomace, and sugar beet pulp	2–7 pH	Swells	Yes	Cold and hot water		0.1%–.5%	HM pectins require a certain level of acid or sugar (55%—80%) to gel
Pectin, LM	Forms firmer thermo-reversible gel with alginate	Citrus peel, apple pomace, and sugar beet pulp	2–7 pH	Swells	Yes	Cold and hot water		0.15%–3%	LM and LMA pectins gel in the presence of calcium ions
Sodium alginate		Brown seaweeds	3.5–10 pH	Yes	Yes	Cold and hot water		0.5%–1%	Forms gel in the presence of calcium, magnesium, and acid
Starch	Iota	Maize, potato, rice, tapioca, and wheat	2.5-7 pH			Cold water		Depending on the starch source	Forms gel in the presence of calcium and acid
Tara gum	Xanthan gum	Tara seeds	4–10 pH			77	25	0.1%–0.75%	Gels strongly with calcium salts
Xanthan gum	LBG, guar gum, tara gum, and konjac Starch and carrageenan for dairy food	Product of bacterial fermentation	1–13 pH	Yes	Yes	Cold and hot water		0.05%–1%	Stable in the presence of sodium

Gel Character (gel strength shown in star ratings of 1 to 5 stars [★])	Appearance	Functions	Applications	Shear Stability	Temperature to Form Gel	Freeze–Thaw Stability	Alcohol Tolerance
Low, medium, and high rigidity (★★★ to ★★★★) HM: Thermo-irreversible.	Clear, bright to opalescent	Gelling agent Thickener Stabilizer Suspension	Jam, jellies, fruit juice, milk, yogurt, bakery products, low-fat mayonnaise	Normally breaks gel	HM: 77°F/25°C to 194°F/90°C Melts above 158°F/70°C	Yes	0%–12%
Brittle and high rigidity (★★★★ to ★★★★★) LM and LMA: thermo-reversible	Clear, bright to opalescent	Gelling agent Thickener Stabilizer Suspension	Jam, jellies, fruit juice, milk, yogurt, bakery products, low-fat mayonnaise	Normally breaks gel	LM: 104°F/40°C to 212°F/100°C LMA: 86°F/30°C to 58°F/70°C and Melting point for both 158°F/70°C	Yes	0%–12%
Strong and brittle (★★★★) Thermo-irreversible	Clear and bright	Stabilizer Thickener Emulsifier Gelling agent Film-forming agent Suspension	Bakery fillings, dairy, sweet drinks, desserts, jams, marmalades, ice creams, meat and poultry processing, vegetables, potato preparations	Normally breaks gel (shear-thinning)	Not affected by temperature	Yes	
Native starches: low resistance Modified starches: increases resistance (★★★★★)	Opaque, hazy, or clear (based on the starch source)	Gelling agent Stabilizer Thickener	Soups, sauces, dressings, dairy, bakery, spreads, bread, pastries, confectionary	Native starches: low resistance Modified starches: greater resistance	Depends on the starch concentration	Modified starches	
Does not form gel on its own Structurally similar to guar gum and locust bean gum	Opalescent	Stabilizer Thickener	Dairy products, breads, pastries, ice creams, emulsions	Decrease viscosity	Cold/hot, thermo-reversible	Stable	
Does not form gel on its own Soft/elastic gels (★) Solution has high yield value Thermo-reversible	Hazy	Thickener Emulsifier Stabilizer Suspension agent Gelling agent (in synergy)	Salad dressings, ice cream, bakery products, sauces, beverages, foams	Decrease viscosity under shear (shear-thinning)	Great synergistic effect with konjac gum to form gel at 40°C/104°F Thermo-reversible at 50°C/122°F	Yes	0%–60%

Food Hydrocolloids: Thickeners, Gelling Agents, Emulsifiers, and Stabilizers

After studying this chapter you should be able to:

- Identify major food hydrocolloids

- Define each food hydrocolloid

- Describe the history and the origins of food hydrocolloids

- Recognize various functions of food hydrocolloids and their culinary uses

- Describe different applications of food hydrocolloids

FUNCTIONS OF ADDITIVES: NEW FOOD HYDROCOLLOIDS

Food science in the kitchen has broadened the possibilities and applications of thickening, gelling, emulsifying, and stabilizing by expanding the use of new food hydrocolloids. One of the key techniques within the modern kitchen is texture control. It is necessary to observe the appearance and textures of gels in order to better understand and properly apply food hydrocolloids. In addition, the flavor, color, and aroma of sauces or foams, and the mouth-feel that each food hydrocolloid can contribute to the final dish, are equally significant. As a result, food hydrocolloids that minimally affect natural flavors and enable easier texture control have become more desirable in the kitchen.

E-numbers are codes for food additives assigned by the European Union that identify food ingredients considered safe for consumption. Although rarely used in North American food labeling, this book will provide E-numbers for applicable food hydrocolloids in Chapters 5 and 6.

In addition to a brief introduction and description of various food hydrocolloids within this chapter, two tables are included at the end of the chapter to better summarize the provided information. Table 5.1 (page 93) lists common usage of the described food hydrocolloids within the categories of gelling, thickening or as a stabilizing agent. Meanwhile, Table 5.2 (page 93) displays the range of Bloom strengths of various gelatin categories. The listed information includes the common name referral of gelatin subsets with its value in units of Bloom and finally followed by a brief description of physical characteristics.

Agar (E406)

Definition

Agar is a water-soluble polysaccharide composed of agaropectin and agarose. It is found in the cell walls of the red algae (seaweed); *Rhodophyceae*, *Gelidium*, and *Gracilaria* are the main species that are commercially utilized. Agar is sold in flake, powder, or bar forms. It ranges from white to semitranslucent in color. Agar is flavorless, and it often is treated with inorganic bleaches and dyes to remove its natural odor and color, which is not desirable for certain applications.

History

Although the word *agar* is derived from the Malaysian word *agar-agar*, it is considered to have its origins in Japan. In the late seventeenth century, the Japanese observed the gelling property of this seaweed and started the production of agar (*kanten* in Japanese). Chinese workers in Malaysia imported the product, which has been widely used as an ingredient in many Asian countries. After its scientific application was discovered in the late nineteenth century, especially in the microbiology field of bacterial cultivation, the use of agar has spread more broadly throughout other disciplines.

Culinary Uses

The most important advantage of agar in food applications is its ability to form unique gels that are firm, brittle, and have a thermo-reversible tolerance to heat. Because agar is insoluble in cold water, heat for hydration is required before sweeteners, colorings, flavorings, or acids can be added and cooled to form a gel. It can serve as a clarifying agent in stocks and brews as a replacement for pectin (see page 87), while it can also act as a stabilizer for emulsions. Agar has a special property known as hysteresis, which refers to the large differences between gelling and melting temperatures. It is used to produce warm gelatin with a firm texture that can withstand temperatures up to 176°F/80°C. It is most commonly used as a gelling agent in items ranging from traditional Japanese desserts to ice creams, pie fillings, and cheeses.

Notes

Two factors can alter the gelling ability of agar: (1) the acidity or alkalinity of the ingredients with which it is mixed, and (2) the season in which the seaweed is harvested, due to its chemical structure affecting the type of postharvest treatments necessary for processing. Acidic foods, such as citrus fruits and strawberries, may require higher concentrations of agar, while highly acidic foods in their raw state (such as kiwis, pineapples, fresh figs, papayas, mangoes, and peaches) contain enzymes that break down the gelling ability of agar, resulting in a gel that will not set properly. In vegetarian and vegan diets, agar is used as a substitute for gelatin (an animal byproduct) because of its great satiation qualities; it also is a common ingredient in diet foods.

Arabic Gum (E414)

Definition

Arabic gum (or *gum arabic*—the terms are used interchangeably) is a polysaccharide composed of arabinose and galactose that is water-soluble. It is a natural gum secretion (resin) extracted from two species of the acacia tree: *Acacia senegal* and *Acacia seyal*. Both species are grown in the sub-Sahelian areas of Africa (or the area south of the Sahara Dessert consisting of most of Africa) and in Sudan (which are also the biggest producers of arabic gum). It is available in powder form for commercial use; and it is also known as gum acacia or gum arabic. It is characterized as having smooth hydration and gentle viscosity that allows it to be a great emulslfier.

History

Since ancient times, *arabic gum* has a history as both a food additive and as a pharmaceutical ingredient. Even though it is called "arabic," it is not completely Arabic in origin. Various species of acacia tree are harvested mainly in Africa but also in the Middle East, India, and Australia. This name originated because arabic gum was traded throughout the Middle East to western Asia and to Europe.

Culinary Uses

Arabic gum is used for various culinary purposes, including as a sweetener in soft drinks and food flavoring. It functions as a thickener, emulsifier, and stabilizer, which are beneficial to the production of foods such as marshmallows, candies, ice creams, and sweetener syrups. Other uses range from acting as a binding agent in chocolate and candy coating to keeping noodles from sticking together during the manufacturing process. Compared with other food hydrocolloids with a similar molecular weight (e.g., guar gum, xanthan gum, lambda carrageenan), arabic gum exhibits low viscosity in water. It can provide a distinctive crispy texture to confectionary treats when used as a dry solid.

Arabic gum is the most popular gum used for flavored oil encapsulations because of its contribution to forming a brittle outer shell that prevents flavors from oxidizing while also enabling water- and oil-based items to combine more easily. The use of arabic gum in the bakery extends shelf life by maintaining moisture levels of the product. The small quantities of proteins (glycoproteins) found within arabic gum are essential for the emulsifying and stabilizing processes.

Carrageenan (E407)

Definition

There are three commercial types of carrageenans. All variations are water-soluble polysaccharides. Each is produced from a different variety of red algae (seaweed): iota carrageenan from *Eucheuma denticulatum*, kappa carragenan from *Kappaphycus alvarezii*; and lambda carrageenan from an expensive species of the red algae, *Gigartina*. Carrageenan is a white or light brown powder and it is most commonly used as an emulsifying, stabilizing, and gelling agent. It is one of the three main algae manufactured, along with sodium alginate and agar.

History

The name carragneenan is derived from the seaweed *Chondrus crispus*, also called Irish moss, found in the Carragheen region along the south coast of Ireland. Carrageenan has been industrially produced for about 80 years. Currently, the Philippines produces the most carrageenan; about 80 percent of the world supply is manufactured there from cultivated seaweed. The use of the seaweed started hundreds of years ago in China, however; its gelling properties have been utilized there since approximately 600 BCE, and in Ireland since approximately 400 CE.

Culinary Uses

Carrageenan

Carrageenan is often used to emulsify or stabilize a wide variety of food items, especially products made from milk. It is utilized for meat products to improve the quality and/or raise the cooking yield of poultry, ham, and sausage products. In addition, it is often used in sauces and salad dressings to provide thickness and to stabilize the emulsion. Carrageenan also helps to stabilize frozen dairy foods by preventing whey from separating and keeping ice cream from becoming crystallized.

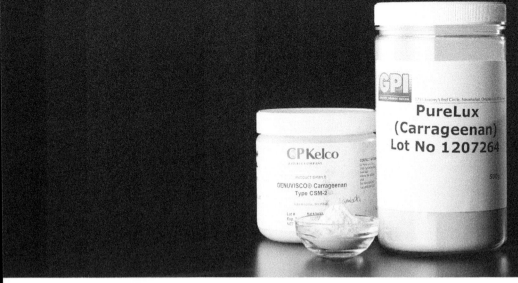

Lambda carrageenan

Because *lambda carrageenan* does not form a gel, it is the least used of the three car- rageenans. Its applications include use as a thickener; an emulsifier; and a stabilizer for foams, suspensions, instant drinks, and dairy desserts. It is exclusively used in combina- tion with kappa carrageenan for adding creaminess to milk-based products.

Iota carrageenan

Iota carrageenan forms a soft and elastic gel, but with the addition of potassium or cal- cium salts it can form a dry, resilient gel that is stable against the freeze–thaw effect. The shear-reversible gel properties can be used to stabilize ingredients such as suspended herbs and vegetables in vinaigrette-style salad dressings. It is also used as a stabilizer in soymilk, gravies, canned meats, and pasta—and often used as the base for foams. Iota carrageenan can be mixed with kappa carrageenan to enhance food structure, creating more resilient gels that are resistant to heat.

Kappa carrageenan

Kappa carrageenan forms a firm, brittle-textured gel, and an even firmer or harder gel can be created with the addition of potassium salts. The key properties are its high gel solid-

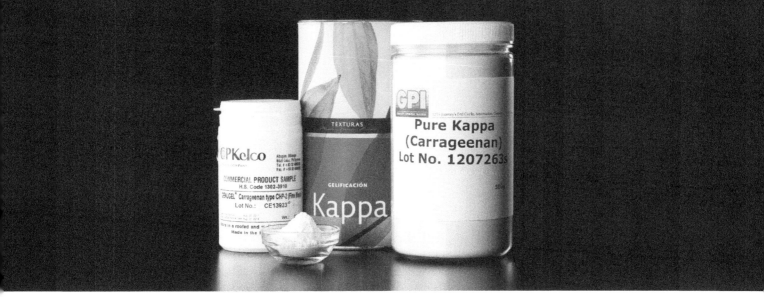

ness and powerful interaction with milk proteins. When cooled, kappa carrageenan gel has the ability to set faster than other hydrocolloids. It is broadly used to increase viscosity in a wide array of foodstuffs including dairy products, desserts, and sauces. Remarkably, it is also used in beer as a clarifier to remove haze-causing proteins. A gel made of kappa carrageenan is slightly opaque but becomes clearer with the addition of sugar. Once gelled, kappa carrageenan can withstand heat higher than ambient temperatures, but note that high acidity can affect gelling ability.

Notes

Similar to gelatin, kappa and iota carrageenan can provide elastic and transparent gelled preparations. Therefore, carrageenan can be a substitute for gelatin in vegan-based diets. Kappa and iota carrageenan are both insoluble in cold water; they require heat to hydrate and must be cooled down to form a gel. The gel or foam made of kappa and iota carrageenan can be served hot because it is able to resist temperatures of up to 140°F/60°C. At this temperature, the created gel reverts back to an aqueous solution due to its thermo-reversible property. Due to a loss of gel strength and viscosity at higher temperatures, for products with a pH lower than 4.3, carrageenan should be added promptly before hydrolysis occurs. Mixing kappa and iota carrageenan can have a synergic effect to create a firmer gel. Kappa carrageenan shows great synergy with other hydrocolloids, especially with locust bean gum, by increasing gel strength and changing gel texture from brittle to elastic with a better mouthfeel. Kappa carrageenan can also be used with konjac, pectin, and xanthan gum.

Gelatin

Definition

Gelatin is derived from a hydrolysis of collagen, a protein found within the skin, bones, tendons, and ligaments of animals such as cattle, hogs, and fish. It is commercially produced in powdered and sheet form; and it is a translucent, colorless, brittle (when dry), and nearly tasteless solid substance. Gelatin does not have an E-number because it is defined as a food ingredient and not as a food additive. It contains 18 amino acids, including 8 of

the 9 essential amino acids. The strength of gelatin is measured in units of Bloom. High bloom refers to a higher molecular weight of gelatin, which results in a product with a stiffer consistency. Gelatin used in foods normally varies from around 125 Bloom to 250 Bloom.

History

Gelatin has been used for more than 4,000 years. In ancient Egypt a gelatin mixture was used as an adhesive for carpentry. In 1682, a French scientist by the name of Denis Papin reported on a cooking process in which he attempted to obtain a jelly-like mixture from animal bones. Around 1875, the emergence of small factories allowed for the mass production of gelatin to become possible. Currently, gelatin is used in various applications ranging from classical aspic recipes to vitamin capsule fillers, which add bulk to the filling to allow better absorption of stronger medicinal components.

Culinary Uses

Gelatin is traditionally the most common cooking agent for gelling, and also acts as a thickener and a stabilizer. It is the most versatile texturing ingredient in the sugar confectionary industry. It also is used in water-based gels, jelly candies, aerated confectionaries, yogurt, dairy desserts, creams, and lowfat spreads. Since gelatin is a source of high-quality protein and does not contain cholesterol or sugar, it is often used in reduced fat foods to simulate the mouthfeel of fat and to create volume without adding calories.

Notes

Gelatin is used in a wide range of items, from terrines to foams. It forms a thermo-reversible gel that melts at 95°F/35°C. This unique property creates an excellent flavor release when placed in the mouth because it melts at body temperature. Gelatin must be hydrated in cold or warm water before being introduced into any other liquid. It must be dissolved in low heat, as boiling inhibits its strengthening power. Freezing should be avoided; due to freeze–thaw instability, gelatin will lose its smooth texture and become brittle once it has been defrosted.

Vegans and vegetarians do not eat foods containing gelatin because it is an animal product. Kosher and other religious customs may require gelatin from nonpork sources such as fish or from animals that were ritually slaughtered.

Gellan Gum (E418)

Definition

Gellan gum is a water-soluble polysaccharide. It is produced by the fermentation of the bacteria *Sphingomonas elodea*. There are two types of gellan gum: one has a high acyl (HA) content, and the other has low acyl (LA) content. High-acyl gellan produces soft, resilient, and stable gels; while low-acyl gellan creates hard, nonresilient, unstable gels. Gellan gum is a light yellow powder that hydrates in hot water, but low-acyl gellan gum can also hydrate in cold water. When both types of gellan gum are used in varying percentages, the final texture of the created gel will vary accordingly.

History

During the 1970s, the company CP Kelco discovered the bacterium *Sphingomonas elodea* in naturally grown plants and fermented it to produce gellum gum. Approval for food usage of gellan gum was established in 1988 in Japan and in 1992 in the United States. Furthermore, the U.S. Department of Agriculture (USDA) National Organic Program (NOP) has approved gellan gum as an organic ingredient under the established guidelines determined by the National Organic Standards Board (NOSB).

Culinary Uses

Gellan gum can be applied to a wide range of foods. The important characteristics of gellan gum are its high gel strength, excellent flexibility, stability, and clarity. Due in part to these properties, gellan gum functions to thicken, emulsify, and stabilize. The most common use of gellan gum is for producing water-based gels. Gels made of gellan gum will not dissolve in higher temperatures, and have superior shrink resistance. Gellan gum also produces excellent transparency, delicacy, a slick taste, and outstanding flavor release in comparison to gels made with sodium alginate, agar, gelatin, or carrageenan. It is also broadly used in the bakeshop (dry mixes, fillings, and glazes), in dairy products, and in beverages as a suspending agent. For example, it maintains the suspension of soy protein particles in soymilk.

In order to produce a firm gel that can be sliced cleanly while also resisting temperatures up to 194°F/90°C, gellan gum should be heated to 185°F/85°C and then allowed to cool to achieve proper gelling effect. However, gellan gum can lose its gelling ability in high-saline content solutions. A pure gellan gum solution can be dropped into an ion-rich water solution to form gelled spheres. Gels can be made into thin sheets that can be rolled or folded with the use of high-acyl gellan. Gellan gum can be used instead of agar as a gelling agent; only approximately half the amount of gellan gum is required to achieve equivalent gel strength.

Guar Gum (E412)

Definition

Guar gum is a water-soluble polysaccharide that it is not adversely affected by salt. In addition, guar gum demonstrates excellent stability during freeze–thaw cycles. It is extracted from the guar bean, which is mainly grown in India and Pakistan. It is typically produced as an off-white powder and is economical because it has almost eight times the water-thickening potency of cornstarch. As a result, only a very small quantity is needed to produce sufficient viscosity. Guar gum can also be used in various multiphase formulations.

History

India accounts for about 80 percent of the global trade in guar products, and the guar plant is typically consumed by humans or used as cattle feed. Since 1944, the guar plant has been grown in the southwest region of the United States. Recently, the cultivation of guar gum has been attempted in Brazil, Argentina, and Colombia, as well as in regions of Africa and Australia.

Culinary Uses

Guar gum has wide applications in the food industry. In the bakeshop, it improves elasticity and texture while extending the shelf life in foods by preventing syneresis of water (refer to Chapter 4) in pastry filling, jellies, and jams. It is used in dairy products as a thickener in milk, yogurt, and aqueous cheeses, and in ice creams to maintain a uniform texture. It also works as a stabilizer in dressings, sauces, and foams to prevent oil droplets from coalescing as an emulsifier. Guar gum also slows ice crystal growth by decreasing mass transfer across the solid/liquid interfaces.

Notes

Guar gum demonstrates viscosity synergy when combined with xanthan gum and is more soluble and an overall better stabilizer than locust bean gum. Unlike locust bean gum, it is not self-gelling; either sodium borate or calcium must cross-link with guar gum for gelling to occur. Guar gum has strong shear-thinning properties unaffected by salts that can remain stable over a wide range of pH. Yet strong acids can cause hydrolysis (or the splitting back

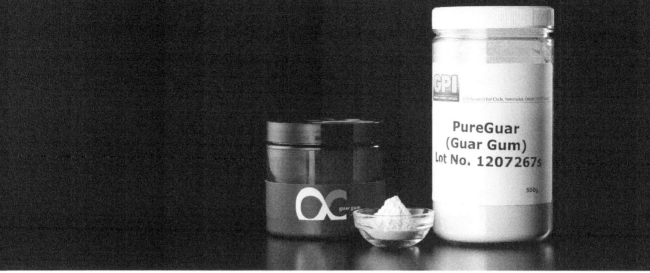

Courtesy of GPI Inc. and Le Sanctuaire

into sugar units), which can result in loss of viscosity, and alkalines in strong concentrations can reduce viscosity when heated (e.g., pH 3 at 122°F/50°C). Overall, guar gum is highly sensitive but has much greater viscosity compared to most other food hydrocolloids.

Konjac (E425)

Definition

Konjac is a viscous water-soluble polysaccharide. Also known as *konjak* and *konjaku*, it refers to a plant of the genus *Amorphophallus* and also to the dietary fiber derived from the root of that plant. Konjac plants are mainly grown in Asia in places such as China, Japan, Korea, India, and Thailand. Normally found as a white to yellow powder, konjac is used for applications that include roles as a gelling agent, thickener, stabilizer, emulsifier, and film former for food applications.

History

Konjac has been used as a gelling agent for more than 2,000 years and is listed in *The Divine Farmer's Herb-Root Classic*, the oldest herbal medicinal book in China. It was introduced in Korea around 550 CE and soon after to Japan with its use spreading widely and rapidly to other Asian countries by the 1800s.

Culinary Uses

Konjac is commonly used as a texturing ingredient in Asia, as it is more valued for its texture than its flavor. In Japanese cuisine, konjac (known as *konnyaku*) appears in many traditional dishes. It is typically mottled gray and firmer in consistency than most gelatins. It is also used in confectionaries such as bakery fillings or pie fillings. Additionally, konjac can be made into Asian fruit jelly snacks typically served in bite-size pieces. It is also often used to prepare food items such as pizza dough, pasta, tortillas, and restaurant confectionaries.

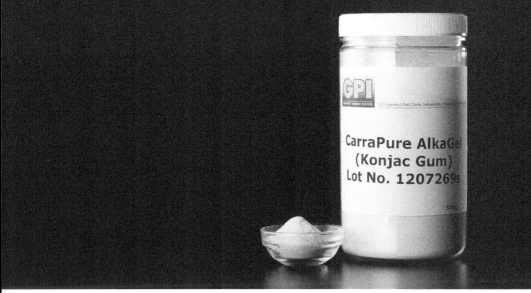

Notes

Konjac is one of the most versatile hydrocolloids. It can create a greasy and chewy mouth-feel similar to that of fat. Konjac gum is not adversely affected by salt, and it can produce both thermo-reversible and thermo-irreversible gels. It interacts with other thickening agents such as carrageenan, xanthan gum, starch, and agar.

Lecithin (E322)

Definition

Lecithin is a fatty substance derived from egg yolks and soy. Lecithin is available as a yellow- or brown-colored powder or in a liquid form that is considered both vegetarian- and vegan-friendly. Lecithin has a variety of uses in commercial products such as cosmetics, paints, and plastics; and it is often used as an emulsifier and antioxidant in foods. Similar to maltodextrin, lecithin is commonly not described as a true food hydrocolloid because it is not a polysaccharide.

History

In 1847, French chemist Nicolas-Theodore Gobley isolated an orange-colored substance in egg yolks for its unique emulsifying properties. Gobley named his discovery "lecithin," a word derived from the Greek *lekithos* (egg yolk). High production costs originally kept lecithin from being produced commercially, but large quantities of lecithin were found in soybeans, resulting in the mass production of the much more desired soy lecithin emulsifier by the 1920s.

Culinary Uses

The naturally present lecithin in egg yolk is traditionally used as an emulsifier in many sauces, such as mayonnaise and hollandaise. Lecithin has a wide variety of applications due to its added nutritional value and essential nutrient content while also reducing fat and egg requirements when used in baking. It also helps to evenly distribute ingredients, stabilize fermentation, increase product volume, and protect yeast cells in dough during freezing. Additionally, lecithin works as a releasing agent to prevent adhesion, thus contribut-

ing toward cleaning practices after the manufacturing process. This unique surface-active property makes the use of lecithin as an emulsifier ideal.

Notes

Lecithin will produce air bubbles and often stabilizes liquids, creating a smooth and creamy mouthfeel in dressings, sauces, airs, foams, and mousses. When applying lecithin to an oil/water emulsion, it first must be dispersed in the oil before the water is added (see Table 7.2, Common Emulsions, on page 124). Currently, researchers are exploring the possibility of other potential applications within the culinary world and in other professional uses.

Locust Bean Gum (E410)

Definition

Locust bean gum is a water-soluble polysaccharide. It originates from a fibrous vegetable gum extracted from the seeds of the long pods of the evergreen locust bean tree, also called a carob tree. The endosperm is extracted from the pod and then milled to produce the final white- to yellow-white colored locust bean gum powder. Nutritionally, these pods are high in protein and sugar.

History

The evergreen locust bean tree bears fruit (called locust beans, carob beans, or St. John's bread), which has been used in herbal medicine within the Mediterranean region. The origin of the name "locust bean gum" is derived from the sweet, pulpy fruit pods of the tree that resemble locusts. In the early nineteenth century, locust bean gum was the principal food item for the British cavalry. Other applications include the bean's use as cattle feed.

Culinary Uses

Locust bean gum is often utilized as a thickening and stabilizing agent in modern culinary applications. The bean powder is sweet in flavor, similar to chocolate, and is used as a chocolate

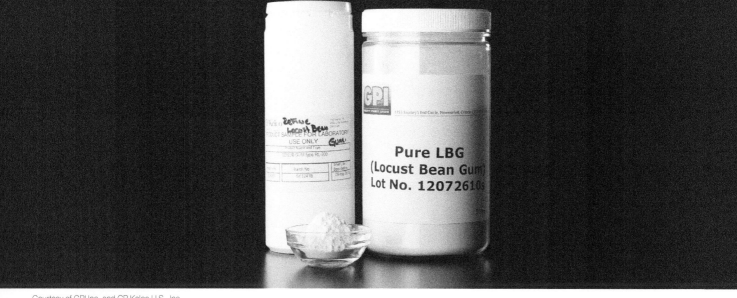

substitute in addition to sweetening food. Locust bean gum is also utilized as a stabilizer in soft drinks, soups, and sauces by maintaining the appropriate clarity within liquids. It stabilizes and controls dough texture in baking and it is often used to create ice cream bases in pastry.

Notes

Locust bean gum can be dispersed in both hot and cold water; however, it will only hydrate in hot water. It has thickening and cohesive properties and is applied as a highly effective viscosity adjuster. Locust bean gum in synergy with kappa carrageenan, agar, or xanthan gum can create a strong and elastic gel; furthermore, it can also stabilize emulsions alone or increase viscosity with xantham gum.

Methylcellulose (E461)

Definition

Methylcellulose consists of inorganic compounds derived from cellulose. It is a water-soluble, hydrophilic (water-friendly), white powder with no taste or smell. Cellulose constitutes the majority of seed plants and is considered as the most plentiful carbohydrate available. It is directly consumed, but the main sources of cellulose in production are wood and cotton.

History

Methylcellulose was first commercially manufactured in Germany in the 1920s and was introduced to the United States in 1938. The use of methylcellulose as a food additive within the food industry began years after its initial production. Currently, the industry is conducting research to explore the different potential applications of cellulose derivatives.

Culinary Uses

Methylcellulose forms a solid, flexible, and transparent film that demonstrates suitable resistance to oil and ester (an organic compound produced by the reaction of alcohol and acid). The tem-

perature of the gel and its precipitation is determined by three factors: the type of product, the concentration of the solution, and the speed with which it is heated. The water solution of the gel will become opaque due to gelling and precipitation properties. Thermal gelation is a unique feature that occurs subsequent to a loss of water during heating, resulting in a product with transparent viscosity; but the created gel will return to its original liquid condition when cooled to a certain degree. In other words, methylcellulose will gel when hot and melt when cooled. Methyl-cellulose is used to thicken sauces and salad dressings. It also is used to coagulate and stabilize ice creams to help prevent ice crystals from forming during freezing or when refreezing after melting. Methylcellulose also functions as an emulsifier by preventing the separation of mixed liquids.

Notes

Methylcellulose forms a thermo-reversible gel that is not soluble in hot water but rather is only soluble in cold water. As a result, the liquid should first be heated and the powder mixed in thoroughly while it is hot in order to avoid the formation of lumps. The solution should be stirred continuously as it cools to allow the methylcellulose to fully dissolve. Methylcellulose is used to create hot or brûlée ice cream. Ice cream can be prevented from melting when heat is applied by dipping the ice cream in a solution of methylcellulose and water to create a thin layer to protect it from the heat.

Pectin (E440)

Definition

Pectin is a water-soluble polysaccharide found within the pits of certain ripe fruits and vegetables. Commercially available as a white- to light brown–colored powder, the majority of pectin is extracted from citrus peel or from fruit pomace (most commonly from sugar beets, potatoes, and pears). When pectin is separated, it creates two commercially available forms: high methyl esterified pectin (HM) and low methyl esterified pectin (LM), where methyl esterification is a resulting reaction of combining acid and methyl alcohol. While HM types can form a gel in an acidic product with the presence of sugar, the LM type can form a gel in a broader pH range with lower concentrations of sugar.

History

The act of using pectin in recipes for jam or marmalade goes back to the 1700s, but it was not until 1825 that chemist Henri Braconnot isolated and described pectin. Originally, high pectin–producing fruits were used for these recipes, but due to Braconnot's research, pectin was added to fruits with lower pectin concentrations to create a greater variety of jams. The commercial production of pectin did not begin until the 1900s. It is typically extracted by adding citrus peels to a mixture of water and acid. The excess water and solids are removed before the addition of alcohol and salt, which dehydrates the pectin before it is crushed into its commonly available powdered form.

Culinary Uses

Traditionally used in jam and marmalade preparations, pectin is usually applied as a stabilizer, thickener, and/or gelling agent for a given solution. Thoroughly mixing dried pectin with sugar and melting it ensures an even distribution of the pectin throughout the product. It is also used in fruit juice beverages to restore a fresh mouthfeel. Yogurt drinks and acidified dairy beverages use pectin to stabilize protein dispersion. LM pectin gels in the presence of calcium ions and it can also be used to create spherifications (similar to sodium alginate).

Notes

Pectin is commonly used as a fat substitute in lowfat cooking, and it also has excellent flavor release capabilities compared with other food hydrocolloids. HM pectin is usually used in high sugar content gels with firm texture, such as jams or pâté de fruit. LM pectin requires less sugar usage; it is thus better suited for the preparation of foods for those with diet restrictions and specific dietary requirements. When using either HM or LM pectin, it is necessary to know the type of sugar content environment in which the pectin will be used in order to achieve the desired outcome. Along with sodium alginate, pectin has a unique property that can create different biopolymers (large molecules; e.g., protein molecules) after a synergetic effect takes place, transforming the structural makeup of the newly created gel.

Courtesy of Texturas - Solegraells; GPI Inc.; and Le Sanctuaire

Sodium Alginate (E401)

Definition

Sodium alginate is a dietary fiber created from the combination of alginic acid with ionic sodium. It is a water-soluble polysaccharide commonly found in brown algae, such as the giant kelp *Macrocystis pyrifera*, *Ascophyllum nodosum*, and in varieties of *Laminaria*. It binds with water to form gel bodies in the seaweed that in effect contribute to its flexibility in seawater. It is normally found as a white- to yellow-colored powder and can be labeled as "algin" or "alginate." Sodium alginate dissolves in both hot and cold water to create a viscous solution.

History

Scottish chemist Dr. E. C. C. Stanford first extracted and identified alginate in 1881, and commercial production of it began around the 1930s. Alginate and its derivatives have been utilized as food hydrocolloids as well as a food additive. It also has applications in the medical field and other industries. Scientists are researching the potential health benefits of sodium alginate, along with its potential to lower cholesterol and blood sugar levels.

Culinary Uses

Sodium alginate has a unique property that modifies only through ion exchange, without heating or cooling, due to gel formation in the presence of calcium ions. This makes sodium alginate exceptionally useful as a thickener, emulsifier, and stabilizer. It can also form a heat-stable gel within a cold solution as an overall gelling agent. Sodium alginate is necessary to create spherifications, or the process consisting of submerging a flavored fluid containing sodium alginate into a bath of calcium chloride. Alternatively, adding sodium alginate to a bath of high calcium–content food creates what is known as reverse spherification. Both processes involve the same mechanism: the creation of a gelled film surrounding the fluid. The thickness of the gel wall of the sphere is dependent on the amount of time it is submerged in the bath of either calcium or alginate before rinsing off with water to stop the

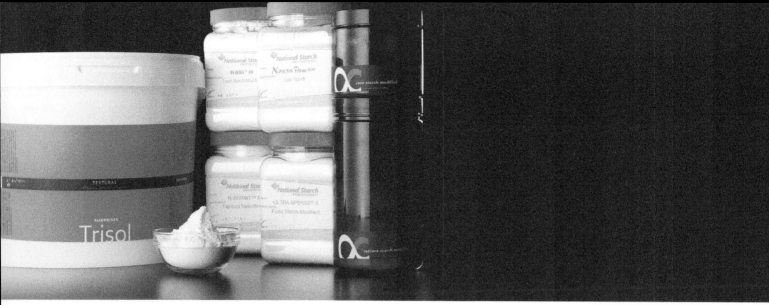

cooking process. This process can create spheres of different sizes (e.g., caviar, gnocchi, eggs), in addition to an array of flavors. Sodium alginate is widely used in the production of gel-like foods or gel stuffing and has been applied to a large number of foods items such as ice creams, lactic drinks, and dressings.

Notes

The difference between spherification and reverse spherification is the dispersion of the sodium alginate and calcium (i.e., within the flavored liquid or within the bath). Furthermore, in synergy with HM pectin (which usually only functions in acidic and high-sugar solutions), sodium alginate can form a firm gel in a wider range of pH levels and at acidic levels of solutions. Along with pectin, sodium alginate is also known as a rare synergic food hydrocolloid.

Starch

Definition

Starch is a digestible complex carbohydrate contained in the seeds, fruits, tubers, roots, and stem pits of plants. Pure starch is normally available as a white, tasteless powder, and it is most abundantly found in corn, potatoes, wheat, rice, and cassava. It is also the primary carbohydrate of the human diet and a common source of energy. Starches, often referred to as modified starches or prehydrated starches, offer new functional benefits and are prepared by changing the ratio of amylose, which contributes to gelling properties, and amylopectin, which provides thickening and viscosity capabilities.

History

The ancient Egyptians created a paste from wheat starch to reinforce cloth while weaving and possibly as an adhesive for papyrus pieces. The Romans applied the use of starch to produce a variety of items, including creams for cosmetic purposes and powders for the hair, as well as to thicken sauces in the kitchen. Other cultures during ancient times used starch to prepare foods. In China, rice starch was utilized during papermaking to smooth out the surface of the pages.

Culinary Uses

Starch, with a wide range of functionality and flexibility, is used in the production of processed foods such as breads, pancakes, cereals, noodles, pastas, and tortillas. Starch is also commonly used as a stabilizer, thickener, and gelling agent in other food items, such as puddings, custards, soups, sauces, gravies, pie fillings, and salad dressings.

Notes

Natural starches have inconvenient characteristics, such as lump formation, when dissolved in a liquid. Modified starches were created to enhance certain functional benefits of starches while removing undesired properties. Modified starches are commonly made from tapioca, potatoes, wheat, or corn sources.

Tara Gum (E417)

Definition

Tara gum (also known as Peruvian carob) is a water-soluble polysaccharide, the properties of which are not adversely affected by salts. Composed of mannose and galactose, it is structurally similar to guar and locust bean gums. Tara trees are native to South America and have been introduced to Morocco and East Africa. Tara beans are harvested when they turn black and the endosperm is extracted and grounded into a white- to yellow-colored powder that has a wide range of food applications.

History

The tara bean pod contains tannic acid, which is often used in the leather industry, and the seeds of the pod were formerly just considered a byproduct. The European Union recognized the use of tara gum as a food additive with culinary applications as a thickener, stabilizer, and gelling agent in foods. It is estimated that around 1,500 to 2,000 tons of tara gum are produced each year for use in the food industry.

Culinary Uses

Although it may not always be listed as an ingredient on food labels, tara gum is often used in dairy products. It improves shelf life by binding water and thus controlling the texture. It can also influence crystallization and prevent the loss of moisture in items such as cheeses, creams, ice creams, pickles, baked goods, cereals, mustards, dried fruits and vegetables, soups, and several food items. Due to this quality, tara gum is probably used and consumed more often than is realized. It works more efficiently as a thickener rather than as a gelling agent and has great synergy with other food hydrocolloids.

Notes

Tara gum interacts synergistically with xanthan gum, agar, and carrageenan to increase gel strength and make these gels less prone to moisture loss.

Xanthan Gum (E415)

Definition

Xanthan gum is a water-soluble polysaccharide with many uses in food applications. Available as a light yellow powder similar to cornstarch, xanthan gum is produced by fermenting glucose or sucrose from the *Xanthomonas campestris* bacterium, which is then dried and ground. It is one of the most common food hydrocolloids and is used as a thickener and to provide viscosity, stabilizing, and emulsifying properties.

History

Studied by chemists Allene Rosalind Jeanes and P. A. Sandford, xanthan gum was brought into the market in the early 1960s in conjunction with the U.S. Department of Agriculture (USDA) and the Kelco Company under the trade name Kelzan. It is approved as a safe food additive by many countries, including the United States, Canada, and the European Union.

Culinary Uses

Xanthan gum demonstrates great thickening power. It is widely used in a variety of items from salad dressings to sauces and is used to stabilize foams and to help prevent the formation of crystals in ice creams. For low- or nonfat dairy products, xanthan gum acts as a fat substitute by adding a textural feeling of fat. As it is vegetable-based, it is great for cooking and baking foods for those who have food allergies (especially to eggs, soy, and gluten) or for those with dietary restrictions.

Notes

Xanthan gum is extremely versatile, although it cannot be gelled on its own. It can be dissolved in hot and cold liquids; it also can thicken alcohol in an acidic solution while being resistant to freezing and thawing. Xanthan gum demonstrates remarkable increase in viscosity when synergized with locust bean gum, guar gum, or konjac. Meanwhile, locust bean gum or konjac can also increase thickness by forming an elastic and cohesive gel. Xanthan gum is compatible with most organic acids, such as acetic, citric, lactic, tartaric, and phosphoric acids. It can also be used in combination with starch and kappa carrageenan.

TABLE 5.1: COMMON USES OF FOOD HYDROCOLLOIDS

Name	Thickener	Gelling	Stabilizer	Emulsifier	Film Forming	Suspension
Agar	x	x	x	x		x
Arabic gum	x		x	x	x	x
Carrageenan, iota	x	x	x	x		x
Carrageenan, kappa	x	x	x	x		x
Carrageenan, lambda	x		x	x		x
Gelatin	x	x	x	x	x	
Gellan gum (high acyl/low acyl)	x	x	x	x		x
Guar gum	x		x	x	x	x
Konjac gum	x	x	x	x	x	x
Lecithin (technically not a hydrocolloid)			x	x		x
Locust bean gum (carob gum)	x		x		x	x
Methylcellulose	x	x	x	x	x	x
Pectin (high methyl esterified/low methyl esterified)	x	x	x			x
Sodium alginate	x	x	x	x	x	x
Starch	x	x	x			
Tara gum	x		x			
Xanthan gum	x	x	x	x	x	x

TABLE 5.2: GELATIN STRENGTH (BLOOM)

Gelatin Type	Gel Strength (Bloom)	Texture
High	220–300	Hard, brittle
Medium	150–220	Firm, springy
Low	50–150	Soft, elastic
Leaf Type	**Gel Strength (Bloom)**	**Grams per Leaf**
Titanium	100	5
Bronze	125–155	3.3
Silver	160	2.5
Gold	190–220	2
Platinum	135–265	1.7

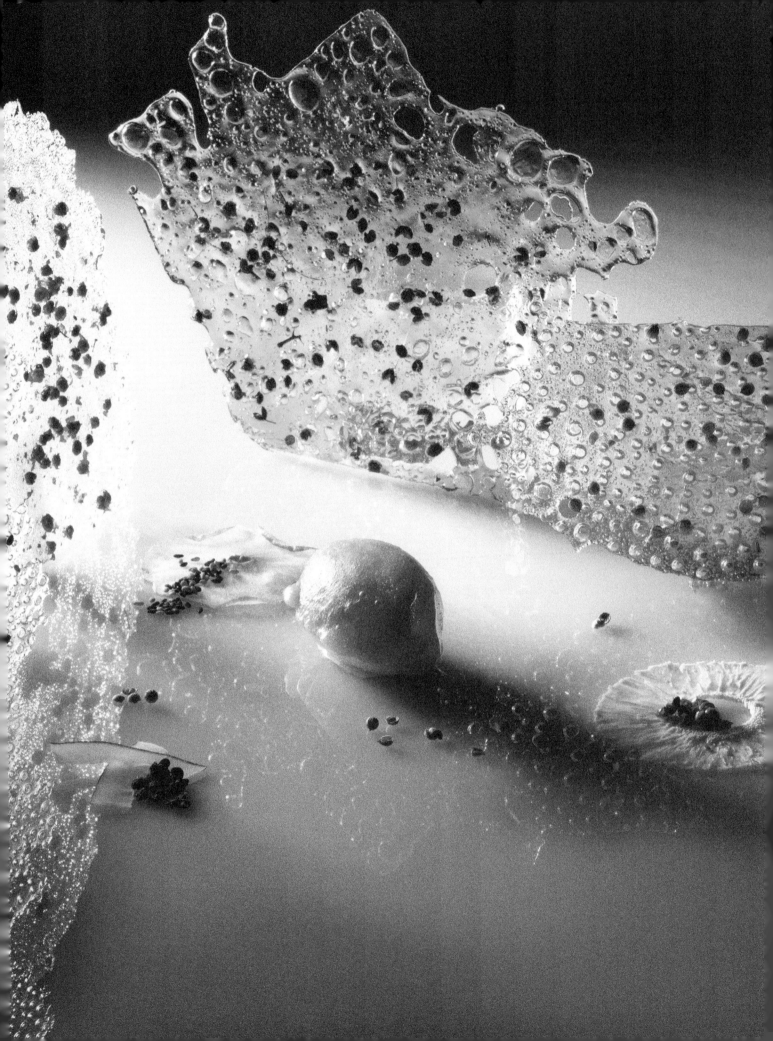

Sweeteners, Antioxidants, and Others

After studying this chapter you should be able to:

- Identify some of the major sweeteners and antioxidants used in cooking

- Define the various types of sweeteners and antioxidants

- Explain the history of sweeteners and antioxidants

- Describe the functionality of major sweeteners and antioxidants, in addition to their culinary usage

- Utilize other ingredients often used in modern cooking applications

SWEETENERS

Sugars are used for flavoring purposes by adding sweetness to food. Sugar is the generic term for edible crystalline carbohydrates, which can be divided into two structural types: simple (monosaccharide) and double (disaccharide). Each structural type of sweetener has unique properties and suitable usages. Once you comprehend the specific properties of sweeteners, you can maximize their effects as well as their different applications in modern cooking.

Dextrose/Glucose:

Definition

Dextrose, or *glucose*, is a monosaccharide found in plants and animal tissues. Commercial dextrose/glucose is obtained from cornstarch in the United States and from potatoes, grapes, or honey sources in Europe. In its final form, dextrose/glucose is a white crystalline powder that provides a moderate degree of sweetness. Dextrose occurs naturally in foods such as maize, rice, wheat, cassava, arrowroot, and sago.

History

Dextrose was isolated in 1747 by Andreas Sigismund Marggraf, a German pharmacist. He did not formally apply a name to his discovery but only referred to it as a type of sugar. In 1811, Constantine Kirchoff was able to produce a sugar syrup from this isolated component; and in 1838 French chemist Jean-Baptiste-André Dumas named the isolated type of sugar "glucose" (a term derived from the Greek language). It was not until 1902 that German scientist Emil Fisher conducted further research on glucose by identifying its primary functions within the human body. For this work he won a Nobel Prize in Chemistry.

Culinary Uses

Dextrose/glucose is commonly used as a substitute for sugar in recipes. It does not leave an aftertaste, and it speeds up browning time for baked goods. It has half the sweetening strength of plain sugar and also helps inhibit large crystal formation in ice creams and sorbets. Commercial processors use dextrose for various treatments, including canning, preserving, brewing, and in meat production to aid in the fermentation process of cured meats.

Notes

Dextrose is often mistaken as glucose syrup, which is a mixture of dextrose, maltose, and other complex carbohydrates. In baking, dextrose helps prevent dough from spreading and also enhances the volume and texture of cakes. Dextrose provides a sensation of coolness when added to mint flavors and provides a strong tart flavor when added to sour ingredients.

Courtesy of Le Sanctuaire

Fructose

Definition

Simple monosaccharides are found in many food items. *Fructose* (also known as fruit sugar) is identified as the sweetest and one of the most water-soluble of all sugar types. Fructose is sold as a yellow- to white-colored crystalline substance. Found naturally in honey, tree fruits, berries, and melons, it is also synthetically manufactured during the process of manufacturing high-fructose corn syrup. In addition, fructose combined with glucose will produce disaccharide sucrose.

History

Augustin-Pierre Dubrunfaut first discovered the organic fructose molecule in 1847. Japanese researchers developed synthetic high fructose corn syrup (HFCS) in the 1970s, and by 1975, HFCS was integrated into many processed foods and manufactured beverages. The crystalline form was made available in the early 1980s. The United States has the highest consumption of HFCS.

Culinary Uses

Due to its low cost and high sweetening power, fructose is more commonly used in soda and candy production than glucose or sucrose. Its sweetening strength is altered by factors such as temperature and pH levels. Fructose can improve the softness and texture of candy or prevent the cell wall structure of frozen fruits from crystallizing. In addition, fructose has the ability to enhance the relative sweetness of other sweeteners when combined.

Notes

Fructose has 125 percent to 170 percent more sweetening power than sucrose. Yet it has a tendency to lose its sweetness at higher temperatures, and it is often not used directly. It is suitable for making ice creams or sorbets due to its ability to inhibit crystallization.

Isomalt (E953)

Definition

Isomalt, or *isomaltitol*, is derived from sucrose, which is composed of two disaccharides: gluco-mannitol and gluco-sorbitol. It functions as a sugar substitute and is sold in white crystalline or powder form. The chemical and enzymatic reactions that occur during the manufacturing of isomalt make its properties more stable compared to those of sucrose. Isomalt is a natural sugar alcohol that is commonly derived from beets.

History

Isomalt was discovered in the 1960s, and in 1990 its use was approved in the United States. It is used in products such as hard candies, toffees, chewing gum, chocolates, baked goods, nutritional supplements, cough drops, and throat lozenges. It has been available in Europe since the early 1980s and is currently used in a wide variety of products in more than 70 countries worldwide.

Culinary Uses

Products made with isomalt have the same texture and appearance as those made with sugar; however, the sweetening power depends on three factors: its type, the concentration of the product in which it is being used, and temperature. Heat will not cause isomalt to caramelize or lose its sweetness; thus it is predominantly used in products that are boiled, baked, or subjected to higher temperatures. Isomalt is almost exclusively used in decorative cake ornaments and sugar sculpture showpieces because it will not crystallize as quickly as sugar. A synergistic effect occurs when it is combined with other sweeteners, often masking bitter elements of other sweeteners while also increasing the sweetening power of the combined sweetener.

Notes

Isomalt has 45 percent to 65 percent of the sweetness of sucrose strength at equivalent amounts. It dissolves more slowly in the mouth; candies made with isomalt have a longer-lasting taste. Shelf life, volume, and flavor are also increased because of isomalt's stabilizing characteristics. When compared to sugar, health benefits include lower caloric content and fewer dental concerns.

Sucrose

Definition

Sucrose is a disaccharide consisting of a carbohydrate formed by glucose and fructose during photosynthesis. The most common form of sucrose is sugar, a white and odorless crystalline powder that is sweet in taste. Most commonly extracted from the juice of sugar cane and sugar beets, sucrose is also produced from date palms, sorghum, and sugar maples.

History

From early as 350 CE, chewing on sugar canes to release sweetness has made this natural resource a valuable product. A technique to crystallize sugar was discovered in India at around 500 BCE in a process called *khanda*; the term "candy" originated from this expression. A luxury item until the eighteenth century, sugar became more commonly available when methods of refining lowered production costs. During this time, experimentation on alternative sources for sugar from beets became popular due to trade restrictions throughout Europe.

Currently the European Union, Brazil, and India are the highest producers of sugar. Sugar is the most widely traded commodity; 100 out of the world's 180-plus countries produce sugar.

Culinary Uses

Sucrose can be found in practically every realm of the culinary spectrum and is perhaps one of the most widely used ingredients in the kitchen. Mostly recognized for its use in confectionaries and desserts, sucrose as sugar used in high proportions can be a preserving agent and has double the sweetening power of glucose. It is essential in the fermentation process for multiple products, such as beer or cider, and also for bread dough by feeding the yeast to create a rise. Sucrose adds bulk and volume as well as affects the texture of a product. It also acts as a thickener in jams and marmalades and can improve the color of baked goods.

Notes

There is no difference between sugar derived from sugar cane and sugar derived from sugar beets. However, the size of the sugar crystals will affect sweetness, receptiveness, and the ability to dissolve in liquids. The types of sucrose or sugars available are: powdered, granulated, cubed, preserving, brown, palm, Demerara, Muscovado, and invert sugar varieties (for further definition, refer to the discussion of trimoline).

Trehalose

Definition

Trehalose is a naturally occurring white crystalline disaccharide found in living organisms such as yeast, crustaceans, and fungi. It is composed of two sugar molecules, both of which are glucose; and it has 45 percent less sweetness than sucrose. It does not have the ability to brown as much as sugar, but it has low water retention and attraction qualities. Trehalose is commercially available in a white powder form.

History

Trehalose was discovered by H. A. L. Wiggers and originates from the fungus ergot, found in rye. It was later isolated for further research and production in 1859 by Marcellin Berthelot; however, the original extraction process made it costly for mass production. Then, in 1994, the Japanese starch-processing company Hayashibara developed an effective way to extract trehalose through enzyme manipulation. Currently its use is spreading to Western countries to partly replace ordinary sugar with what is being viewed as a "healthy" sugar alternative.

Culinary Uses

Trehalose is a highly valuable resource, with its wide commercial applications. These applications include protein stability, water retention, freeze–thaw advantages, shelf life extension, lowering of freeze-points, and the ability to partially simulate the mouthfeel of alcohol in non-alcoholic beverages. In professional kitchens, avant-garde techniques are being applied with trehalose because of its low sweetness levels combined with its sucrose-like properties. In Japan, trehalose is used in a wide spectrum of dishes from surumi to confections, and it is also used to prevent starches from hardening—making the freezing of ingredients such as udon noodles possible, because trehalose can be thawed without breaking down the food item.

Notes

Mixing trehalose with water and bringing it to a frying temperature can simulate "frying" texture without the use of oil. This technique is still being refined, and it is a promising method for a healthier and attractive new cooking technique. Trehalose can be applied to reduce the natural bitterness of certain foods and also can be used as an antioxidant. In natural applications, trehalose can protect plants, animals, and fungi from drying out by forming a gel wall around vital cells that allows normal cell function to occur after rehydration.

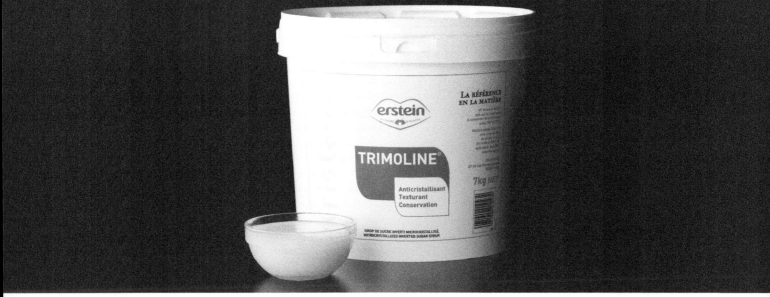

Trimoline

Definition

Trimoline is concentrated inverted sugar syrup. Inverted sugar syrup is created by heating sucrose and then adding an acid to break down the sucrose into its simplest forms of glucose and fructose. This usually white and thick stabilizer syrup is mainly used in baking, pastries, and ice creams.

History

As an inverted sugar, trimoline origins tie with the history and production of sucrose/sugar. Refer to the section on sucrose for further information.

Culinary Uses

Trimoline is used for a wide variety of effects and is applied mainly within commercial kitchens. In baking, shelf life is extended due to an increase in water retention. The texture, flavor, and colors of products with trimoline are well enhanced and preserved. Crystallization is almost nonexistent, making trimoline ideal when creating high/noncream-liquid-ratio ice creams or sorbets (i.e., an ice cream base that has more parts noncream sources compared to the actual cream source).

Notes

Soaking syrup can be omitted when using trimoline to bake cakes. Trimoline can also partially replace the quantity of sugar needed in many recipes. Honey and maple sugar are examples of natural forms of inverted sugar.

ANTIOXIDANTS

Antioxidants are substances that prevent oxidation or the discoloration and the deterioration of food. Oxygen is a vital element necessary for any form of life; however, it also causes oxidation or the loss of electrons, which causes discoloration and deterioration. While oxidation can occur naturally and artificially, antioxidants from natural origins, with the effects and different applications of antioxidants in food and modern cooking applications will be discussed in the following section.

Ascorbic Acid (E300)

Definition

Ascorbic acid is highly water-soluble and is found as a white crystalline powder composed of carbon, hydrogen, and oxygen molecules. It is a reductone (acid-reducing agent) and has high antioxidant properties. Ascorbic acid is usually synthesized from organic vitamin C and is often referred to as vitamin C because it has similar benefits; however, it does have a different chemical structure.

History

In 1907, Axel Holst and Theodor Frølich stumbled across the cause and the cure for scurvy, a vitamin C deficiency illness, while investigating the cause of beriberi in guinea pigs. It was discovered that scurvy could be avoided by incorporating fresh foods and fruits (in particular, citrus) into a regular diet. In 1937, the Nobel Prize for Chemistry was awarded to Walter Norman Haworth for his work in determining the structure of ascorbic acid. (It was shared with Paul Karrer, who received his award for his work on vitamins.) That same year, the Nobel Prize for Physiology or Medicine went to Albert von Szent-Györgyi for his studies of the biological functions of L-ascorbic acid. At the time of its discovery in the 1920s, it was called hexuronic acid by some researchers, but it was later renamed by Szent-Györgyi for its antiscorbutic properties. Now, through a technique called the Reichenstein process, vitamin C or ascorbic acid can be synthetically processed through conventionally bred microorganisms.

Culinary Uses

The primary use of ascorbic acid is retaining the freshness and color of meats, fruits, and vegetables after extended oxygen exposure. In addition, this antioxidant trait is used to keep oils and fats from spoiling and changing color. When applied to dough, ascorbic acid can also improve texture and loaf volume.

Notes

All animals must consume vitamin C; it cannot be produced within the body, and it prevents scurvy. During the pasteurization process, natural vitamin C is lost in many fruit drinks, but during the production process the fruit drinks are later fortified with ascorbic acid as a supplementary added health benefit. The term "ascorbic acid" is derived from a- ("not") and *scorbutus* ("scurvy"). Exposure to oxygen, metals, light, or heat sources destroys ascorbic acid. It must be stored in a dark, cold, and nonmetallic container to maintain its properties.

Citric Acid (E330)

Definition

Formed from the natural fermentation of sugar or from the commercially cultured *Aspergillum niger*, *citric acid* is sold as a crystalline powder or as a liquid solution. It is commonly known to be responsible for the tartness in fruits, but it should not be confused with vitamin C due to its difference in structure and function. Citric acid is also known as sour salt.

History

Persian alchemist Jābir ibn Hayyān discovered several naturally occurring acids, including citric acid, which was one of his findings during the eighth century. Citric acid was then isolated in 1784 by Swedish chemist Carl Wilhelm Scheele, who was able to crystallize the acid from lemon juice. This resulted in the industrialization of citric acid by companies such as Pfizer in 1874. The acid was sold as an antiseptic to sterilize products. Now fungus cultures such as the *Aspergillum niger* are fed inexpensive sugars, then fermented and precipitated to produce large quantities of citric acid.

Courtesy of Le Sanctuaire

Culinary Uses

Citric acid is soluble in liquid. It is commonly used as an acidity regulator and as a preservative, including acidifying and preserving oils and fats. Furthermore, citric acid is an important preservative in chocolate, milk, and dairy products in addition to its use in jams, marmalades, and fruit-based spreads. It lends itself as a tenderizer in meats by breaking down meat proteins before cooking. When gelling with pectin, citric acid will enhance the gel strength. Citric acid is also used to enhance existing acidic flavors in recipes.

Notes

Citric acid is used in food coloring to balance the pH level of the normally basic properties of dye. Other applications include its use as an odorless alternative to white vinegar for cleaning. Citric acid is solid at room temperature, with a melting temperature of 262°F/152°C; it decomposes at higher temperatures. Nearly all organisms can metabolize the citrate in citric acid.

Potassium Citrate (Natrium Citrate) (E332)

Definition

Potassium citrate is a mineral and electrolyte produced from evaporated citric acid. High amounts are naturally occurring in fruits such as bananas, melons, and dried prunes. Leafy vegetables, salmon, flounder, and poultry are also natural high-quality sources of potassium citrate. Potassium citrate is salty in taste, and for cooking purposes, it is available as a white, odorless, crystalline powder. Along with citric acid, potassium citrate is at times referred to as a "sour salt."

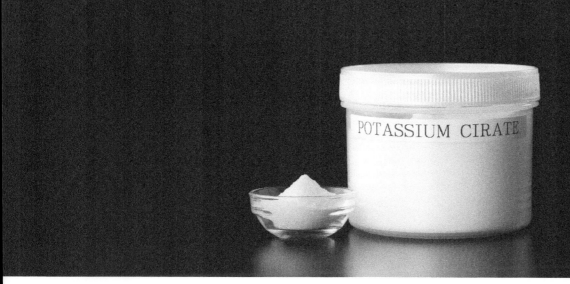

History

In 1702, Georg Ernst Stahl suspected the existence of potassium. In 1736, Henri-Louis Duhamel du Monceau established a difference between the element potassium and sodium salts. In 1807, Sir Humphry Davy successfully isolated potassium. But before its identification and theories of existence, potassium was mixed with ash and pigmented substances by Nigerian tribes to create textile dyes. Currently, the medical industry produces numerous potassium extract pills to fight various illnesses affecting the kidneys. Potassium citrate is also used in the fertilization of plants and is considered vital for a healthy life.

Culinary Uses

As a food additive, potassium citrate is used to regulate acidity and to enhance flavor. It is frequently incorporated into soft drinks such as 7UP and Sprite for acidity balance. Furthermore, potassium citrate works as an antioxidant, stabilizer, and emulsifier.

Note

Potassium citrate, similar to sodium citrate (see opposite), can be used as a sequestering agent to keep calcium ions from gelling too quickly.

Sodium Citrate (E331)

Definition

Sodium citrate is soluble in water but not in alcohol. It is produced by neutralizing citric acid through the use of sodium hydrate or sodium carbonate. There are three kinds of sodium citrate that differ in chemical formulations: monosodium citrate, disodium citrate, and trisodium citrate. Trisodium citrate is often referred to simply as sodium citrate, and it is this variety of sodium citrate that is most commonly used in food. It possesses a salty, mildly tart flavor and is available in a crystalline white powdered form. Sodium citrate is the salt of citric acid; it is also commonly known as sour salt.

Courtesy of Texturas – Solegraells and Le Sanctuaire

History

In 1911, sodium citrate was first used to manufacture processed cheese in Switzerland. By 1914 it was used as an anticoagulant in a blood transfusion by Albert Hustin and Luis Agote. Currently, beverage companies such as Ocean Spray and Red Bull use sodium citrate in their recipes to enhance product flavoring.

Culinary Uses

Sodium citrate and citric acid are both naturally found in foods and are both considered to be a safe ingredient to use in cooking. They are typically used to enhance flavor, or as a preservative in cooking. Sodium citrate is commonly used as an antioxidant and as a pH adjuster. Sodium citrate is employed as a flavoring agent in certain varieties of club sodas and citrus soft drinks and can also be found in energy drinks, to which it contributes the tartness in taste. It is also used as an emulsifier in dairy products such as processed cheese.

Notes

Sodium citrate can also be used to control acidity in gelatin desserts. In modern cooking applications, sodium citrate acts as a sequestering agent by attaching to calcium ions in liquid and keeping the solution from forming a gel too quickly.

Tartaric Acid (E334)

Definition

Tartaric acid is soluble in water and is an organic acid that shares its composition with four other acids: dextro, laevo, racemic, and mesotartaric acid. Found most abundantly in grapes, it also exists in bananas, tamarind, and other plant sources. Additionally, it is collected from wine barrels. Tartaric acid is sold as a crystalline white powder and is also known as tartar.

History

The early Roman and Greeks were familiar with tartar; the acid was noticed during the production of wine and later identified by Jabir ibn Hayyan around the year 800 CE. In 1769, Carl Wilhelm Scheele carried out further research on tartaric acid. Other scientists, such as Jean-Baptiste Biot in 1832 and Louis Pasteur in 1847, expanded research by noticing tartaric acid's ability to polarize light movement and by identifying the crystalline structure that defines this acid.

Culinary Uses

Tartaric acid is used in wine production for maintaining proper pH levels to keep unwanted bacteria from developing, while it also works to preserve the wine. It adds intense sourness or tart flavors to recipes that lack these aspects. It is natural to mention one of its potassium salt derivatives, cream of tartar, when discussing tartaric acid in food. Cream of tartar is an active ingredient in baking powder and is used to make confections such as taffy and hard candies. Cream of tartar acts as a leaving agent in baking, a stabilizer in meringues, and a creaming additive in candies and frosting.

Notes

Tartaric acid is also used as a cleaning agent for copper and as a polishing agent for other metals.

OTHERS

The label "others" is very useful in modern cuisine because it includes components such as minerals, enzymes, and food hydrocolloids with unique properties. These constituents are necessary in the development of recipes in combination with food hydrocolloids and essential techniques discussed in this book.

Calcium Chloride (E509)

Definition

Calcium chloride is a naturally occurring salt that results from calcium and chlorine combining and then evaporating. Calcium chloride can absorb and retain liquid and it is commonly found in a solid white form at room temperature, but it is also sold in flake, powder, and pebble forms.

History

Sir Humphry Davy discovered the calcium element in 1808 and was able to isolate calcium chloride while running electrical currents through other elements. It is very probable that people had been using calcium and calcium chloride in different applications before its classification. Currently, the processes involved in producing calcium chloride are refining limestone within natural brines or through a neutralization process using hydrochloric acid.

Culinary Uses

For commercial use, calcium chloride finds its way into a plethora of food items. Tofu production utilizes calcium chloride as a firming agent to curd soybeans, while the canned vegetable industry uses the same effect to maintain their products' texture rigidity. The low sodium content lends itself to pickling brines that maintain high salinity while keeping health concerns low. Sports drink and milk producers take advantage of calcium chloride by using it as a calcium and electrolyte fortifier after the pasteurization process has extracted the naturally occurring calcium. Brewers correct mineral deficiencies and adjust flavor profiles with calcium chloride, while cheese artisans use it to balance the natural calcium and protein in casein during cheese production. Lately, in modern professional kitchens calcium chloride is being used with alginate to produce "caviar" or spherical creations using purées and juices.

Notes

Calcium chloride must be kept in a tightly sealed, airtight container due to its ability to absorb and retain moisture. Common applications include brine for refrigeration plants, ice and dust control on roads, and desiccation. Precaution should be taken when handling calcium chloride in order to prevent skin rash or irritation. Chloride fumes are gradually emitted from this product and the material must be handled within a well-ventilated area.

Calcium Lactate (E327)

Definition

A crystalline powdered salt called *calcium lactate* is produced when calcium carbonate is combined with lactic acid. Milk itself has a highly soluble calcium salt and is a great source of calcium. Natural calcium is found in milk; and calcium is essential for proper bone growth and to stimulate muscle contractions.

History

In 1789, Carl Wilhelm Scheele isolated the acid found in sour milk, and the term "lactic" was applied to his discovery. During the 1800s, several scientists determined the existence of lactic acid in other organic tissues such as fresh milk, meat, and blood. The chemical formula for lactic acid was diagrammed in 1833, and this understanding of lactic acid has made the identification of calcium lactate possible in other food processes. Currently, calcium lactate is applied to the medical, food, and research industries.

Culinary Uses

Calcium lactate is a natural antioxidant. Application on cut fruits and vegetables to retain color and freshness is similar to the effects of calcium chloride, but it does not leave a bitter aftertaste. Its higher pH inhibits mold and maintains low bacteria levels during food processing. Within modern cuisine, calcium lactate is used in the reverse spherification process, which involves submerging a purée or liquid mixed with calcium lactate into a bath of sodium alginate.

Notes

Calcium lactate is combined with gluconate to prevent calcium lactate crystal formation when producing aged cheese. It is commonly added after the cheese has solidified and has been cut into portions. Calcium lactate can prevent tooth decay by remineralizing the tooth enamel, and it can also be used with calcium gluconate to form a calcium-rich product.

Maltodextrin

Definition

Maltodextrin is a water-soluble polysaccharide that is produced from cooking down the starch from products such as corn, potatoes, tapioca, and rice. Carbohydrates transform into maltodextrin when the dextrose equivalence is below 20. Its taste ranges from slightly sweet to almost no taste at all, and it has the ability to thicken fats. Maltodextrin is highly processed; its protein and gluten have been removed. It is found in a white and extremely lightweight powdered form.

History

Similar to many discoveries, an accident played a role in the discovery of dextrin. An 1821 fire in a potato factory in Dublin, Ireland, produced a brown-colored powder. In 1833, when starch was reduced in an iron pan by physician Jean-Baptiste Biot and chemist Jean-François Persoz, this substance was labeled as dextrin. The commercialization and mass production of dextrin by the AVEBE Company began in 1873.

Culinary Uses

As a food additive, maltodextrin adds savory or sweet coatings to fried snack foods. It is often blended with artificial sweeteners in various sodas and sports drinks. It is found in cheese spreads and salad dressings and is used as a coating for confections when mixed with glucose syrup. In addition, it is used as a bulking agent to increase the volume of foodstuff without obvious changes to its original flavor.

Courtesy of Texturas - Solegraells and Le Sanctuaire

Notes

Tapioca maltodextrin is used to dry fats into powders and to replace fats in cheese, ice cream, and dessert products. Fats should be liquefied, chilled, and mixed with a starting ratio of 60 percent fat to 40 percent tapioca maltodextrin. Mixing fat product and maltodextrin together in a Robot Coupe and passing it through a tamis will result in a finer and fluffier texture.

Monoglyceride (E472)

Definition

Monoglyceride, or *monoacylglycerol*, is a fatty acid derived from a glyceride ester. It is white to off-white in color and is available as a powder or in liquid form. Commercial monoglycerides are made from vegetables, from animal origins (cattle or pig), or can also be synthetically produced.

History

It was known that natural oils contain glycerin fatty acid ester. French chemist Marcellin Berthelot achieved a synthesized glycerin fatty acid ester from glycerine and fatty acids in 1854. Its commercial application was initiated as an additive to margarine during the 1930s.

Culinary Uses

Monoglyceride is used as an emulsifier, to help mix ingredients that would not otherwise blend well together (i.e., oil and water). It is often applied to ice creams, oils, chocolates, jams, and jellies to maintain their shape and to prevent dampening. Monoglycerides can also be found in bakery products, beverages, chewing gum, shortening, whipped toppings, margarine, and varieties of other confectionary items.

Notes

Monoglyceride can create foams at lower temperatures, but it has a tendency to collapse at higher temperatures. This foaming property aids in cake baking, while the collapsing or de-foaming property is utilized when making tofu or jelly. Monoglyceride also prevents candies and caramels from sticking and inhibits excess moisture from being absorbed and expelled. In restaurants, monoglyceride is often used to keep whipped cream and ice creams stable for service.

Transglutaminase (Activa)

Definition

Transglutaminase (often abbreviated as TG) is a food enzyme obtained from natural sources such as plants, animals, and microorganisms. It has the unique ability to improve the physical properties of various protein-containing foods. It is an enzyme that can catalyze the formation of a stable bond between atoms known as covalent bonds. When using transglutaminase, the bond between the amino acids lysine and glutamine within proteins become residual and are then created.

History

Food enzymes have been used for centuries in items such as beer, cheese, and wine. Research on transglutaminase has been conducted for its usage in food; it was first identified in 1959 and fully diagrammed in 1968. After testing more than 5,000 strands of microbes, researchers at the Japanese company Ajinomoto discovered a strain of soil bacteria, *Streptoverticillium mobaraense*, that produces large quantities of easily purified TG. Currently, Ajinomoto is the only producer of food grade TG, marketed under the brand name Activa.

Culinary Uses

Transglutaminase is used in processed meat production such as emulsified sausages and cooked ham. TG improves texture and increases connectivity, thus decreasing loss during the manufacturing process. TG minimizes product loss by allowing the chef to incorporate all parts of the animal into the production of meat and fish dishes. It also replaces binding agents such as salt and allows consumers to benefit from a lower salt intake. Additionally, TG can be used in bakery and milk products to improve texture. TG will also remain stable under heat and physical stress applications.

Transglutaminase

Notes

TG is used to bond meat together, similar to an adhesive. It can be used to bind meat mixtures such as sausages without casings, thicken egg yolks, strengthen dough mixtures, and increase yield in tofu production. In modern cooking applications, it also allows the possibility of inventing something unique, such as pasta made from a variety of proteins rather than starch, by binding together food items that would not normally be fused together. TG will bond within a few hours, but bond strength will be substantially higher after 4 or 5 hours of refrigeration. Note that highly acidic environments (below pH 4) can inhibit binding efficiency.

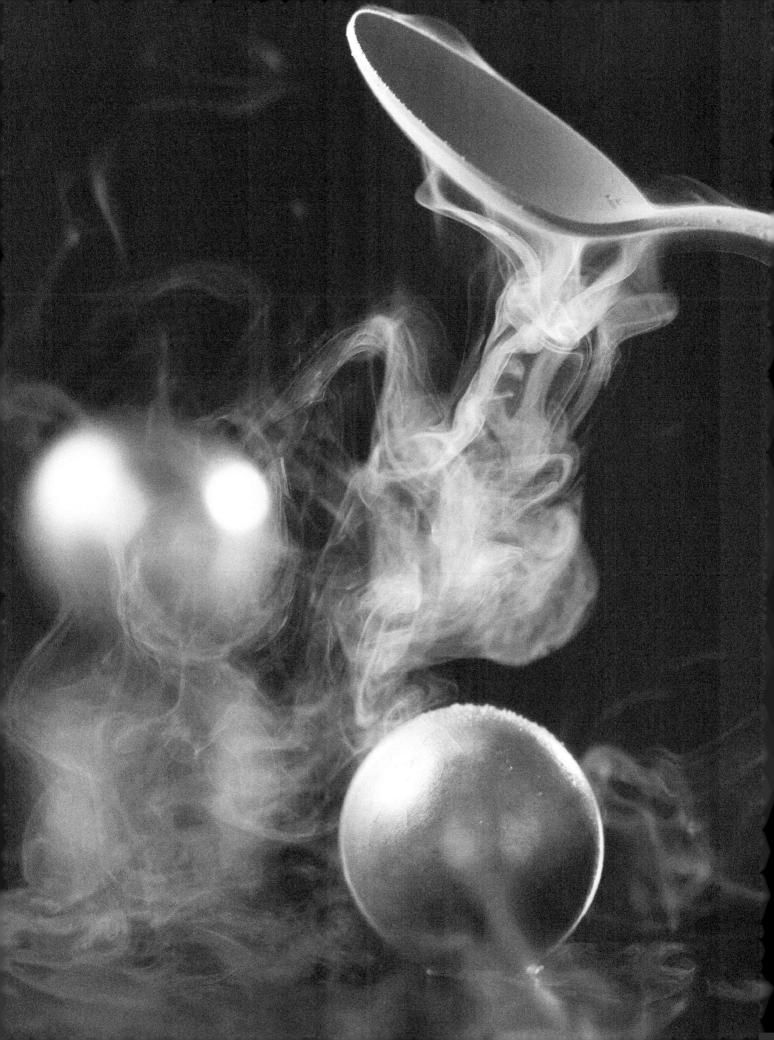

Overview of Techniques

After studying this chapter you should be able to:

- Explain the basic method of each technique
- Explain the basic functionality of each technique
- Name different cooking applications for each technique

7

This chapter presents a synopsis of the most commonly used techniques in the current modern culinary world. It provides a different approach to conventional methods, utilizing some of the most advanced equipment and tools found in modern kitchens.

The techniques described within this chapter will allow one to gain the knowledge to apply specific methodologies to ingredients and food hydrocolloids. The simple guidelines will serve as a foundation to create the standard for chefs in the kitchens.

Some of these methods are directly used in the test kitchen. Useful visuals will be provided in order to better explain the process in practical applications in Chapters 8 through 11. An alternative method will be provided for equipment not accessible in a given working kitchen. For instance, there are substitute methods to clarify stock in a traditional manner if a centrifuge is unavailable.

DRYING

Drying is a technique that has been used for thousands of years as a method to manipulate certain foods. It has seen many improvements, and devices have been created to control variations in texture, water content, and stability for an extended shelf life. As the techniques for drying are described, note the reasons why foods are dehydrated:

1. To concentrate flavors
2. To preserve the food
3. To create a casing that seals in moisture, as used in traditional baking
4. To create textures ranging from chewy to crispy

The next step is to recognize the ways that foods are dried. Several traditional drying techniques have been applied across time and cultures. Salt and sugar cures, the application of low heat, sun-drying processes, and the use of alcohol (via osmosis) are a few examples of the methods used for drying or dehydration in a practical or a home kitchen environment.

Basic dehydration is defined as the process of drying out a given food item through the use of heat only (including sun-drying). More recently, the drying techniques applied in laboratories and industrial kitchens have inspired chefs to utilize advanced equipment to attain the desired effects. Listed below are the most common techniques used and their outcomes:

Vacuum-drying: An alternative to achieve basic dehydration by applying pressure in a vacuum tube that alters the boiling point of the water. The temperature of the product is lowered, which also allows it to vaporize at a lower temperature without cooking or degrading the product being dehydrated. Commercial beef jerky is a common product of vacuum-drying; it enables a longer shelf life while concentrating the flavors developed during the curing process.

Spray-drying: This technique involves a shower misting device and a warmed or heated tube to disperse vapor-size droplets of a soluble liquid into a chamber tube. The mist from the head of a spraying device is comprised of tiny particles that dry quickly. The dehydrated product is collected in a compartment that is connected to the main chamber. The spray-drying technique concentrates the majority of the flavoring powders and is often used for commercial production of dried goods, such as milk powder, which is created by spray-drying raw milk into a crystalline powder form.

Freeze-drying/lyophilization: Completely freezing a product and then applying high-vacuum pressure allows only the ice crystals within the food to vaporize or sublimate. After pressure is applied, heat is used to accelerate the sublimation, then the use of low-temperature condenser plates removes the vaporized/sublimated moisture from the chamber. The freeze-drying technique requires a greater understanding of when foods are completely frozen, and recognition of the critical temperatures to correctly dry out the item completely. A properly freeze-dried food item does not require refrigeration in order to keep the product from spoiling. Freeze-drying is often utilized to create dried fruits in cereals and instant noodles, and most commonly to freeze-dry coffee.

> **Recipe Reference:** Freeze-Dried Fruit (Freeze-Dried Fruit served with Freeze-Dried Milk and Cereal)

Tips for proper drying:

1. Shape or cut the food to a suitable size so it will dry within the time needed or to achieve the desired texture.

2. Airflow must be kept at an even level in order for the product to dry uniformly and to speed up drying time when using common dehydrating techniques.

3. Avoid high temperatures that may lead to scorching and affect the flavor or the texture of the final dried product.

4. After drying, keep the food items in a dry environment and use desiccants such as silica gels. Store using vacuum packing or keep in an airtight container.

5. Pasteurization of the food item after drying is sometimes still required to remove any bacteria that may have formed during the drying process. Steaming, quick-blanching, and highly diluted bleach solutions can be used to attain proper sanitation levels.

These varied drying techniques allow an array of outcomes. Refining basic drying techniques while looking to apply one of the more advanced methods to the same product may help refine the process by achieving a higher level of production value.

> **Recipe Reference:** Perfect Huevos Rancheros Serve with Hot Bean Foam, Dehydrated Jalapeño and Tortilla Powders

ESSENCE AND FLAVOR EXTRACTION

The aromatic qualities of foods can perhaps be as important as the actual flavor. The sense of smell greatly affects how a person can react to the taste that will follow after eating the item such as smelling coffee before tasting it—what begins as a sweet aromatic is usually followed by bold, tannic taste and enhancing the overall sensory experience. Harnessing these aromas and applying them to oil concentrates and extracts allows further use of flavor-layering perceptions.

Several techniques have been developed and refined to isolate the essence of flavors of aromatics:

Ingredient		Prefreezing Temperature before Freeze Dry Stage		Freezing— First Stage				Heating— Second Stage		Total Drying Time (hour)	Example of Use
				Holding Tray		Condenser		Holding Tray			
		F°	C°	F°	C°	F°	C°	F°	C°		
Meat	Beef	-13	-25	-4	-20	-49	-45	86	30	4 to 8	instant consomeé, soup, flavor powder, noodle
	Pork	-13	-25	-4	-20	-49	-45	86	30	6 to 12	instant consomeé, soup, flavor powder, noodle
Poultry	Chicken	-13	-25	-4	-20	-49	-45	86	30	6 to 12	instant consomeé, soup, flavor powder, noodle
Dairy	Eggs	-40	-40	-31	-35	-76	-60	140	60	12	Instant soup, instant noodle
	Milk	-4	-20	5	-15	-40	-40	158	70	12 to 16	Instand milk
Seafood	Lobster	5	-15	14	-10	-31	-35	68	20	120	instant consomeé, soup, flavor powder
	Scallops	5	-15	14	-10	-31	-35	68	20	8 to 48	instant consomeé, soup, flavor powder
Vegetables & Fruits	Fruits	-49	-45	-40	-40	-85	-65	86	30	4 to 64	cereal, freeze-dry package fruits, yogurt topping
	Green leaves	-13	-25	-13	-25	-58	-50	104	40	12	Instant soup, instant noodle
	Vegetables	-22	-30	-13	-25	-58	-50	104	40	4 to 24	Instant soup, instant noodle
Others	Noodles	-4	-20	5	-15	-40	-40	158	70	12	Instant noodle
	Stocks, broths, and sauces	-4	-20	5	-15	-40	-40	158	70	8 to 36	Powdered stock

Steam distillation: Steam is applied to aromatics, which are then filtered to a cold tank, creating condensation and allowing two types of the essence (known as distillates and essential oils) to be collected. The first type, distillates, is a water-soluble solution, while the residuals of the aromatic flavor collect on the bottom of the tank. The second type isolates essential oils that will not dissolve in water, and has a higher concentration of aromatic compounds. The negative aspect to steam distillation is the amount of heat that is applied, which may change the overall flavor perception of the essence. Spices are an ideal ingredient to use because they can attribute their aromatic properties to this process quite readily and more efficiently than fresh ingredients.

Solvent extraction: Applying water-rejecting solvents such as ether or hexane will cause the oils of the ingredient to be expelled, creating a pasty, almost solid product called concrete or oleoresin. These concrete or oleoresin substances contain the concentrated resins of the aromatic compounds, which are then washed with an absolute alcohol (ethyl alcohol). This isolates the aromatic flavor and then filters it to create a solution with the flavor infused within the alcohol. This technique eliminates the need to apply heat, hence, keeping the original essence intact.

Enfleurage: This is a technique that uses fats or oils to absorb the aromatic essence of plant-based ingredients. The process involves a single aromatic or a crushed mix of aromatics mixed with unscented fat. The fat is melted and then strained after several days of applying fresh aromatics to the original batch. Absolute alcohol is applied, followed by distillation or evaporation to isolate the desired essence. This is perhaps the oldest technique in fragrance extraction; however, although it is very labor intensive, it is a direct way to extract essence flavors.

All of these methods are reproduced efficiently with laboratory equipment now often used by chefs. While specialized equipment is costly, it provides less labor-intensive methods to perform specific needs with consistent results.

All aromatics and essences play an important role in how food is perceived. Even the most basic of extraction techniques (such as placing fresh rosemary in olive oil) can create an expanded flavor profile. Caution should be applied when creating such essences due to the botanical nature of most compounds. Allergies, adverse reactions, and toxins should be carefully reviewed when creating any botanical-based essence.

Recipe Reference: Ras el Hanout Essence Gelatin Served with Wakame Granité

Clarifying

The classic approach to clarifying liquids such as stocks involves creating a raft by whipping a protein such as egg whites or meat purée into the stock and cooking it slowly. The raft gathers fatty clouding agents and leaves a clearer stock below the floating raft. The clear liquid is then ladled out of a hole made in the center of the raft.

Clarity is sought not only in stocks but also in juices, soups, and sauces. Clarity in modern kitchens is achieved by several different means. Food hydrocolloids such as methylcellulose and other gelling agents allow chefs to clarify liquids by two different approaches.

The first technique involves using methylcellulose and is similar to the classic approach of creating a raft. First, the food hydrocolloid is whipped into a foam state, and then it is mixed with the liquid to create the raft. It is then slowly cooked before ladling out the clarified liquid.

The second method is a gel-clarifying technique that applies gelling food hydrocolloids such as gellan gum, agar, or gelatin. These food hydrocolloids are dissolved in the liquid to be clarified and then cooled or frozen. Then the mixture is warmed or thawed, allowing the gelled liquid to release the clarified liquid. The cooled or frozen liquid is placed in a cheesecloth or strainer, and the gelling food hydrocolloid clings to the sediments while the clear liquid is gathered below the strainer in a process known as syneresis. This gel-clarifying technique requires syneresis to occur at a temperature warm enough to release the liquid but also cool enough to keep the gelatin gelled. Gel clarification can take days to finish, but it is an inexpensive alternative when compared to using a centrifuge machine.

The centrifuge allows the chef to utilize lab equipment in order to separate sediments within liquids. The centrifuge utilizes the force of gravity and centripetal force to push down and separate the denser materials within a liquid, allowing the concentrated clear liquids to be accessible on the upper layer. The use of the centrifuge begins with loading a given liquid that requires clarification into specialized canisters. These canisters are then placed in the designated rotor holders, and a time and rpm (revolutions per minute) setting is selected. The resulting liquid will be concentrated, with layers of differentiating density, as well as having pristine clarity. The variety of liquids that can be clarified in a centrifuge is endless and can range from juices to stocks to butter to chocolate. The precision of clarity resulting from the centrifuge is equivalent to and at times better than that obtained by traditional clarifying methods.

> **Recipe Reference:** Flavor Gels: Lemon, Cola, Coconut, Orange, Plum, Basil, Chocolate, Salsa, and Strawberry

FLAVOR ENHANCEMENTS

Flavor enhancement is essential in any type of cooking. It heightens and prolongs flavors by generating an overall flavor experience. Flavor is the sensory impression determined by the combination of taste, smell, texture, sight, temperature, and even sound. Modern cooking allows the chef to play with the customer's predetermined thoughts. For instance, melon caviar takes the customer's taste expectation and completely surprises the palate by releasing concentrated flavors within a unique vessel. These illusions, combined with the techniques introduced in this book, can offer a unique and unforgettable dining experience. This chapter introduces different applications and techniques to bring out the possibilities of flavor in contemporary cooking.

Smoking

Smoking was originally used to preserve food by dehydrating the food product through utilizing the antimicrobial and antioxidant property of smoke to prevent the development of pathogenic microorganisms. The most traditional method involves the use of wood chips, burning them to create smoke. After the creation of modern refrigeration, smoking was used less commonly to preserve foodstuff and more to add aromatic flavor. The following are a few examples of new smoking methods that do not require the use of fire:

- **Electrostatic smoking** involves smoking an item using infrared radiation. This technique shortens the time normally needed to smoke fish or other meat.
- A **smoking gun** only adds a final aroma and atmosphere to a dish that has been previously smoked. It is often used to garnish a smoked dish.
- **Liquid smoke** (distilled smoke vapor) can be added to almost any braise or sauce to simulate the smoking technique without the act of actual smoking.

These new methods can be used in cooler temperatures without drying or cooking the food. Smoked salt or smoked spices can be used to add smoky flavor without using actual fire. They are also used with products that cannot usually be smoked (e.g., butter, raw seafood, liquids, and ice cream). These smoking methods will not result in a strong color or texture change compared with conventional smoking techniques.

What seems like a simple idea or technique is in actuality a very detailed and precise science in modern cuisine. The following is provided to guide any chef to make the correct choices when smoking.

1. **Choosing the food item to be smoked:** Factors such as thickness, weight, and fat content can affect which type of smoking method to utilize. Items with low fat content will not absorb the smoke flavor as readily as food items with high fat content. Larger cuts of meat, for example, require a lengthier amount of time for the smoke to penetrate to the center, while small absorbent mushrooms require only short exposure to smoke.

2. **Method of smoking:** Hot, cold, dry, or wet are a few choices available when preparing to smoke foods. The temperature of the smoke determines which flavors will be imparted to the food. For example, if the desired effect is to flavor food but not cook it, then the cold-smoke technique is the best option. Hot smoke will ultimately cook the food item, which will result in less smoking time and a more direct method of cooking (such as in a barbecue pit). Moisture control in the product is also an imperative factor to consider. An already dry piece of meat will not only become drier and tough but also will not effectively capture the smoke vapor flavors that are emitted.

   Liquid smoke (distilled smoke essence) is another method applied in industrial and commercial kitchens alike and is commonly used for convenience and consistency.

3. **Wood selection:** The source and species of wood can provide deep flavor profiles when used for smoking. The chosen wood variety can be bought in pellet, chip, or natural raw form. It is important to note that the wood must undergo a complete drying process before usage.

   Recipe Reference: Puffed Chicken Skin

Herbs, Spices, and Condiments

It is common to use herbs and spices to add rich flavor and/or to minimize undesirable flavor in cooking. Culinary herbs are usually distinguished from vegetables because they are used in small quantities and their purpose is to provide flavor rather than to be directly consumed as food. Spices, on the other hand, are dried aromatic parts of plant seeds, roots, pods, buds, and bark. The purpose of spices is to add flavor and color through the use of trivial amounts that are irrelevant to nutritional value.

Herbs and spices (including salt and garlic) can easily overpower the flavor of the main product during the sous-vide process. This is in part because the sous-vide process can infuse flavors very efficiently; thus, dried powders usually provide a better result. Herb- and spice-infused oil used for finishing can be an alternative approach to direct use, while salt and pepper can be added after cooking. Alcohol used for flavor enhancement should be well cooked by either sautéing, boiling, or flambéing beforehand to avoid an uneven finish due to alcohol not evaporating during the sous-vide cooking process or a possible metallic aftertaste.

Marinating

Marinating is the process of soaking food in a seasoned liquid prior to cooking. Marinating has two main functions: to tenderize the ingredient and to infuse flavor. Marinating liquids can range from simple to complex based on a given recipe. In terms of equipment, using the vacuum sealer to help marinate expedites the process while keeping the food safe from external bacteria. Adding an acid to the marinade can tenderize meats by breaking down connective tissues. In addition, some foods containing certain enzymes (e.g., papaya, pineapple, onion, fig, and kiwi) are often used to tenderize meats as an acid alternative. In general, vacuum-pack pouches are useful for keeping the food covered and allowing the content to be easily refrigerated.

Dry Rubs and Paste

Dry spices and herbs to infuse flavor to food can also be applied instead of using a liquid marinade. The thickness of the rub applied on the food and the amount of time that it is left to set determine the intensity of the flavor. Water, oil, or lemon juice is added to the dry herbs and spices for a paste or a wet rub, which better adheres to the surface of the product than a dry rub. For the best result, apply the rub or paste evenly and with enough pressure to penetrate the protein. After the rub or paste is applied, it should be covered and kept refrigerated. Vacuum-pack pouches or bags can be convenient when applying rubs to speed up the flavoring process and provide a barrier against bacteria. Dry rubs are typically used for grilling, pan-frying, or broiling cooking methods, while wet rubs are typically applied just before cooking in order to have the greatest impact on flavor. Food items that have been wet-rubbed can also be grilled, broiled, or pan-fried.

Brining/Osmosis

Brining was originally a method used to preserve meats, fish, poultry, and vegetables by soaking in highly concentrated salt solutions. It is now widely used for food preparation to add flavor, tenderize meats, and help retain moisture in the product. The use of smaller quantities of salt mixed with sugar and other spices and herbs is the base for brines that permeate the food item with flavor by a process called osmosis. The process may take an extended amount of time, depending on the type and size of the food intended for brining. Brines should be kept cold, both before immersing the food and also during the brining process. Instead of saltwater, any other variety of liquid (e.g., fruit juice, beer, or wine) can be used as a brining liquid. Since the brining process often determines the flavor bases, controlling brining time and liquids is essential for a successful result.

Powders

The creation of powders is a new approach that is applied in modern cooking. Powders are commonly characterized as having flavors that are dried to a dust form and then sprinkled or served alongside food as a garnish. There are several modern ways of preparing powders.

Maltodextrin: An innovative way to prepare powders is the use of hydrocolloids to mix an oil-based liquid with maltodextrin (physiochemical modified starch). The oil and maltodextrin combine until a powder of preferred consistency is achieved. The end result is a powder with intense flavor.

> **Recipe Reference:** Ants on a Log Served with Nutella Powder, Caesar Salad Soup Served with Bacon Powder and Sous Vide Quail Egg

Freeze-Dried Powders: A flavorful powder without discoloration or loss in taste can be created by removing all the liquid from a food product by using a freeze dryer that applies high pressure to food. (Refer to freeze drying/lypholization in "Drying Techniques.")

> **Recipe Reference:** Yuzu Marshmallow Served with Freeze-Dried Beet Powder

Liquid Nitrogen Powders: By adding LN2 to fresh food, the ingredients are immediately frozen without loss of aroma and flavor. The product can be ground into a fine powder with a food processor after freezing. Pastes or sauces can be easily created by adding oil or water to these powders without loss of nutritional value and flavor. This process preserves the nutrients and flavors of the product by instantly freezing the food item because of the extremely low temperature of LN2.

> **Recipe Reference:** Sugar Candy Ball Served with White Chocolate Powder, Olive Oil Gelatin Served with Beet Air and Chorizo Powder

EMULSIONS

Extensively utilized within the kitchen, emulsions are characterized as two types: water in oil (W/O) and oil in water (O/W). Common examples are mayonnaise (a liquid-in-oil emulsion) and solid butter (an oil-in-liquid emulsion). In modern cuisine, emulsions are highly advantageous because they can adjust mouthfeel, control viscosity of liquids, and combine products that would not ordinarily be combined, to create a sauce, dressing, or vinaigrette. The desire to sustain a suspended emulsion for hours, days, or weeks for extended shelf-life has led to the merging of science and food. This collaboration of new food hydrocolloids and stabilizers developed into what are called "surfactants" (also known as surface acting agents or simply emulsifiers). Surfactants create a bond between the ever-repelling natures of oils and liquids. Using the correct emulsifier while making an emulsion can lead to the creation of a truly unique concoction.

In general, restaurants have normally utilized one stage of an emulsion: the primary emulsion (e.g., beurre blancs and vinaigrettes). However, the growing relationship between science, technology, and food has caused a second stage of emulsions to become common. This secondary stage ensures that the oil and liquid parts are broken down into minute droplets, thus creating longer-lasting emulsions using modern equipment designed for this process.

Recipe Reference: Farmer's Market with Eggless Pistachio Mayonnaise, Caviar Tempura Served with Instantly Frozen Crème Fraîche

TABLE 7.2: COMMON EMULSIONS: OIL-IN-WATER (O/W) AND WATER-IN-OIL (W/O)

Ingredient	Type	Emulsifier or Stabilizer
Beurre blanc	O/W	Casein from butter
Butter	W/O	Casein from dairy
Chocolate	W/O	Lecithin and/or casein (from milk powder), sometimes polyglycerol polyricinoleate
Egg yolk	O/W	Lecithin
Espresso crema	O/W	Coffee polysaccharides
Hollandaise and mayonnaise	O/W	Lecithin from egg yolk
Ice cream	O/W	Casein, egg yolk, semisolid fat droplets
Margarine and shortening	W/O	Monoglyceride, lecithin
Milk	O/W	Casein
Soda drink	O/W	Arabic gum
Vinaigrette	W/O	Polysaccharides and proteins

TABLE 7.3: EMULSIFIERS

Hydrocolloid	Examples of Common Use	Observations
Agar	Meringue, icing, fondant, dairy (ice cream, cream, milk, yogurt)	Works in wide range of viscosity
Arabic gum	Soda drink, syrup, flavored oil, pasta	Great emulsifying ability
Carrageenans	Dairy, meat, dressings	Good for cold dairy application
Gelatin	Dairy, yogurt, confectionary	Works mainly in cold temperatures
Gellan gum	Soy milk, beverage, filling, glaze	Loses ability to emulsify in acid medium
Guar gum	Dressings, dairy (cheese, ice cream, yogurt), soups	Not recommended for use in high concentrations
Konjac	Seasoning powder, sauce, fat substitutes	Works in hot and cold temperatures
Lecithin	Mayonnaise, hollandaise, margarine	Found naturally in egg yolk and soy
Methylcellulose	Ice cream, filling, dressings, sauces	Stable at high temperatures
Monoglyceride	Eggless mayonnaise, chocolate, ice creams	Shows good stability
Sodium alginate	Sausage, meat, dairy, sauce	Good for dairy application in low concentrations
Xanthan gum	Mayonnaise, dressings, sauce	Works in hot and cold temperatures, with wide range of viscosity

FOAM, AIR, BUBBLE: GAS IN WATER

An invaluable technique in kitchens today is the creation of foams that provide the chef with innumerable ways to present flavor, textures, and aromas. Foam in its most basic elements is both a liquid and a gas. The variation of these two ingredients defines its unique characteristics. What holds true for the majority of foams are that smaller bubbles created by the gas produce greater structural integrity. When the gas is created or introduced into the liquid, two particular structures are at play: the continuous liquid surrounding the gas and also the dispersed element (most commonly air). To stabilize foam, several agents can be added to support the structure: fats, proteins, gums, starches, and surfactants are examples of common types of foam stabilizers.

The traditional technique of foam creations customarily involves a whisk or the introduction of oven heat to a batter (steam is released when the water evaporates, as in a soufflé). Recently, a surge in techniques to develop frothy creations has led to the development and usage of several devices such as immersion blenders, whipping siphons, rotor stator homogenizers, vacuum chambers, and electric aquarium air pumps.

Types of Foams

It is important to understand the different classifications of foams before setting up to create a product.

Froths, Airs, or Bubbles: Can be wet or dry, depending on the foaming agent, but are usually considered coarse in texture. Commonly used to balance rich sauces with a light sharp flavor, or to add a dimension of texture that only popping gasses can provide.

Light Foams: Possess a greater mouthfeel and can hold a peak compared to froths, airs, or bubbles. Flavor can be added without considerable increase of substance to the dish.

Thick Foams: Maintain their airy texture, but also have a greater visual presence when served on the plate. The bubble structure is very dense and enhances the overall mouthfeel of the foam.

Set Foams: Depending on the selected stabilizer, these foams are set by either heating or chilling the mixture. The liquid between the bubbles solidifies by upholding the bubbles in place and allowing prolonged foaming reactions to occur.

> **Recipe Reference:** Caviar Tempura Served with Instantly Frozen Crème Fraîche; Hot Lobster Tokoroten Served with Sous Vide Lobster, Truffle Oil Encapsulation, and Pernod Air; Hot Truffle Gel Served with Sous Vide Sea Bass and Hot Corn Foam; Perfect Huevos Rancheros Served with Hot Bean Foam, Dehydrated Jalapeño and Tortilla Powders, and Salsa Gel; Olive Oil Gelatin Served with Beet Air and Chorizo Powder

Hydrocolloid	Foaming Agent	Foam Stabilizer	Application	Recipes
Agar	x	x	Hot foam, fluid gel foam, light foam	Perfect Huevos Rancheros (Hot Bean Foam)
Arabic gum		x	Set foam	Yuzu Marshmallow
Carrageenans	x	x	Hot foam, thick foam, works well with dairy	Caviar Tempura (Instantly Frozen Crème Fraîche)
Gelatin	x		Light foam, cold foam, set foam	Frozen Macarons
Gellan gum (LA)	x	x	Hot and cold foam	n/a
Guar gum	x	x	Hot foam, works well in acid mediums	n/a
Konjac		x	Hot and cold foam	n/a
Lecithin	x		Hot and cold foam	Olive Oil Gelatin (Beet Air)
Locust bean gum		x	Hot and cold foam	n/a
Methylcellulose	x	x	Hot foam	n/a
Pectin (HM, LM)		x	Hot foam, works well with dairy	n/a
Sodium alginate		x	Hot and cold foam, works well in high-calcium medium	n/a
Xanthan gum	x	x	Light foam, thick foam	Frozen Macaron, Hot Truffle Gel (Hot Corn Foam)

GELLING

Creating gels is possibly one of the most-utilized techniques in the kitchen, varying from the reduction of collagen in animal-based stocks to more advanced applications of clarifying these stocks. Gelling is a classical technique that has progressed into an ever-refining practice due to a better understanding of its nature and its tendencies. The following are explanations and a brief definition of several types of gelling techniques.

Cold Gels: Examples range from panna cotta to gelatin molds. As the name implies, these gels are cold and result in a refreshing yet concentrated flavor. A cold gel can be clear, cloudy, or have suspended items within it.

> **Recipe Reference:** Foie Royale, Hot Lobster Tokoroten, Jaleas, Konnyaku Jelly, Olive Oil Gelatin, Ras el Hanout Essence Gelatin

Hot Gels: These gels are made possible by the study of food hydrocolloids that resist heat, such as xanthan gum, agar, carrageenan, and methylcellulose. Hot gels allow flavors to be enjoyed at warm or hotter temperatures. In addition, they can alter how foods are identified and viewed, which allows chefs the ability to express flavor-texture combinations with a new spectrum.

> **Recipe Reference:** Fried Béarnaise, Hot Truffle Gel

Serving Temp	Texture	Firmness	Gelling Hydrocolloids	Observations	Recipes
Cold	Elastic	Very Soft	160 Bloom gelatin	Not stable in room temperature, recommended to keep cold, good flavor release	
			Iota carrageenan Kappa carrageenan	Highly stable in dairy application	
			HA gellan Kappa carrageenan	Stable, springiness texture	
		Soft	160 Bloom gelatin	Not stable in room temperature, recommended to keep cold, good flavor release	
			Iota carrageenan Kappa carrageenan	Works well in dairy applications	
		Firm	Locust bean gum Agar Xanthan gum	Texture and mouthfeel is like gelatin but doesn't melt in the mouth	
			160 Bloom gelatin	Not stable in room temperature, recommended to keep cold	
			HA gellan	Shows springiness in texture	Olive oil gelatin
			LM pectin Calcium gluconate	Firm texture develops when made with liquid of 18° Brix	
			Iota carrageenan Kappa carrageenan	Highly stable in dairy application	
		Very Firm	160 Bloom gelatin	Not stable in room temperature, recommended to keep cold, good flavor release	Red wine jelly
			LA Gellan Modified starch (Tapioca)	Stable to high temperatures	Fried béarnaise (before fried)
			Konjac	Highly stable, chewy mouthfeel	Konnyaku jelly
			Sucrose HM pectin Citric or tartaric acid	Firm texture develops when made with liquid of 75° Brix	Jaleas (pâté de fruit)
	Brittle	Firm	Low-acyl gellan High-acyl gellan	Highly stable	
			Kappa carrageenan Pottacium citrate	Transparency increased with sugar	Beer gel
			Iota carrageenan 160 Bloom gelatin	Creamy mouthful, show stability	Foie Royal
			Agar	Works well with all liquids but tends to weep over time	
			180 Bloom gelatin	Not stable in room temperature, recommended to keep cold, good flavor release	Ras el hanout gel
			Locust bean gum Kappa carrageenan	Highly stable when used with dairy liquids	
		Very Firm	Agar	Works well with all liquids but tends to weep over time	
			Low-acyl gellan	50% alcohol tolerant	

Serving Temp	Texture	Firmness	Gelling Hydrocolloids	Observations	Recipes
Hot	Very Elastic	Soft	Xanthan gum Low-acyl gellan	Greasy and creamy texture	
			Sorbitol High-acyl gellan Agar	Firm and stable	
			High-acyl gellan Xanthan gum Low-acyl gellan	Creamy mouthfeel	
	Elastic	Soft	Xanthan gum Locust bean gum Low-acyl gellan	Highly stable, clear	
			High-acyl gellan Low-acyl gellan	Less brittle, calcium will help to gel	
	Elastic	Firm	Locus bean gum Agar	Not recommended for dairy gels; best with non-dairy gels	Gel noodles
			Methylcellulose	Gelation occurs when heated	Hot truffle gel
			High-acyl gellan Low-acyl gellan Xanthan gum	Springiness in texture	
	Elastic	Very Firm	Konjac	Thermo-irreversible; highly stable; can be flavored after gelled	Konnyaku jelly
	Semi Brittle	Firm	Agar Guar gum	Resistant, clear	
			Iota carageenan Agar	Creamy mouthfeel	Foie Royal
			High-acyl gellan Agar	Firm; cohesive; thermo-irreversible	
	Brittle	Very Firm	Agar	Syneresis tends to occur over time	
			Low-acyl gellan High-acyl gellan	Thermo-irreversible; firm and clear	

Coating Gels: This classic technique is being rechanneled due to new food hydrocolloids that allow better viscosity–flow control. The effects of warmer temperatures when creating hot coating gels can enhance the experienced aromas. Typically, coating gels are used to glaze and preserve an item, such as a whole fish or a roulade that can be served in its entirety.

Fluid Gels: This technique utilizes the effect of shear thinning, normally by agitating (shearing) a set gel to the point that the gel is no longer solid but has the viscosity of a liquid. Agar, carrageenan, and gellan gum are often used to create fluid gels. Other applications involve suspending small particles such as chopped herbs in a fluid gel. Fluid gels are capable of being hot or cold depending on the applied hydrocolloid.

Gelling has evolved from simple gelatin powders or sheets to incorporate natural hydrocolloids that allow greater variety and control that was not previously available. In order to maximize the quality of the envisioned product, one must consciously apply these hydrocolloids to create intended results.

Recipe Reference: Flavor Gels

Temperature	Gelling Hydrocolloids	Observations	Recipes
Cold	Agar	Highly stable in most liquids; clear appearance	Flavor gels (Fluid Gels)
	160 Bloom gelatin	Clear; smooth mouthfeel; elastic	n/a
	Iota Carrageenan	Can achieve higher viscosity in dairy application; can be used with kappa carrageenan	n/a
	Kappa Carrageenan	Can achieve higher viscosity in dairy application; can be used with iota carrageenan	n/a
Hot	Agar	Losses ability to gel with acidic liquids	n/a
	Low-acyl gellan	Acidic liquids may require a sequestrant to hydrate	n/a
	Agar Xanthan gum	Xanthan gum aids stability in acidic liquids	n/a

THICKENING

Overall, "thickening" is a broad term used to describe the effects of food hydrocolloids on viscosity. Thickening can be seen in emulsions (e.g., vinaigrettes, or in sauces made with yolks such as hollandaise), yet emulsions and thickeners generally both emulsify but are viewed as separate processes in the kitchen.

Methods or Types of Thickening

Starches: The most basic Western thickening application involves producing a roux. This flour and fat mixture is practical for thickening sauces and soups. Other starches such as potato, corn, and tapioca typically provide the same functions but vary in the final taste and texture.

Modified Starches: With advanced control of product design, starch manufacturers are personalizing starches to transform oil, egg yolk, or milk into powders. These powders are then rehydrated with a liquid and can provide thickening qualities.

   Recipe Reference: Ants on a Log, Caesar Salad Soup

Oil: Oil is generally used in thickening of dressings. Although the majority of oil relies on water to thicken, oil can also thicken other fats or oils. Two oils that have different melting temperatures (e.g., cocoa butter and peanut oil) will combine and thicken to create a mixture that will solidify at lower temperatures.

New Food Hydrocolloids: One impressive trait of food hydrocolloids is the fact that cooking is not required and often requires far lesser quantities than those needed to achieve the same results with flour. Food hydrocolloids such as xanthum gum offer the ability to maintain a thick consistency at varying temperatures. With proper dispersion and hydration of food hydrocolloids, thickening can be realized very efficiently and effectively.

Name	Source	Gel Appearance	Application	Recipes
Flojel 60/Flojel 65	Corn	Hazy	Confectionary	n/a
Novation Prima 600	Corn	Hazy	Frozen and refrigerated entrée, soup or dessert, dairy product and fruit preparation	n/a
Pure-Cote B790	Corn	Clear	Film-forming	Ants on a Log (Celery Film)
Maltrin	Corn	Clear	Bakery, beverage, candy, purée	n/a
N-Zorbit M	Tapioca	Hazy	Oil powder	Caesar Salad Soup (Bacon Powder) Ants on a Log (Nutella Powder)
Ultra-Sperse 3	Tapioca	Hazy	Instant pudding, sauce, fruit filling, and instant Bavarian cream	Fried Béarnaise
Ultra-Tex 8	Tapioca	Hazy	Pastry filling and Bavarian cream	n/a
Wondra	Barley malt, wheat	Hazy	Purée, sauce	n/a

Gel: Thickening is possible without creating a solid gel with the correct ratio of liquid to gelling agent. When gelatin is added to warmed pastry cream and then cooled, the result creates a more stable and thickened pastry cream that can hold its shape when piped. This is beneficial when the cream needs to be held on display for an extended amount of time. It also reduces the need for costly cream and extra egg yolks to maintain the firmness of the cream.

Dairy: Whipped or plain cream can thickened (depending on the liquid that is being added) and is a practical method to thicken and reduce a solution. Butter is clearly the better choice when making beurre blancs because it relies on the fat solids to draw out the liquid and create viscosity and a lasting mouthfeel.

Thickening demands balance and technique, which requires practice and familiarity with the products used to thicken a product. A common result of an unbalanced recipe yields products that exudes liquid from within in a process known as syneresis (which can occur over time). This negative result can be avoided by the addition of a stabilizer to control the weakening nature of the original thickener. Gums such as guar gum, locust bean gum, and xanthan gum are typically used to avoid syneresis.

Recipe Reference: Beer Pork and Cotton Candy Cooked in the Gastrovac; Fried Béarnaise Served with Sous Vide Beef Steak and Soufflé Potato; Kuromame Bean Ice Cream; Puffed Chicken Skin Served with Red Wine Sauce and Sous Vide Chicken; Stained Glass Served with Cucumber Sorbet; Uni Caviar-Dashi Broth Served with Seaweed Cracker

SPHERIFICATION/ENCAPSULATION

Spherification or encapsulation is one of most popular techniques in modern cooking applications. The purpose is to create a sphere or a droplet enclosed in an edible capsule. In most cases, a thin layer of gel or film formation is created to enclose the sphere. It can be created in different sizes and can range in resemblance from fish eggs to olives to egg yolks.

The most common applications and associated typical setups are listed below:

Direct Spherification: The most common process involves mixing a flavored liquid solution with sodium alginate and, if necessary, a calcium-reducing sequestrant. This mixture is then dropped, dipped, or spooned into a solution containing a calcium product, such as calcium chloride or calcium lactate. The droplet comes in contact with the calcium and causes the outer skin of the alginate solution to harden, thus containing the liquid inside the created sphere. The length of time that the sphere is in the calcium solution determines the hardness of the outer shell and the cooking process within the capsule. A fresh water bath is used to rinse away the calcium and to slow the hardening process. Another form of spherification utilizes a solution involving gellan gum being dropped into a highly ionic water solution or into a low methyl pectin mixture with a calcium salt bath.

Reverse Spherification: This is a relatively new technique where the calcium is added to the flavored liquid and placed into a bath of water and sodium alginate or another gelling food hydrocolloid. The benefit of this method is the ability to keep the outer skin gelled, while the interior aspect is not affected by the gelling food hydrocolloid.

> **Recipe Reference:** Blood Orange Spheres (Sodium Alginate), Uni Caviar, Olives and Cheese (Xanthan Gum)

Cryospherification: Used to freeze a liquid in a mold in order to have better control of the shape and size of the created sphere. This frozen liquid is then dropped into a bath, which creates a gelled exterior while it starts to thaw. While reverse technique is typically applied, direct spherification can also be prepared for cryospherification.

TABLE 7.8: SPHERIFICATION

Method	For the Spherification*		For the Setting Bath*		Observations	Recipes
	Hydrocolloid	Usage	Hydrocolloid	Usage		
Direct	Sodium alginate	1.0%	Calcium chloride	0.5%	Xanthan gum can be used to thicken liquid to achieve even spheres.	Blood Orange Spheres; Uni Caviar
			Calcium gluconate	2.5%		
	Iota carrageenan	2.0%	Potassium phosphate	5.0%	Can also be made in reverse method.	n/a
	Low-acyl gellan	0.2%	Calcium gluconate	6%	Recommended to use in low-acid liquid with medium calcium concentration. By freezing in a mold, any shape can be created in a water bath at 176°F/80°C. Can also be made in reverse method.	n/a
	Sodium hexametaphosphate	0.1%	Lactic acid	0.1%		
Reverse	Calcium lactate	3.0%	Sodium alginate	0.5%	Use sodium citrate when liquid is acidic or high in calcium. Xanthan gum can be used to thicken liquid to achieve even spheres.	Olives and Cheese (Green Olive Sphere)
			Sodium citrate (optional)	1.2%		
	Calcium lactate	5.0%	Low methyl (LM) pectin	2.0%	Direct spherification method can be used.	n/a

*Proper hydration is recommended for both liquid and water bath.

FREEZING/CARBONATION

Commonly abbreviated as LN2, liquid nitrogen is simply nitrogen in a liquid state. Over 78 percent of atmospheric air consists of nitrogen: a colorless, odorless, nontoxic, and non-flammable gas. To preserve nitrogen in a stable liquid form, LN2 has to be kept at extremely low temperatures. It has a unique boiling point of –321°F/–196°C, or 77 Kelvin, meaning it will evaporate instantly at room temperature and can freeze practically anything on contact with its liquid state.

LN2 has been widely used in various industries as a cryogenic coolant for more than 100 years. It has been applied in medical science and modern physics, and now has a wide field of applications and has been developed for use in a number of areas. Within the food industry, LN2 has been used to freeze foods for preservation and storage purposes, as it preserves the flavors and textures of both sweet and savory foods. The idea of using LN2 in cooking is not new. There are accounts suggesting that LN2 was used to make ice cream in the 1800s. Despite its volatile characteristics, LN2 is fairly safe for culinary purposes because nitrogen will evaporate after the freezing process and will not linger by the time the food is consumed. LN2 allows chefs to prepare food in unique ways by using its extremely low temperatures. It can be poured into a mixing liquid of alcohol to create unique sorbets, or help provide food items such as foie gras with an exceptionally cold outer shell (i.e., cryo-poaching). It can also be used to create an LN2-chilled version of a plancha or a cold version of a hot griddle in a process called cryo-searing or freeze-planching. This technique helps to create extremely crispy outer layers before actual cooking begins. Also, combining LN2 using the foam technique described earlier within the chapter can create the possibility of frozen foams.

> **Recipe Reference:** Blood Orange Spheres (Cryo-poached Blood Orange Teardrops), Frozen Chocolate Eggs, Kuromame Bean Ice Cream

Techniques Using LN2

One can freeze practically anything by utilizing the cold and freezing nature of liquid nitrogen. Once frozen, modification and control of the texture or the shape of the food that would not normally freeze can be easily achieved.

Shaving: A fine powder can be made by using a grinder on an LN2-frozen food item. It will begin to melt once it hits the plate, releasing flavor.

Powdering: A delicate powder can also be made using LN2 and an electrical grinder (see the powder section in Flavor Enhancers section).

Cryo-searing: Similar to searing with a heated pan, a crispy layer on the surface of meats can be created using extremely low boiling temperature of LN2.

> **Recipe Reference:** Caesar Salad Soup Served with Bacon Powder and Sous Vide Quail Egg, Sugar Candy Ball Served with Frozen White Chocolate Powder

Other Freezing Techniques

Anti-griddle: This is a machine with a cold griddle that is crafted to quickly freeze foods at −30°F (−34 °C). It is an ideal device to instantly freeze sauces or purées while maintaining flavor, shape, and texture.

    Recipe Reference: Caviar Tempura (Instantly Frozen Crème Fraîche), Frozen Macaroons

CARBON DIOXIDE (CO2)

Similar to LN2, carbon dioxide (CO2) can be used at low temperatures as a cooking tool or to add a fizz (or carbonation) to food products. Dry ice is CO2 in its solid state with temperatures around −173°F/−78°C. At room temperature, dry ice will begin to evaporate immediately or sublimate into the air. Adding dry ice to a mixing liquid will create creamy sorbets unlike that of sorbets made with LN2 nitrogen. The low sublimating point enables food to be frozen safe for consumption because the dry ice particles disappear from the food by the time it is ingested.

Carbonation

Two methods are available to create carbonated food items. One is to add a certain amount of dry ice and water to a compact container with the intended carbonated item. The other method involves using a siphon that is filled with the ingredients (for example blackberries, water, and syrup) and charging it with CO2 canisters before leaving it to set for several hours. After the gas has dissolved into the berries, the product will be safe for consumption. The carbonation effect will hold for about two hours and is prolonged by cooler temperatures. In addition, the effect will last longer if the item being carbonated is larger.
While carbonation is a common experience in many soft drinks, its application can be appreciated in many forms. For instance, carbonation is used to create the candy Pop Rocks, an iconic candy from the 1970s and the 1980s.

    Recipe Reference: Fizzy Grapes

VACUUM AND LOW-TEMPERATURE COOKING

What many chefs have come to realize is that temperature and pressure play an important role in cooking. Pressure cookers, gastrovacs, immersion circulators, and vacuum-pack machines are revolutionizing cooking approaches that can directly manipulate temperature and pressure factors. The following are some of the low-temperature and vacuum-cooking machines available on the market:

Gastrovac: Gastrovac is a cooking tool with a sealed pot and a vacuum pump with a heat control device. By lowering the boiling temperature with the vacuum system, it can preserve the nutrients, texture, and flavor of the food. For this reason, it is considered within the category of low-temperature cooking. The vacuum system reduces the air between the food cell structures and the liquid is then infused between the cell walls when the pressure returns to a normal state. This technique preserves the texture of fruits and vegetables and can also be used in a preparation to infuse flavors and juices while keeping a fresh and firm texture.

Recipe Reference: Beer Pork and Cotton Candy Cooked in the Gastrovac

Sous Vide: The basic concept of sous vide is sealing food in pouches in which all of the air has been removed through a process commonly known as vacuum packing. The vacuum-pack pouch is then cooked in a water bath using a precisely controlled heating technique. This type of cooking is normally performed at much lower temperatures and for longer periods of time compared with conventional cooking.

Chefs often relate the sous vide method with low-temperature cooking technique; however, sous vide is French for "under vacuum." Simply stated, anything associated with a vacuum machine can be called sous vide.

TABLE 7.9: GASTROVAC COMMON USES

Category	Ingredient	Temperature		Cooking Time (minutes)	Notes
		°F	°C		
Meat	Beef filet	131°F (red); 140°F (pink)	55°C (red); 60°C (pink)	25	Flavor of liquid permeates meat while cooking at a low temperature. Sear on surface if you want to add flavor before cooking in Gastrovac. Sear afterward for a nice presentation.
	Pork shoulder	143°F	62°C	20	Pork does not get dry; keep juicy by infusing seasoning liquid fully. Sear on surface if you want to add flavor before cooking in Gastrovac. Sear afterword for a nice presentation.
	Foie gras	149°F	65°C	20	Sear for a nice caramelized presentation.
Fish	Sardine	104°F	40°C	60	Although almost raw, has moist mouthfeel with condensed flavor, just like after brining.
	Prawn	77°F	25°C	45	Gastrovac only permeates stock flavor; prawns need to be sautéed afterward.
	Tuna (lean)	77°F	25°C	10	Unpleasant fishy smell is removed and can add lightly seasoned flavor instead. Can be used for carpaccio preparation.
Vegetables	Tomato	149°F	65°C	15	Skin should be blanched beforehand.
	Cucumber			25	Peel and cut. Appearance becomes translucent.
	Zucchini flower	77°F	25°C	35	Retains crispy texture and absorbs flavor. Appearance becomes translucent.
	Onion	77°F	25°C	45	Retains moisture and crispy texture. Can hold seasoning flavor. Appearance becomes semitransparent.
	Carrot	77°F	25°C	45	
	Lettuce and other green leaf	77°F	25°C	45	
Fruits	Peach	104°F	40°C	40	Color of skin also permeates to flesh. There is no enhanced sweetness peculiar to cooked fruits. Can be used as sauce and a garniture.
	Apricot	77°F	25°C	60	Cooked in syrup, flavor is enhanced just like perfectly ripe apricot. Texture is similar to fresh apricot.
	Strawberry	77°F	25°C	10	Becomes slightly softer than raw, but retains original flavor and texture. Becomes translucent with even color distribution. The smaller the cut, the faster the liquid permeates.
	Apple	77°F	25°C	10	
	Pear	77°F	25°C	10	
	Melon	77°F	25°C	10	

In addition to the vacuum sealer, an immersion circulator is needed to complete the sous vide cooking method by cooking the item at an even and low temperature setting. The immersion circulator was originally developed for laboratory use to heat water to a very precise temperature. The machine agitates the water bath and evenly distributes the temperature. Some immersion circulators come with insulated water tanks and some have clamps so that they can be transferred from pot to pot.

This cooking method has been around since the early 1970s. It has slowly been spreading around professional kitchens and is finally making its way into home kitchens.

The unique properties of the sous-vide process have inspired a cooking movement that aims solely to increase the quality of food to achieve special culinary effects. The sous-vide process enables chefs to achieve textures and refinements not found in other cooking techniques. When food is cooked in this manner, the sous-vide process preserves the flavor and moisture in the food and helps to improve the "organoleptic" quality of the product. Major examples of the uses of sous vide include texture modification (or compression), flash pickling, vacuum marinating, forming, and de-airing.

Vacuum packaging has been used to enhance the storage life of cooked products. Vacuum packaging can remove the air from foods where most bacteria cultures are destroyed by the lack of oxygen; hence, spoilage is drastically slowed when the proper steps are taken. Oxidation is also greatly reduced by utilizing vacuum packaging. This provides organizational advantages in preparing, serving, and storing foods in large quantities.

Basic Steps for Sous Vide Cooking

Sous-vide cooking typically consist of the following steps:

1. **Preparation:** Cleaning, portioning, seasoning, brining, searing (if needed), and/or tying the intended protein.
2. **Vacuum packaging:** Almost all—99.9 percent—of the air must be removed from the packaging.
3. **Cooking:** Achieve the established cooking temperatures of the ingredients (refer to Table 7.10 on page 126 for appropriate temperatures).
4. **Finishing:** Searing, grilling, salamander (if needed), and assembly.
5. **Serving:** Must be served immediately.

If the food is not served immediately, steps 4 and 5 are omitted and the following extra steps after cooking must be followed:

6. **Cooling:** Cool quickly in ice water bath or blast cooler.
7. **Storage:** Store between the temperatures of 34°F/1°C to 41°F/5°C or freeze at −4°F/−20°C with proper label identifications of the products.
8. **Reheating:** When reheating an item that was previously cooked by the sous vide process, avoid bringing the product above the temperature at which it was originally cooked by sous vide. Microwaves and double-cooking (sous vide in combination with traditional methods) can also be used.
9. **Finishing:** Searing, grilling, salamander (if needed), and assembly.
10. **Serving:** Must be served immediately.

In addition to a immersion circulator, a combi-oven can be used, especially if a bigger capacity is needed, but many believe a water bath works better due to its flexibility and heat conductivity.

Basic Cooking Temperature

These are cooking guidelines that will be affected by thickness, density, and fat content as well as by the starting temperature of the product being sous vided (thaw–frozen). The chef's preferences should be considered when applying these techniques. See Table 7.10.

Recipe Reference: Caesar Salad Soup Served with Bacon Powder and Sous Vide Quail Egg; Fried Béarnaise Served with Sous Vide Beef Steak Soufflé Potato; Hot Truffle Gel Served with Sous Vide Sea Bass and Hot Corn Foam; Perfect Huevos Rancheros Served with Hot Bean Foam, Dehydrated Jalapeño and Tortilla Powders; Puffed Chicken Skin Served with Red Wine Sauce and Sous Vide Chicken

TABLE 7.10: BASIC SOUS VIDE TEMPERATURES

	Ingredient	Weight		Cooking Temperature	Cooking Temperature	Estimated Time (min./hrs.)
		Ounces	Grams	°F	°C	
Fish	Atlantic turbot	6	170.1	132.8°F	56°C	10 min.
	Cod	6	170.1	122°F	50°C	16 min.
	Hake	6	170.1	140°F	60°C	11 min.
	Lobster	8	226.8	139°F	59.5°C	15 min.
	Mackerel	6	170.1	109°F	43°C	13 min.
	Monkfish	6	170.1	140°F	60°C	11 min.
	Octopus	32	907.2	171°F	77°C	5 hrs.
	Salmon	6	170.1	122°F	50°C	14 min.
	Sea bass	6	170.1	122°F	50°C	16 min.
	Skate	6	170.1	131°F	55°C	10 min.
	Stingray	6	170.1	131°F	55°C	11 min.
	Tuna	6	170.1	122°F	50°C	11 min.
Meat	Beef cheek	32	907.2	151°F	66°C	48 hrs.
	Beef sirloin	16	453.6	139°F	59.5°C	45 min.
	Beef tenderloin	16	453.6	144°F	62°C	30 min.
	Beef tongue	32	907.2	158°F	70°C	24 hrs.
	Boudin noir	32	907.2	176°F	80°C	30 min.
	Brisket	32	907.2	147°F	64°C	48 hrs.
	Calf's heart	28	793.8	175°F	79.4°C	24 hrs.
	Calf's liver	32	907.2	145°F	63°C	60 hrs.
	Filet mignon	6	170.1	149°F	65°C	16 min.
	Flat iron steak	32	907.2	131°F	55°C	24 hrs.
	Lamb loin	8	226.8	129°F	54°C	20 min.
	Lamb shoulder	32	907.2	149°F	65°C	24 hrs.

(continued)

	Ingredient	Weight		Cooking Temperature	Cooking Temperature	Estimated Time (min./hrs.)
		Ounces	Grams	°F	°C	
Meat (continued)	Oxtail	32	907.2	185°F	85°C	24 hrs.
	Pork belly	32	907.2	180°F	82.2°C	12 hrs.
	Pork chop	10	283.5	150.8°F	66°C	35 min.
	Pork leg and shoulder confit	32	907.2	176°F	80°C	8 hrs.
	Rack of lamb	12	340.2	129.2°F	54°C	25 min.
	Roast beef	40	1134	131°F	55°C	24 hrs.
	Rabbit leg	12	340.2	185°F	85°C	60 min.
	Rabbit loin	16	453.6	147.2°F	64°C	12 min.
	Rabbit shoulder	32	907.2	149°F	65°C	12 hrs.
	Piglet shoulder	16	453.6	150.8°F	66°C	48 hrs.
	Veal breast	32	907.2	150.8°F	66°C	48 hrs.
	Veal calotte	12	340.2	140.9°F	60.5°C	15 min.
	Veal cheeks	32	907.2	179°F	82.2°C	8 hrs.
	Veal kidney	16	453.6	179.6°F	82°C	60 min.
	veal knuckle	32	907.2	150.8°F	66°C	48 hrs.
	Veal loin	32	907.2	141.8°F	61°C	35 min.
Poultry	Chicken breast	8	226.8	149°F	65°C	30 min.
	Chicken legs	32	907.2	147.2°F	64°C	60 min.
	Duck breast	8	226.8	140.9°F	60.5°C	30 min.
	Duck confit	32	907.2	179.9°F	82.2°C	8 hrs.
	Duck tongue	8	226.8	158°F	70°C	8 hrs.
	Eggs (egg white soft/egg yolk semlhard)	1 pc		154.4°F	68.0°C	75 min.
	Foie gras	11	311.85	149°F	65°C	30 min.
	Guinea fowl	32	907.2	161.6°F	72°C	72 hrs.
	Poulard breast	6	170.1	149°F	65°C	30 min.
	Poulard	32	907.2	143.6°F	62°C	90 min.
	Quail breast	6	170.1	139.1°F	59.5°C	25 min.
	Quail egg (egg white semihard/egg yolk hard)	1 pc		147.2°F	64.0°C	90 min.
	Squab breast	8	226.8	149°F	65°C	35 min.
	Squab leg	16	453.6	154.4°F	68°C	2 hrs.
Fruits	Apricots, peeled, pitted	16	453.6	190.4°F	88°C	15 min.
	Apples, peeled, pitted	16	453.6	190.4°F	88°C	40 min.
	Bananas, skin on	16	453.6	190.4°F	88°C	12 min.
	Cantaloupes, peeled, seeded	16	453.6	127.4°F	53°C	15 min.
	Cherries, whole	16	453.6	190.4°F	88°C	7 min.
	Cranberries, whole	16	453.6	190.4°F	88°C	45 min.
	Grapes, whole	16	453.6	181.4°F	83°C	10 min.

(continued)

	Ingredient	Weight		Cooking Temperature	Cooking Temperature	Estimated Time (min./hrs.)
		Ounces	Grams	°F	°C	
Fruits *(continued)*	Mangoes, peeled, pitted	16	453.6	167°F	75°C	10 min.
	Nectarines, peeled, pitted	16	453.6	190.4°F	88°C	12 min.
	Peaches, peeled, pitted	16	453.6	190.4°F	88°C	16 min.
	Pears, peeled, cored	16	453.6	190.4°F	88°C	60 min.
	Persimmons	16	453.6	190.4°F	88°C	20 min.
	Pineapples	16	453.6	167°F	75°C	60 min.
	Plums	16	453.6	167°F	75°C	20 min.
Vegetables	Asparagus, peeled	16	453.6	185°F	85°C	15 min.
	Bamboo shoots, fresh, peeled	16	453.6	176°F	80°C	6 hrs.
	Beets, baby	16	453.6	185°F	85°C	60 min.
	Beets, large	16	453.6	179.6°F	82°C	60 min.
	Carrots, baby	16	453.6	185°F	85°C	40 min.
	Carrots, large	16	453.6	185°F	85°C	45 min.
	Celery roots, peeled	16	453.6	185°F	85°C	90 min.
	Chard stems	16	453.6	190.4°F	88°C	25 min.
	Corn on cob	16	453.6	140°F	60°C	15 min.
	Daikon radishes, peeled	16	453.6	185°F	85°C	25 min.
	Endive, Belgian	16	453.6	190.4°F	88°C	50 min.
	Fennel bulbs	16	453.6	185°F	85°C	30 min.
	Hearts of palm, peeled	16	453.6	185°F	85°C	90 min.
	Kohlrabi	16	453.6	190.4°F	88°C	75 min.
	Leeks	16	453.6	185°F	85°C	50 min.
	Mushrooms	16	453.6	194°F	90°C	10 min.
	Onion, cipollini, peeled	16	453.6	194°F	90°C	2 hrs.
	Onion, pearl, peeled	16	453.6	185°F	85°C	50 min.
	Onion, sweet, peeled	16	453.6	190.4°F	88°C	45 min.
	Rutabagas, peeled	16	453.6	185°F	85°C	60 min.
	Salsify, peeled	16	453.6	190.4°F	88°C	15 min.
	Shallots, peeled	16	453.6	185°F	85°C	85 min.
	Jerusalem artichokes, peeled	16	453.6	185°F	85°C	60 min.
	Squash, summer type, peeled	16	453.6	149°F	65°C	40 min.
	Squash, firm autumn type	16	453.6	194°F	90°C	15 min.
	Squash, tender autumn type	16	453.6	185°F	85°C	25 min.
	Turnips, peeled	16	453.6	185°F	85°C	35 min.

Small Treats, Hot and Cold

RECIPES

Blood Orange Spheres

SERVED WITH MINT OIL AND CRYO-POACHED BLOOD ORANGE TEARDROPS

NUMBER OF PORTIONS	INGREDIENT	TECHNIQUE/METHOD	TEMPERATURE
18	Sodium Alginate	Spherification	Cold
	Calcium Lactate	Cryo-poaching	

	Ingredients	Amount (g)	Amount (oz)	%	Amount per portion (g)
Water Bath for Blood Orange Spheres	**Total amount**	**2007.0 g**	**70.8 oz**	**100.0%**	**n/a**
	Calcium chloride	7.0 g	0.2 oz	0.3%	n/a
	Water	2000.0 g	70.5 oz	99.7%	n/a
Blood Orange Spheres 28 g or 1 oz per portion size	**Total amount**	**506.5 g**	**17.9 oz**	**100.0%**	**28.1 g**
	Blood orange purée	500.0 g	17.6 oz	98.7%	27.8 g
	Sodium alginate	6.5 g	0.2 oz	1.3%	0.4 g
Mint Oil 8 g or 0.3 oz per portion size	**Total amount**	**150.0 g**	**5.3 oz**	**100.0%**	**8.3 g**
	Mint leaves	50.0 g	1.8 oz	33.3%	2.8 g
	Olive oil	50.0 g	1.8 oz	33.3%	2.8 g
	Grapeseed oil	50.0 g	1.8 oz	33.3%	2.8 g
Cryo-poached Blood Orange Teardrops	**Total amount**	**1 piece**	**1 piece**	**100.0%**	
	Blood orange	1 piece	1 piece	100.0%	
	Liquid nitrogen	As needed			

EQUIPMENT			
	Blender	Liquid nitrogen Dewar flask	Superbag
	Coffee filter	Measuring spoons	Syringe with a fine needle (φ 0.7 mm)
	Cutting board	Parchment paper	
	Goggles	Rubber gloves	Three medium-size plastic containers
	Immersion blender	Rubber spatula	Timer
	Induction burner	Kitchen scale + analytical scale, high precision to 0.001 g	Tongs
	Insulated bowl		Vacuum pack machine
	Knife	Slotted spoon	Vacuum pack pouches

1. A fine sieve or a chinois can also be used if a Superbag is not available.

2. Other fruit purée can be used, but those with higher acidity may require more alginate.

3. Other types of oils can be used.

4. Increase the cooking time in the calcium chloride bath for larger-size spheres.

5. If an insulated bowl is not available, it can be replace by a Styrofoam container.

6. For a mint oil alternative, you can use LN2 to create a frozen powder which is then mixed with oils. Refer to Chapter 7 "liquid nitrogen powders" (pg. 113).

Method

WATER BATH FOR BLOOD ORANGE SPHERES

1. Disperse the calcium chloride in 1000 g of water.

2. Mix with a stirrer or an immersion blender until fully dissolved.

3. Vacuum pack for 4 hours or overnight for proper hydration to occur.

4. Place the remaining 1000 g of water in a separate container and set aside.

BLOOD ORANGE SPHERES

1. Place the blood orange purée in a deep container, and disperse the sodium alginate in the purée.

2. Sheer with an immersion blender.

Blood Orange Spheres Served with Mint Oil and Cryo-poached Blood Orange Teardrops

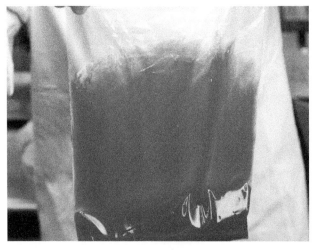

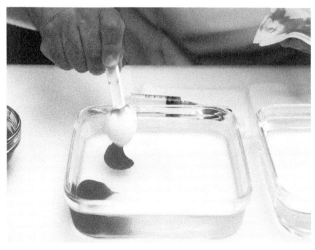

3. Strain using a Superbag, then place in a vacuum pack pouch and vacuum seal for 4 hours or overnight for proper hydration to occur.

4. Prepare the spherification bath set of calcium chloride solution and clean water.

5. Carefully spoon the blood orange purée into the calcium chloride bath.

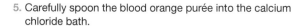

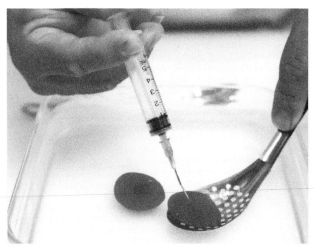

6. Let the sphere set for 2 minutes in the calcium chloride bath until a surface gel forms.

7. Fill the injector with mint oil and inject about 1 ml (0.9582 g/0.0338 oz) into the center of the sphere.

8. Turn over the sphere in the bath and leave for another 2 minutes to seal the injection site (for a total cooking time of 4 to 5 minutes).

9. Scoop the sphere with a spoon and rinse it in the clean water bath.

10. Remove excess water and serve.

MINT OIL

1. Blanch the mint leaves in boiling water for 30 seconds.

2. Quickly place the mint leaves in an ice bath and dry the leaves using a paper towel.

3. Place the mint leaves and oils in a blender and blend into a fine purée.

4. Strain with a coffee or paper filter into a plastic container.

5. Fill the injector with mint oil and inject about 1 ml (0.9582 g/0.0338 oz) into the center of each sphere.

CRYO-POACHED BLOOD ORANGE TEARDROPS

1. Peel and segment the blood orange.

2. Pour the liquid nitrogen into an insulated bowl and cryo-poach the segments for 2 to 3 minutes, or until the pulp begins to break apart.

3. Place the cryo-poached segments between two sheets of parchment paper and lightly crush to separate.

4. Serve immediately.

Caviar Tempura

SERVED WITH INSTANTLY FROZEN CRÈME FRAÎCHE

NUMBER OF PORTIONS	INGREDIENT	TECHNIQUE/METHOD	TEMPERATURE
15	Soy Lecithin/Obrato Sheet	Crispy Texture	Hot/Cold
	Trisol	Foam	
	Lambda Carrageenan		
	Calcium Lactate		

	Ingredients	Amount (g)	Amount (oz)	%	Amount per portion (g)
Tempura Batters 15 g or 0.5 oz per portion size	**Total amount**	**226.9 g**	**8.0 oz**	**100.0%**	**15.1 g**
	All-purpose flour	65.0 g	2.3 oz	28.6 %	4.3 g
	Trisol	60.0 g	2.1 oz	26.4 %	4.0 g
	Salt	0.2 g	0.0 oz	0.1 %	0.0 g
	Baking powder	1.5 g	0.1 oz	0.7%	0.1 g
	Sugar	0.2 g	0.035oz	0.1 %	0.0 g
	Vodka	20.0 g	0.7 oz	1.3 %	1 .3 g
	Water	80.0 g	2.8 oz	35.3 %	5.3 g
Caviar Tempura	**Total amount** (applicable to Caviar only)	**210.0 g**	**7.4 oz**	**100.0%**	**n/a**
	Frying oil	2000 g	70.5 oz		n/a
	Obrato sheets (soy lecithin)	as needed			
	Caviar	210 g	7.4 oz	100.0%	n/a
Instantly Frozen Crème Fraîche 27 g or 1 oz per portion size	**Total amount**	**411.2 g**	**14.6 oz**	**100.0%**	**27.4 g**
	Heavy cream	400.0 g	14.1 oz	97.3%	26.7 g
	Lambda carrageenan	1.6 g	0.1 oz	0.4%	0.1 g
	Calcium lactate	1.6 g	0.1 oz	0.4%	0.1 g
	Water	8.0 g	0.3 oz	1.9%	0.5 g
	Lemon juice	To taste			
	Salt	To taste			

For ingredients that have "0.0 oz" as an amount, please refer to the metric measure as the oz quantity is too small to measure.

Anti-griddle	NO2 chargers	Spider
Bowls in various sizes	Kitchen scale + analytical scale, high precision to 0.001 g	Strainers
Fryer		Superbag
Induction burner	Siphon	Thermometer
Measuring spoons	Spatula	

NOTES

1. Do not fry the tempura caviar for more than 45 seconds or the caviar eggs will over-cook and become dry.

2. The crème fraîche can be dispensed into LN2 and reserved for service if an anti-griddle is not available, or it may also be served directly as foam.

3. If caviar is not available, salmon roe or flying fish roe can be substituted.

4. The obrato paper can be adjusted and modified to the preferred shape.

5. Obrato paper sheets can be found in specialty stores or at drugstores (often used as an alternative method to ingest powered medication to avoid leaving bad aftertastes from medication).

6. A fine sieve or chinois can also be used if a Superbag is not available.

Method

TEMPURA BATTER AND CAVIAR TEMPURA

1. Combine the flour, trisol, salt, baking powder, and sugar in one bowl and set aside.

2. Combine the vodka and water in a separate bowl.

3. Using an immersion blender, stirrer, or whisk, pour the liquid into the dry ingredients until a smooth batter is formed.

4. Pass the mixture through a Superbag and reserve.

5. Heat the oil to 356°F/180°C.

6. Layer three obrato sheets (lecithin sheets) together and create a cone shape.

7. Scoop one small spoonful of caviar (3 g) into the cone and fold the cone to close the open end.

8. Quickly dip into the prepared tempura batter.

9. Carefully place into the hot cooking oil for approximately 30 seconds, until crisp but still light golden color and the batter is opaque.

10. Remove the tempura from the oil and place on a paper towel or on a sheet tray with a rack to let the excess oil drain.

INSTANTLY FROZEN CRÈME FRAÎCHE

1. Pour the heavy cream into a saucepan and heat to 104°F/40°C.

2. Once at temperature, remove the saucepan from the heat and disperse the lambda carrageenan using an immersion blender.

3. In a separate bowl, dissolve the calcium lactate in water and then add to the warm cream using the immersion blender.

4. Add lemon juice and salt to taste.

5. Strain the mixture using a Superbag and chill.

6. Pour the chilled mixture into a siphon and charge with NO2 (one cartridge).

7. Prechill the anti-griddle for about 15 minutes.

8. Dispense the crème fraîche onto the surface of the frozen griddle and let it freeze for approximately 10 minutes, or until frozen but still creamy in texture.

9. Serve immediately or reserve in the freezer in a plastic or stainless-steel container until use.

Farmer's Market With Eggless Pistachio Mayonnaise

SERVED WITH SOUS VIDE VEGETABLES

NUMBER OF PORTIONS	INGREDIENT	TECHNIQUE/METHOD	TEMPERATURE
12	Monoglyceride	Emulsion	Room Temperature
		Sous Vide	

	Ingredients	Amount (g)	Amount (oz)	%	Amount per portion (g)
Eggless Pistachio Mayonnaise 65 g or 2 oz per portion size	**Total amount**	**784.5 g**	**27.7 oz**	**100.0%**	**65.4 g**
	Monoglyceride	12 g	0.4 oz	1.5%	1.0 g
	Grapeseed oil	22.5 g	0.8 oz	2.9%	1.9 g
	Pistachio paste	375 g	13.2 oz	47.8%	31.3 g
	Black truffle juice	375 g	13.2 oz	47.8%	31.3 g
	Salt	To taste			
Sous Vide Vegetables 300 g or 11 oz per portion size	**Total amount**	**3600.0 g**	**127.0 oz**	**100.0%**	**300.0 g**
	White mushrooms	300 g	10.6 oz	38.2%	25.0 g
	Red pearl onions	300 g	10.6 oz	38.2%	25.0 g
	White pearl onions	300 g	10.6 oz	38.2%	25.0 g
	Baby corn	300 g	10.6 oz	38.2%	25.0 g
	Baby carrots	300 g	10.6 oz	38.2%	25.0 g
	Micro tomatoes	300 g	10.6 oz	38.2%	25.0 g
	Macro radishes	300 g	10.6 oz	38.2%	25.0 g
	White asparagus	300 g	10.6 oz	38.2%	25.0 g
	Brussels sprouts	300 g	10.6 oz	38.2%	25.0 g
	Vegetable stock	900 g	31.7 oz	114.7%	75.0 g

EQUIPMENT			
	Adhesive tape	Piping tip	Stirrer
	Induction burner	Rubber gloves	Thermometer
	Measuring spoons	Rubber spatula	Vacuum pack machine
	Pacojet	Saucepan	Vacuum pack pouches
	Pastry comb	Kitchen scale + analytical scale, high precision to 0.001 g	Whisk
	Piping bag		

Farmer's Market With Eggless Pistachio Mayonnaise Served With Sous Vide Vegetables

1. If a Pacojet is not available, using an immersion blender or a stirrer for the mayonnaise can also produce a similar effect without freezing.

2. The monoglyceride acts as an egg substitute and is ideal for vegetarians and vegans.

3. Any type of vegetables can be used for this crudités-style dish.

4. It is recommended that the mayonnaise is placed in a pastry bag with a pastry tip to disperse it on the plate. A pastry comb can also be used for a decorative effect.

Method

EGGLESS PISTACHIO MAYONNAISE

1. Disperse the monoglyceride into the oil in a small saucepan.

2. Heat the monoglyceride oil to 140°F/60°C for proper hydration to occur.

3. Once at temperature, remove the saucepan from the heat and whisk in the pistachio paste.

4. Slowly add the truffle juice to the saucepan and keep whisking until combined, maintaining the temperature of 113°F/45°C.

5. Whisk until emulsified.

6. Place the mixture into a Pacojet canister and freeze until solid.

SOUS VIDE VEGETABLES

1. Peel, wash, and trim all vegetables.

2. Group each vegetable in separate vacuum pack pouches with 100 g of vegetable stock.

3. Vacuum seal the pouches.

4. Cook each vacuum pack pouch sous vide. See Table 7.10, Basic Sous Vide Temperatures (pages 126–129) for appropriate temperatures and cooking times.

5. Immediately cool the cooked vegetables in an ice water bath and reserve.

7. Insert the frozen canister in the Pacojet and operate to produce a creamy texture.

8. Reserve in the refrigerator until use.

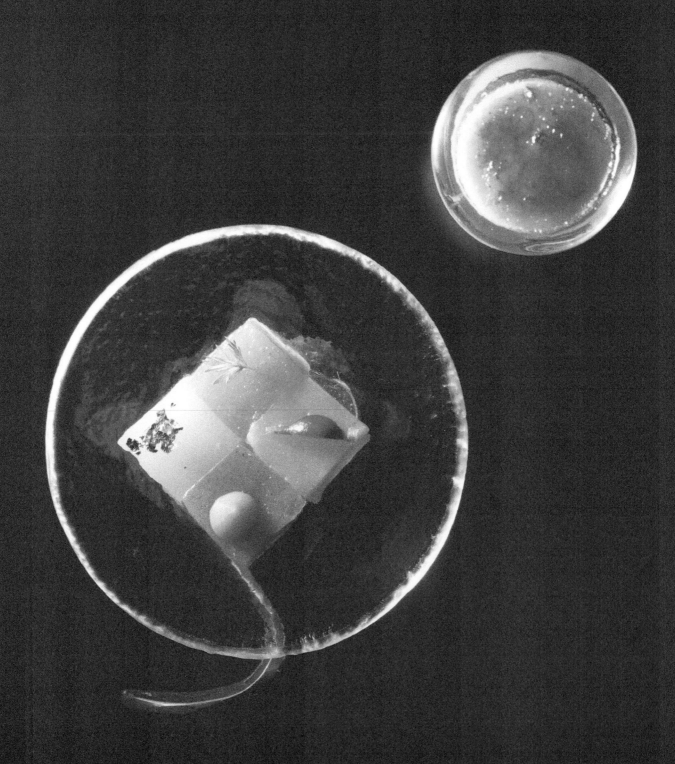

Konnyaku Jelly
SERVED WITH DENGAKU MISO

NUMBER OF PORTIONS	INGREDIENT	TECHNIQUE/METHOD	TEMPERATURE
15	Konjac	Gel, Emulsion	Hot/Cold

Konnyaku Jelly

160 g or 6 oz per portion size

Ingredients	Amount (g)	Amount (oz)	%	Amount per portion (g)
Total amount	**2,397.0 g**	**84.5 oz**	**100.0%**	**159.8 g**
Water (to mix with Konjac powder)	2000 g	70.5 oz	83.4%	133.3 g
Konjac powder	50 g	1.8 oz	2.1%	3.3 g
Water (to mix with calcium hydroxide)	300 g	10.6 oz	12.5%	20.0 g
Calcium hydroxide	3 g	0.1 oz	0.1%	0.2 g
Hijiki paste or seaweed (optional)	20 g	0.7 oz	0.8%	1.3 g
Paprika	4 g	0.1 oz	0.2%	0.3 g
or				
Tosaka	20 g	0.7 oz	0.8%	1.3 g
Water (for boiling the konjac mixture)	10,000 g	352.5 oz	n/a	n/a

Dengaku Miso

9 g or 0.5 oz per portion size

Ingredients	Amount (g)	Amount (oz)	%	Amount per portion (g)
Total amount	**129.0 g**	**4.5 oz**	**100.0%**	**8.6 g**
Yellow miso paste	75 g	2.6 oz	58.1%	5.0 g
Mirin	15 g	0.5 oz	11.6%	1.0 g
Sake	20 g	0.7 oz	15.5%	1.3 g
Sugar	15 g	0.5 oz	11.6%	1.0 g
Egg yolks	1 g	0.0 oz	0.8%	0.1 g
Ginger (grated)	3 g	0.1 oz	2.3%	0.2 g

For ingredients that have "0.0 oz" as an amount, please refer to the metric measure as the oz quantity is too small to measure.

EQUIPMENT			
Bowls and containers in various sizes	Measuring spoons	Superbag
	Rubber gloves	Thermometer
Bucket or deep container	Rubber spatula	Thermomix
Grater	Kitchen scale + analytical scale, high precision to 0.001 g	Large stockpot
Large whisk		Spider
	Spoon	

1. If a Thermomix is not available, a heating element such as a gas burner or an induction burner can be used in conjunction with a thermometer and an immersion blender.

2. Konjac is a strong alkali; it is advised to wear rubber gloves when mixing by hand.

3. To extend shelf life: Mix ½ teaspoon of calcium hydroxide with 500 ml of water and place the konnyaku in the mixture to maintain moisture. Then vacuum pack the konnyaku with the sekkai solution and boil to 185°F/85°C for 15 minutes.

4. The konnyaku can also be served hot or boiled in a flavored stock or soup.

5. A fine sieve or chinois can be used if a Superbag is not available.

Method

KONNYAKU JELLY

1. Place the 2000 g/70.5 oz of water and konjac powder in a Thermomix and set it to 99°F/37°C at the lowest stirring setting.

2. Once at temperature, set the Thermomix to speed 3 for 30 seconds and then to speed 8 for an additional 30 seconds.

3. Transfer the mixture into a deep-set plastic bowl or a bucket.

4. Mix with your gloved hands in order to incorporate air.

5. Add water if the consistency is too stiff, and continue mixing until a soft but stable gel forms.

6. Combine the 300g/10.6 oz of water with calcium hydroxide in a separate bowl and reserve.

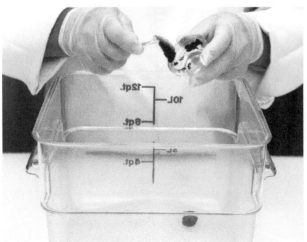

7. Add hijiki paste (or paste of the desired flavor/color) to the konjac gel.

8. Mix together with your hands.

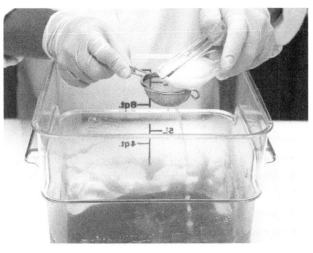

9. Add the calcium hydroxide mixture to the konjac mixture by passing it through a strainer.

10. Mix first with a whisk, then furiously with your gloved hands for about 3 minutes until fully incorporated.

11. Place in a heat-resistant mold of the desired shape.

13. Then take the konnyaku out of the molds and boil for another 20 minutes in the same water until lightened and hard to the touch.

14. Let the konnyaku rest in the cooking water overnight.

12. Pour the 2.6 gallons/10 liters of water into a stockpot and bring it to a boil. Add the konjac mixture in the molds and boil them for 20 minutes.

DENGAKU MISO

1. Place the miso, mirin, sake, and sugar into a Thermomix and set the temperature to 176°F/80°C on the lowest stirring setting.

2. Once at temperature, add the egg yolks and ginger and increase the Thermomix to speed 3 for 30 seconds.

3. Then set the Thermomix to speed 8 for an additional 30 seconds.

4. Pass the mixture through a Superbag or small strainer and reserve in an airtight container.

Olives and Cheese Served with Red Wine Jelly and Mozzarella Balloon

Olives and Cheese

SERVED WITH RED WINE JELLY AND MOZZARELLA BALLOON

NUMBER OF PORTIONS	INGREDIENT	TECHNIQUE/METHOD	TEMPERATURE
8	Sodium Alginate	Reverse Spherification	Cold
	Xanthan Gum		
	Calcium Lactate	Gel	
	Gelatin		

	Ingredients	Amount (g)	Amount (oz)	%	Amount per portion (g)
Water Bath for the Green Olive Sphere	**Total amount**	**2005.0 g**	**70.7 oz**	**100.0%**	**250.6 g**
	Sodium alginate	5.0 g	0.2 oz	0.2%	0.6 g
	Water	2000.0 g	70.5 oz	99.8%	250.0 g
Green Olive Sphere	**Total amount**	**705.6 g**	**24.9 oz**	**100.0%**	**88.2 g**
88 g or 3 oz per portion size	Green olives (pitted)	500 g	17.6 oz	70.9%	62.5 g
	Green olive juice (liquid from the olives)	200 g	7.1 oz	28.3%	25.0 g
	Xanthan gum	1.6 g	0.1 oz	0.2%	0.2 g
	Calcium lactate	4 g	0.1 oz	0.6%	0.5 g
Red Wine Jelly	**Total amount**	**577.0 g**	**20.4 oz**	**100.0%**	**72.1 g**
72 g or 3 oz per portion size	Gelatin sheets (160 Bloom)	16 g	0.6 oz	2.8%	2.0 g
	Ice water (for soaking gelatin)	220 g	7.8 oz	38.1%	27.5 g
	Port wine or pinot noir	316 g	11.1 oz	54.8%	39.5 g
	Sugar	20 g	0.7 oz	3.5%	2.5 g
	Black peppercorns	5 g	0.2 oz	0.9%	0.6 g
Mozzarella Balloon	**Total amount**	**500.0 g**	**17.6 oz**	**100.0%**	**62.5 g**
62 g or 2 oz per portion size	Buffalo mozzarella cheese	500 g	17.6 oz	100.0%	62.5 g
	Water (to melt cheese)	1000 g	35.3 oz	n/a	n/a

Air pump	Rubber gloves	Timer
Bowls in various sizes	Rubber spatula	Three medium-size containers
Immersion blender	Kitchen scale + analytical scale, high precision to 0.001 g	
Measuring spoons		Vacuum pack machine
Perforated spoon		Vacuum pack pouches
	Scissors	Chinois
	Superbag	

1. A blender can be used instead of an immersion blender to apply shear force.

2. If the olive mixture is not at desired thickness after hydration, add xanthan gum in 0.2 g increments and check consistency.

3. A fine sieve or chinois can be used if a Superbag is not available.

4. The percentage of gelatin to red wine is increased due to alcohol and pH and tannic acid content.

5. Once placed in the alginate bath, the olive sphere will not sink on its own and will need to be pushed below the surface with the aid of the spoon to allow the outer layer to form.

6. If the mozzarella cheese begins to harden while softening it, return the cheese to the warm water and avoid overworking or the consistency of the cheese will become rubbery.

Method

WATER BATH FOR THE GREEN OLIVE SPHERE

1. Disperse the sodium alginate in 1000 g of water.

2. Mix with a stirrer or an immersion blender until fully dissolved.

3. Vacuum pack for 4 hours or overnight, until proper hydration occurs.

4. Place the remaining 1000 g of water in a separate container and set aside.

1. Place the pitted green olives and olive juice in a deep container and disperse the xanthan gum and calcium lactate in the olive mixture.

2. Shear with immersion blender or a mixer.

3. Strain using a Superbag and then vacuum pack and refrigerate for 4 hours or overnight, until proper hydration occurs.

4. Prepare the reverse spherification bath set of sodium alginate in one container and the reserved clean water in another.

5. Carefully spoon the olive purée into the alginate bath.

6. Let the olive purée cook in the alginate bath for 2 minutes, or until a surface gel forms.

7. Turn the sphere over in the bath and leave for another 2 minutes.

8. Scoop out the sphere with a perforated spoon and rinse in the clean water bath.

9. Drain excess water and place the sphere in olive oil with the aromatic ingredients.

10. Reserve until use.

RED WINE JELLY

1. Soak the gelatin in the ice water until it softens.

2. Place the wine, sugar, and peppercorns into a saucepan and bring to a boil.

3. Once the sugar has dissolved, remove from the heat and add the gelatin.

4. Strain the wine mixture using a fine sieve or a chinois.

5. Cool the mixture down to 104°F/40°C.

6. Pour into a mold of the desired shape (e.g., 3-oz silicon molds).

MOZZARELLA BALLOON

1. Place the cheese in hot water at 131°F/55°C until it softens.

2. Tear off a small amount of cheese and place it on the tip of the air pump.

3. Fill the mozzarella balloon with air until it is the desired size.

4. Twist the ends to keep the air in the balloon, and trim with scissors.

5. Serve immediately.

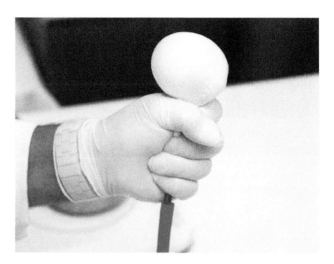

Olive Oil Gelatin

SERVED WITH BEET AIR AND CHORIZO POWDER

NUMBER OF PORTIONS	INGREDIENT	TECHNIQUE/METHOD	TEMPERATURE
10	High Acyl Gellan	Gel	Cold
	Monoglyceride	Aeration	
	Lecithin	Liquid Nitrogen	

	Ingredients	Amount (g)	Amount (oz)	%	Amount per portion (g)
Olive Oil Gelatin 51 g or 1.8 oz per portion size	**Total amount**	**549.5 g**	**19.4 oz**	**100.0%**	**55.0 g**
	Monoglyceride	1.5 g	0.1 oz	0.3%	0.2 g
	Olive oil	150 g	5.3 oz	27.3%	15.0 g
	High acyl gellan	6 g	0.2 oz	1.1%	0.6 g
	Water	350 g	12.3 oz	63.7%	35.0 g
	Salt	2 g	0.1 oz	0.4%	0.2 g
Beet Air 30.2 g or 1 oz per portion size	**Total amount**	**302.0 g**	**10.7 oz**	**100.0%**	**30.2 g**
	Beet juice	300 g	10.6 oz	99.3%	30.0 g
	Lecithin	2 g	0.1 oz	0.7%	0.2 g
Chorizo Powder 20 g or 0.7 oz per portion size	**Total amount**	**200.0 g**	**7.1 oz**	**100.0%**	**20.0 g**
	Chorizo	200 g	7.1 oz	100.0%	20.0 g
	Liquid nitrogen	As needed			

Olive Oil Gelatin Served with Beet Air and Chorizo Powder

EQUIPMENT	Aquarium air pump	Insulated bowl	Rubber gloves
	Containers and bowls in various sizes	Kitchen scale + analytical scale, high precision to 0.001 g	Rubber spatula
	Dewar flask		Saucepan
	Immersion blender	Measuring spoons	Spoon
	Induction burner	Protective gloves and eyewear	Whisk
			Zester

NOTES

1. The gel can be served hot (up to 194°F/90°C).

2. Caution should be taken when the oil is combined with the gellan paste due to the heightened sensitivity of the mixture, which should be quickly placed in prepared molds.

3. Olive oil can be replaced with other oils of the same density.

4. For better results, warm approximately 20% of the juice to 113°F/45°C and add the lecithin to it. Then pour that portion back into the remaining juice before adding shear force.

5. An electronic aquarium air pump or an immersion blender may be used to create bubbles or air.

Method

OLIVE OIL GELATIN

1. Combine the monoglyceride with the olive oil in a saucepan and heat to 140°F/60°C; set aside.

2. Disperse the high acyl gellan gum in water in a separate saucepan.

3. Bring the gellan gum mixture to a boil at 194°F/90°C until fully hydrated.

4. Whisk consistently to create a paste, and add salt.

5. Pour the olive oil mixture into the gellan gum mixture and whisk to combine.

6. Whisk constantly until combined, and bring the temperature back up to 194°F/90°C.

7. Quickly remove from the heat and pour into a container.

8. Allow the olive oil gelatin to cool for two hours in the refrigerator, then cover with plastic wrap and continue letting it set until firm (about 8–10 hours).

BEET AIR

1. Combine the beet juice and lecithin in a deep container.

2. Use an immersion blender or aquarium pump to create air.

3. Serve immediately.

CHORIZO POWDER

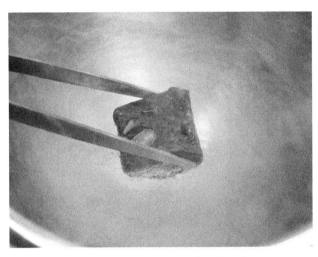

1. Carefully place the LN2 into an insulated bowl.

2. Poach the chorizo until frozen.

3. Using protective gloves, immediately grate the chorizo into a fine powder.

4. Serve immediately.

Perfect Huevos Rancheros Served with Hot Bean Foam, Dehydrated Jalapeño and Tortilla Powders, and Salsa Gel

Perfect Huevos Rancheros

SERVED WITH HOT BEAN FOAM, DEHYDRATED JALAPEÑO AND TORTILLA POWDERS, AND SALSA GEL

NUMBER OF PORTIONS	INGREDIENT	TECHNIQUE/METHOD	TEMPERATURE
15	Agar	Sous Vide	Hot
		Hot Foam	
		Dehydration	

	Ingredients	Amount (g)	Amount (oz)	%	Amount per portion (g)
Huevos Rancheros	**Total amount**	**15**	**15**	**100.0%**	**1**
1 egg per portion size	Eggs	15	15	100.0%	1 egg
Hot Bean Foam	**Total amount**	**503.0 g**	**17.7 oz**	**100.0%**	**33.5 g**
34 g or 1 oz per portion size	White beans	200 g	7.1 oz	39.8%	13.3 g
	Bean cooking liquid	300 g	10.6 oz	59.6%	20.0 g
	Agar	3 g	0.1 oz	0.6%	0.2 g
Jalapeño Powder	**Total amount**	**350.0 g**	**12.3 oz**	**100.0%**	**23.3 g**
23 g or 0.8 oz per portion size	Jalapeño	350 g	12.3 oz	100.0%	23.3 g
Tortilla Powder	**Total amount**	**300.0 g**	**10.6 oz**	**100.0%**	**20.0 g**
20 g or 0.7 oz per portion size	Tortilla	300 g	10.6 oz	100.0%	20.0 g

EQUIPMENT			
	Bowls in various sizes	Knife	Siphon
	Cutting board	Measuring spoons	Spice grinder
	Dehydrator	NO2 canister chargers	Spider
	Funnel	Rubber gloves	Strainer
	Immersion circulator	Kitchen scale + analytical scale, high precision to 0.001 g	Thermometer
			Thermomix

NOTES

1. If a Thermomix is not available, a heating element such as a gas burner or an induction burner can be used in conjunction with a thermometer and an immersion blender.

2. For softer egg yolks, see Table 7.10, Basic Sous Vide Temperatures (pages 126–129) for specific cooking times for eggs.

3. If an immersion circulator is not available, the egg may be cooked in the conventional poaching style; however, the texture will be altered.

4. Any other bean variety can be substituted for the white beans.

5. Xanthan gum can be substituted for agar due to its heat-resistant properties.

Method

HUEVOS RANCHEROS

1. Cook the eggs sous vide at 154°F/68°C for 75 minutes.

2. Cool the cooked eggs in an ice water bath.

3. Peel the eggs and remove the egg white, leaving only the yolk. Reserve in an airtight container.

4. Serve immediately or keep in the refrigerator.

HOT BEAN FOAM

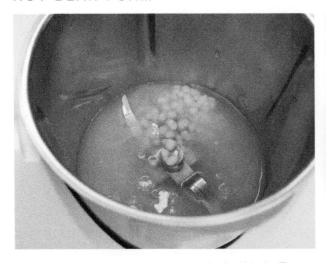

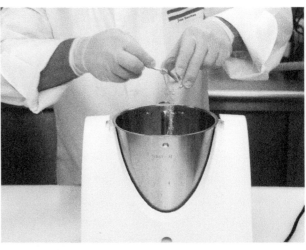

1. Placed the cooked white beans and the liquid in the Thermomix.

2. Disperse the agar into the beans and hydrate fully by setting the Thermomix to 194°F/90°C on the lowest stirring setting.

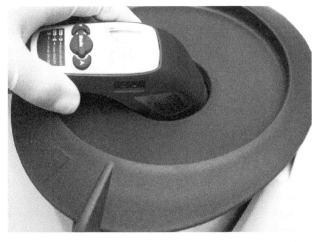

3. Once at temperature, increase the Thermomix speed to 8 for 4 minutes and purée the bean mixture.

4. Strain the mixture through a sieve.

JALAPEÑO POWDER

5. Pour the hot strained mixture into an espuma canister and charge with NO2.

6. Keep the canister warm in a hot water bath at 108°F/42°C until ready to use.

1. Remove the seeds from the jalapeño and slice the flesh.

2. Place the sliced peppers in a dehydrator set at 125°F/52°C for 16 to 18 hours, or until dry.

3. Grind the dehydrated jalapeños using a spice grinder, then pass them through a sieve.

TORTILLA POWDER

1. Cut the tortilla into small pieces.

2. Place the tortilla pieces in a dehydrator set at 125°F/52°C for 12 to 14 hours, or until dry.

3. Grind the dehydrated tortilla using a spice grinder, then pass it through a sieve.

4. Store the tortilla powder in an airtight plastic container until use.

4. Store the jalapeño powder in an airtight plastic container until use.

SALSA GEL

1. See Flavor Gel recipe (page 179).

Uni Caviar–Dashi Broth Served with Seaweed Cracker

Uni Caviar–Dashi Broth

SERVED WITH SEAWEED CRACKER

NUMBER OF PORTIONS	INGREDIENT	TECHNIQUE/METHOD	TEMPERATURE
12	Lambda Carrageenan	Spherification	Cold/Warm
	Potassium Citrate	Thickening	
	Calcium Chloride		
	Sodium Alginate		
	Tapioca Starch		

	Ingredients	Amount (g)	Amount (oz)	%	Amount per portion (g)
Dashi Broth	**Total amount**	**507.6 g**	**17.9 oz**	**100.0%**	**42.3 g**
42 g or 1.5 oz per portion size	Lambda carrageenan	2.5 g	0.1 oz	0.5%	0.2 g
	Potassium citrate	1.8 g	0.1 oz	0.4%	0.2 g
	Bonito stock	250 g	8.8 oz	49.3%	20.8 g
	Kombu stock	250 g	8.8 oz	49.3%	20.8 g
	Calcium chloride	0.3 g	0.0 oz	0.1%	0.0 g
	Water	3 g	0.1 oz	0.6%	0.3 g
Water Bath for the Uni Caviar	**Total amount**	**2007.0 g**	**70.8 oz**	**100.0%**	**167.3 g**
	Calcium chloride	7 g	0.2 oz	0.3%	0.6 g
	Water	2000 g	70.5 oz	99.7%	166.7 g
Uni Caviar	**Total amount**	**302.6 g**	**10.7 oz**	**100.0%**	**25.2 g**
25 g or 0.9 oz per portion size	Uni (roe of sea urchin)	100 g	3.5 oz	33.0%	8.3 g
	Bonito stock	200 g	7.1 oz	66.1%	16.7 g
	Sodium alginate	2.6 g	0.1 oz	0.9%	0.2 g
Seaweed Crackers	**Total amount**	**385.0 g**	**13.6 oz**	**100.0%**	**32.1 g**
32 g or 1 oz per portion size	Tapioca starch	200 g	7.1 oz	51.9%	16.7 g
	Seaweed nori sheets (ground)	65 g	2.3 oz	16.9%	5.4 g
	Salt	To taste	13.6 oz	100.0%	32.1 g
	Warm water	120 g	4.2 oz	31.2%	10.0 g
	Frying oil	As needed			
Garnish for Dashi Broth	**Total amount**	**50.0 g**	**1.8 oz**	**100.0%**	**4.2 g**
4 g or 0.15 oz per portion size	Junsai (water shield)	50 g	1.8 oz	100.0%	4.2 g

For ingredients that have "0.0 oz" as an amount, please refer to the metric measure as the oz quantity is too small to measure.

EQUIPMENT

Blender	Rubber gloves	Thermomix
Caviar kit	Rubber spatula	Three medium-size containers
Fryer	Slotted spoon	
Kitchen scale + analytical scale, high precision to 0.001 g	Spider	Vacuum pack machine
	Steamer	Vacuum pack pouches
Measuring spoons	Superbag	
Robot Coupe	Thermometer	

NOTES

1. If a Thermomix is not available, a heating element such as a gas burner or an induction burner be used in conjunction with a thermometer and an immersion blender.

2. The bonito liquid can be served warm or cold due to the heat-resistant properties of lambda carrageenan.

3. A reverse spherification can be made with similar results using an alginate water bath with xanthan gum and calcium lactate dissolved in the uni and bonito mixture.

4. Increase the cooking time in the calcium chloride bath for larger-size caviar droplets.

5. A fine sieve or chinois can be used if a Superbag is not available.

6. It is recommended to serve the caviar immediately, or the product will dry out due to the continuing reaction of the calcium chloride overcooking the droplets.

Method

DASHI BROTH

1. Mix the lambda carrageenan and potassium citrate together in a small bowl.

2. Pour the bonito stock and kombu stock into the Thermomix.

3. Disperse the carrageenan powder mixture into the stock solution.

4. Set the Thermomix to 194°F/90°C and on the lowest stirring setting.

5. Once at temperature, increase the setting to speed 3 for 30 seconds and then to speed 8 for an additional 30 seconds.

6. In a separate small bowl, dissolve the calcium chloride with water and add it to the hot stock solution.

7. Strain the solution using a fine sieve.

8. Cool to the desired temperature.

WATER BATH FOR THE UNI CAVIAR

1. Disperse the calcium chloride in 1000 g of water.

2. Mix with a stirrer or immersion blender until fully dissolved.

3. Vacuum pack the broth for 4 hours or overnight, or until proper hydration has occurred.

4. Place the remaining 1000 g of water into a separate container and set aside.

UNI CAVIAR

1. Place the uni (sea urchin roe) and stock into a blender.

2. Disperse the sodium alginate into the sea urchin mixture and blend for 1 to 2 minutes, or until combined.

3. Strain using a Superbag and vacuum pack for 4 hours or overnight, or until proper hydration has occurred.

4. Prepare the spherification bath set of sodium chloride and clean water.

5. Place the caviar cream in a syringe or a caviar dropper.

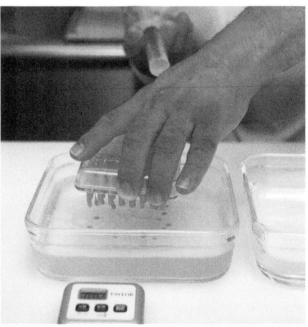

6. Slowly draw out the uni cream into round droplets 1 cm in diameter into the calcium chloride solution.

7. Let the droplets cook in the calcium chloride solution for 2 to 3 minutes.

8. Scoop the caviar with a perforated spoon and remove any excess solution.

9. Rinse the caviar in the clean water bath.

10. Serve immediately.

SEAWEED CRACKERS

1. Combine all the dry ingredients in a Robot Coupe.

2. Add water to form a paste-like dough.

3. Place the dough on a large sheet of plastic wrap.

4. Roll the dough into a cylindrical shape.

5. Steam the dough at 122°F/50°C for 3 hours or until dry.

6. Place in the freezer until firm but not fully frozen.

7. Slice the cylindrical dough lengthwise into strips 1 mm wide.

8. Fry in oil (356°F/180°C to 365°F/185°C) for about 1 minute, or until the strips are crispy.

Surprises

RECIPES

Fizzy Grapes

SERVED WITH GRAPE-FLAVORED BUBBLES

NUMBER OF PORTIONS	INGREDIENT	TECHNIQUE/METHOD	TEMPERATURE
7	Texturas Fizzy	Carbonation	Cold
	Sucrose	Bubbles	
	CO2		
	Lecithin		

	Ingredients	Amount (g)	Amount (oz)	%	Amount per portion (g)
Fizzy Grapes 153 g or 5 oz per portion size	**Total amount**	**1073.0 g**	**37.8 oz**	**100.0%**	**153.3 g**
	Peeled grapes	1000 g	35.3 oz	93.2%	142.9 g
	Grape Syrup	70 g	2.5 oz	6.5%	10.0 g
	Texturas Fizzy	3 g	0.1 oz	0.3%	0.4 g
Grape Syrup 12 g or 0.4 oz per portion size	**Total amount**	**85.0 g**	**3.0 oz**	**100.0%**	**12.1 g**
	Grape juice	70 g	2.5 oz	6.5%	10.0 g
	Sugar	10 g	0.4 oz	0.9%	1.4 g
	Lemon juice	5 g	0.2 oz	0.5%	0.7 g
Grape-Flavored Bubbles 10 g or 0.4 oz per portion size	**Total amount**	**72.0 g**	**2.5 oz**	**100.0%**	**10.3 g**
	Lecithin	2 g	0.1 oz	0.2%	0.3 g
	Grape Syrup (from the Fizzy Grapes marinade)	70 g	2.5 oz	6.5%	10.0 g

EQUIPMENT			
	Bowls in various sizes	Funnel	Measuring spoon
	Cutting board	Induction burner	Rubber gloves
	Electronic aquarium air pump	Kitchen scale + analytical scale, high precision to 0.001 g	Rubber spatula
	Espuma canister		Saucepan
	Espuma chargers (CO2)	Knife	Strainer

■ **Fizzy Grapes** Served with Grape-Flavored Bubbles

1. Use a seedless grape variety and avoid using ripe grapes.

2. The grapes can be placed back in the espuma canister and charged with CO2 to prolong the carbonation effect.

3. Cherry tomatoes and cherries can be used instead of grapes.

4. If an electronic aquarium air pump is not available, an immersion blender can be used to create bubbles.

Method

FIZZY GRAPES

1. Blanch the grapes in boiling water for 20 to 45 seconds.

2. Place the blanched grapes in an ice water bath and proceed to peel the grapes and dry them using a paper towel.

3. Divide the grapes into thirds and place in three espuma canisters.

4. Place one-third of the grapes and 23 g of grape syrup into each canister.

5. Add 1 g of Texturas Fizzy per espuma canister with the grapes.

6. Charge each canister with two charges of CO_2.

7. Let the grapes marinate in the espuma canisters for a minimum of 4 hours and maximum of 12 hours to achieve maximum carbonation.

8. Release the gas from the canisters and strain the contents, reserving the juice.

9. Serve immediately.

GRAPE SYRUP

1. Combine all the ingredients in a bowl and mix.

2. Reserve for use in Fizzy Grapes recipe.

GRAPE-FLAVORED BUBBLES

1. Combine the lecithin and the grape syrup together in a bowl.

2. Apply shear force using a stirrer, whisk, or immersion blender for proper hydration to occur.

3. Insert the plastic tube of the electronic aquarium air pump machine into the syrup solution and operate the machine.

4. Allow the machine to produce air bubbles for 1 to 2 minutes.

5. Scoop up the air bubbles using a spoon and serve immediately.

Flavor Gels

LEMON, COLA, COCONUT, ORANGE, PLUM, BASIL, CHOCOLATE, SALSA, AND STRAWBERRY

NUMBER OF PORTIONS	INGREDIENT	TECHNIQUE/METHOD	TEMPERATURE
25	Agar	Fluid gels	Hot/Cold

	Ingredients	Amount (g)	Amount (oz)	%	Amount per portion (g)
Lemon Gel 24 g or 0.8 oz per portion size	**Total amount**	**588.0 g**	**20.7 oz**	**100.0%**	**23.5 g**
	Agar	8 g	0.3 oz	1.4%	0.3 g
	Simple syrup	280 g	9.9 oz	47.6%	11.2 g
	Lemon juice	300 g	10.6 oz	51.0%	12.0 g
	Salt	To taste			
Cola Gel 15 g or 0.5 oz per portion size	**Total amount**	**384.0 g**	**13.5 oz**	**100.0%**	**15.4 g**
	Agar	4 g	0.1 oz	1.0%	0.2 g
	Simple syrup	80 g	2.8 oz	20.8%	3.2 g
	Cola-flavored soda	300 g	10.6 oz	78.1%	12.0 g
Coconut Gel 14 g or 0.5 oz per portion size	**Total amount**	**358.0 g**	**12.6 oz**	**100.0%**	**14.3 g**
	Agar	3 g	0.1 oz	0.8%	0.1 g
	Simple syrup	100 g	3.5 oz	27.9%	4.0 g
	Coconut milk	200 g	7.1 oz	55.9%	8.0 g
	Lemon juice	5 g	0.2 oz	1.4%	0.2 g
	Water	50 g	1.8 oz	14.0%	2.0 g
	Salt	To taste			
Orange Gel 11 g or 0.4 oz per portion size	**Total amount**	**263.0 g**	**9.3 oz**	**100.0%**	**10.5 g**
	Agar	3 g	0.1 oz	1.1%	0.1 g
	Simple syrup	60 g	2.1 oz	22.8%	2.4 g
	Orange juice	200 g	7.1 oz	76.0%	8.0 g
Plum Gel 13 g or 0.5 oz per portion size	**Total amount**	**334.0 g**	**11.8 oz**	**100.0%**	**13.4 g**
	Agar	4 g	0.1 oz	1.2%	0.2 g
	Plum wine	200 g	7.1 oz	59.9%	8.0 g
	Plum juice	80 g	2.8 oz	24.0%	3.2 g
	Water	50 g	1.8 oz	15.0%	2.0 g
Basil Gel 15 g or 0.5 oz per portion size	**Total amount**	**384.0 g**	**13.5 oz**	**100.0%**	**15.4 g**
	Basil purée	35 g	1.2 oz	9.1%	1.4 g
	Water	180 g	6.3 oz	46.9%	7.2 g
	Simple syrup	165 g	5.8 oz	43.0%	6.6 g
	Agar	4 g	0.1 oz	1.0%	0.2 g
	Salt	To taste			

Flavor Gels Lemon, Cola, Coconut, Orange, Plum, Basil, Chocolate, Salsa, and Strawberry

Ingredients	Amount (g)	Amount (oz)	%	Amount per potion (g)
Total amount	**361.0 g**	**12.7 oz**	**100.0%**	**14.4 g**
Dark chocolate (61%), chopped	57 g	2.0 oz	15.8%	2.3 g
Milk	250 g	8.8 oz	69.3%	10.0 g
Agar	4 g	0.1 oz	1.1%	0.2 g
Sugar	50 g	1.8 oz	13.9%	2.0 g
Total amount	**243.0 g**	**8.6 oz**	**100.0%**	**9.7 g**
Spicy salsa	200 g	7.1 oz	82.3%	8.0 g
Agar	3 g	0.1 oz	1.2%	0.1 g
Simple syrup	40 g	1.4 oz	16.5%	1.6 g
Total amount	**283.0 g**	**10.0 oz**	**100.0%**	**11.3 g**
Strawberry consommé	200 g	7.1 oz	70.7%	8.0 g
Simple syrup	80 g	2.8 oz	28.3%	3.2 g
Agar	3 g	0.1 oz	1.1%	0.1 g

Chocolate Gel
14 g or 0.5 oz per portion size

Salsa Gel
10 g or 0.3 oz per portion size

Strawberry Gel
15 g or 0.5 oz per portion size

EQUIPMENT

Cheesecloth	Measuring spoon	Stainless-steel bowl
Deep hotel pan	Perforated hotel pan	Superbag
Immersion blender	Rubber gloves	Thermometer
Induction burner	Rubber spatula	Whisk
Kitchen scale + analytical scale, high precision to 0.001 g	Saucepan	
	Spoon	

NOTES

1. Re-melt the set gel and add more of the flavored liquid if the gel is too brittle.

2. If shear force has already been applied to a gel that is too stiff, add hot liquid (from the same source).

3. If the gel is too soft, re-melt and add more agar.

4. It is advisable to pass all gels through a Superbag or fine tamis for a smoother consistency.

5. Cold Fluid Gels: can also use 160 Bloom gelatin, iota, or kappa carrageenan as a gelling agent.

6. Hot Fluid Gels: can also use agar, lactic acid, gellum, and xanthum gum as a gelling agent.

7. Avoid incorporating air when using the immersion blender to purée the flavor gels.

8. Plum wine and plum juice are available in specialty stores or in Asian grocery stores.

Method

1. Sprinkle the agar into the simple syrup and mix well to disperse the powder.

2. Pour the syrup into a saucepan and bring the mixture to a boil to fully hydrate the agar for 30 seconds at 194°F/90°C.

3. Heat the desired flavored liquid, and the water and salt if specified in the ingredients list, to 194°F (90°C). Do not bring the liquid to a boil.

4. Add the warmed flavored liquid to the hot syrup.

5. Mix well using a whisk or an immersion blender.

6. Strain the mixture using a Superbag or a chinois.

7. Let it cool to set.

8. Once set, mix with an immersion blender into a smooth purée.

9. Note: The plum gel doesn't need syrup as the plum wine is sweet enough. In steps 1 and 2, heat the plum wine, plum juice, and water. Sprinkle the agar and follow steps 4 to 7.

Follow the above steps 1 to 8 with slight modifications for Basil, Chocolate, Salsa, and Strawberry gels.

BASIL GEL

1. Mix the basil and water and create a purée; strain using a Superbag.

2. Follow steps 1 and 2 from the Lemon, Cola, Coconut, Orange, and Plum Gels method.

3. Omit step 3 from above as heating the flavor liquid is not needed; instead it will be add to the warm syrup.

4. Continue following steps 4 to 7 from the above method.

CHOCOLATE GEL

1. From the Lemon, Cola, Coconut, Orange, and Plum Gels method steps 1 and 2, replace the syrup with milk as the milk and sugar will substitute for the simple syrup in this gel.

2. Omit step 3 from above as heating the flavor liquid is not needed; instead the chopped chocolate will be added to the warm milk.

3. Add chopped chocolate to a saucepan containing milk, sugar, and the agar mixture.

4. Continue following steps 4 to 7 from above method.

SALSA GEL

1. Purée prepared salsa, and strain it through a Superbag.

2. Follow steps 1 to 7 from the Lemon, Cola, Coconut, Orange, and Plum Gels method.

STRAWBERRY GEL

1. Freeze the strawberry juice. Defrost over a cheesecloth overnight in the refrigerator to collect the strawberry consommé.

2. Follow steps 1 to 7 from the Lemon, Cola, Coconut, Orange, and Plum Gels method.

Freeze-Dried Fruit

SERVED WITH FREEZE-DRIED MILK AND CEREAL

NUMBER OF PORTIONS	INGREDIENT	TECHNIQUE/METHOD	TEMPERATURE
16	Frooze-Dried Fruit	Freeze-Drying	Room Temperature

	Ingredients	Amount (g)	Amount (oz)	%	Amount per portion (g)
Freeze-Dried Fruits 156 g or 5.5 oz per portion size	**Total amount**	**3500.0 g**	**123.4 oz**	**100.0%**	**218.8 g**
	Mango	500 g	17.6 oz	20.0%	31.3 g
	Kiwi	500 g	17.6 oz	20.0%	31.3 g
	Dragon fruit	500 g	17.6 oz	20.0%	31.3 g
	Beets	500 g	17.6 oz	20.0%	31.3 g
	Raspberries	500 g	17.6 oz	20.0%	31.3 g
	Blackberries	500 g	17.6 oz	20.0%	31.3 g
	Blueberries	500 g	17.6 oz	20.0%	31.3 g
Freeze-Dried Milk 125 g or 4.4 oz per portion size	**Total amount**	**2000.0 g**	**70.5 oz**	**100.0%**	**125.0 g**
	Whole milk	2000 g	70.5 oz	100.0%	125.0 g

EQUIPMENT			
	Acetate sheets	Kitchen scale + analytical scale, high precision to 0.001 g	Scissors
	Bowls in various sizes		Sheet trays of various sizes
	Cutting board	Knife	Tweezers
	Dry packs/silicone packs	Mandolin slicer	
	Freeze-drying machine with glass flask attachment	Plastic storage containers	

Freeze-Dried Fruit Served with Freeze-Dried Milk and Cereal

1. Prepared fruits and vegetables must be prefrozen to extract excess water from the product before placing them in the freeze-dry machine.

2. As an alternative if a freeze-dry machine is not available, a dehydrator can be used to remove excess water from the ingredients. The texture will be slightly different.

3. Freeze-drying whole berries requires more time compared to sliced fruit due to the larger surface area and higher water content.

4. Milk should be poured in the glass flask and frozen before the glass flask is attached to the freeze-dry machine.

5. As an alternative, the milk can be frozen using LN2 and then powdered using a blender. Refer to Frozen Chocolate Powder in the Sugar Candy Ball recipe.

Method

FREEZE-DRIED FRUITS

1. Prepare preferred fruit and vegetables by peeling, slicing, parboiling, and cutting them into desired shapes.

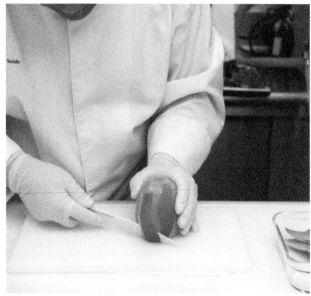

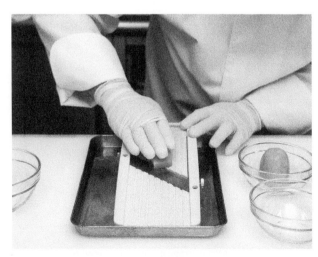

2. Use a mandolin slicer or a sharp knife to cut the fruit into slices 1/10th inch/2–3 mm thick. Set aside.

3. Use acetate sheets or other plastic sheets to line the inside of the freeze-dry chamber and set the temperature to −54°F/−48°C.

4. Place the prepared sliced fruit and whole berries in the freeze-dry chamber, turn on the vacuum pump function, and set the pressure to 11 Pa.

5. Let the slices freeze-dry for 24 to 36 hours (time will vary based on water density of the product).

6. Once the sliced fruit and whole berries appear dried, release the pressure and turn off the vacuum pump function.

7. Remove the slices and place in an airtight container with a dry pack to maintain freshness.

FREEZE-DRIED MILK

1. Place the milk in the freeze-drying flask and freeze until solid.

2. Connect the frozen flask to the freeze-drying machine and set the temperature to –54°F/–48°C.

3. Turn on the vacuum pump and set to 11 Pa, or refer to the manufacturer's manual.

4. It will take about 8 to 10 hours to produce freeze-dried milk powder.

Frozen Chocolate Eggs Dark, Milk, and White Chocolate Variety

Frozen Chocolate Eggs

DARK, MILK, AND WHITE CHOCOLATE VARIETY

NUMBER OF PORTIONS	INGREDIENT	TECHNIQUE/METHOD	TEMPERATURE
30	Liquid Nitrogen	Freeze	Cold

	Ingredients	Amount (g)	Amount (oz)	%	Amount per portion (g)
Dark Chocolate Eggs	**Total amount**	**1500.0 g**	**52.9 oz**	**100.0%**	**50.0 g**
50 g or 1.8 oz per serving portion	Dark chocolate (56%)	330 g	11.6 oz	22.0%	11.0 g
	Cacao butter	170 g	6.0 oz	11.3%	5.7 g
	Liquid nitrogen (LN2)	1000 g	35.3 oz	66.7%	33.3 g
	Rubber balloons	10 pieces			
Milk Chocolate Eggs	**Total amount**	**1380.0 g**	**48.9 oz**	**100.0%**	**46.0 g**
46 g or 2.8 oz per portion size	Milk chocolate (41%)	300 g	10.6 oz	21.7%	10.0 g
	Cacao butter	80 g	2.8 oz	5.8%	2.7 g
	Liquid nitrogen (LN2)	1000 g	35.5 oz	72.5%	33.3 g
	Rubber balloons	10 pieces			
White Chocolate Eggs	**Total amount**	**1365.0 g**	**48.1 oz**	**100.0%**	**45.5 g**
45 g or 1.6 oz per portion size	White chocolate (41%)	300 g	10.6 oz	22.0%	10.0 g
	Cacao butter	65 g	2.3 oz	4.8%	2.2 g
	Liquid nitrogen (LN2)	1000 g	35.3 oz	73.3%	33.3 g
	Rubber balloons	10 pieces			

EQUIPMENT			
	Air pump	Goggles	Rubber balloons
	Bowls in various sizes	Insulated bowl	Rubber gloves
	Chocolate tempering machine	Kitchen scale + analytical scale, high precision to 0.001 g	Rubber spatula
	Dewar flask		Small ladle
	Dispenser bottle	Measuring cup	
	Funnel	Protective gloves	

1. If the chocolate is not at proper temperature when poured into the balloon, uneven coating of the chocolate inside the balloon will result.

2. Chocolate that is too hot will result in spotted, brittle, and fragile eggs.

3. Over-freezing the chocolate in LN2 for an extended amount of time can cause the eggs to shatter.

4. Always wear protective gloves and goggles when handling LN2.

5. Wear gloves when handling the chocolate eggs to prevent fingerprints on the final product.

6. If a chocolate tempering machine is not available, a double boiler (bain-marie) can be used to melt the chocolate and cacao butter.

7. If an insulated bowl is not available, it can be replaced by a Styrofoam container.

Method

CHOCOLATE EGGS

1. Temper chocolate and cacao butter together in chocolate tempering machine to 86°F/30°C.

2. Maintain the melted chocolate at the proper temperature.

3. Invert the rubber balloon inside out and wash off the latex powder with water, allowing it to dry, and reinvert the balloon.

4. Carefully pour LN2 from the Dewar flask into an insulated bowl and set aside.

5. Pour the melted chocolate into a plastic dispenser bottle and fill the balloon with chocolate until it is half full.

6. Use an air pump to inflate the balloon to the desired size and tie a secure knot.

7. Roll the balloon in the insulated bowl containing the LN2 until the chocolate is evenly distributed and hardened.

8. Allow the balloon to rest for 1 to 2 minutes, then carefully peel the balloon away from the chocolate.

9. Store peeled eggs in the freezer in an airtight container until use.

Paletillas de Dulce (Polenta, Isomalt, and Chocolate Tuiles Variety) Served with Edible Earth

Paletillas de Dulce
(Polenta, Isomalt, and Chocolate Tuiles Variety)

SERVED WITH EDIBLE EARTH

NUMBER OF PORTIONS	INGREDIENT	TECHNIQUE/METHOD	TEMPERATURE
16	Isomalt	Tuile	Room Temperature
	Glucose	Powder	
	Pectin		
	Maltodextrin		

Ingredients	Amount (g)	Amount (oz)	%	Amount per portion (g)
Polenta Tuile				
8 g or 0.3 oz per portion size				
Total amount	**127.9 g**	**10.6 oz**	**100.0%**	**8.0 g**
Pectin	0.4 g	0.0141	0.3%	0.0 g
Sugar	37.5 g	1.3 oz	29.3%	2.3 g
Butter	30 g	1.1 oz	23.5%	1.9 g
Fresh cream (47%)	12.5 g	0.4 oz	9.8 %	0.8 g
Polenta	35 g	1.8 oz	27.4%	2.2 g
Glucose	12.5 g	0.4 oz	9.8%	0.8 g
Pistachios (optional garnish)				
Isomalt Tuile				
10 g or 0.35 oz per portion size				
Total amount	**158.0 g**	**5.6 oz**	**100.0%**	**9.9 g**
Isomalt	150 g	5.3 oz	94.9%	9.4 g
Pink peppercorns	8 g	0.3 oz	5.1%	0.5 g
Red food coloring	3 drops			
Chocolate Tuile				
25 g or 0.9 oz per portion size				
Total amount	**405.0 g**	**14.3 oz**	**100.0%**	**25.3 g**
Pectin	25 g	0.9 oz	6.2%	1.6 g
Sugar	150 g	5.3 oz	37.0%	9.4 g
Cocoa powder	10 g	0.4 oz	2.5%	0.6 g
Butter	50 g	1.8 oz	12.3%	3.1 g
Glucose	40 g	1.4 oz	9.9%	2.5 g
Water	80 g	2.8 oz	19.8%	5.0 g
Cacao paste (chocolate chips)	50 g	1.8 oz	12.3%	3.1 g
Edible Earth				
60 g or 2 oz per portion size				
Total amount	**967.0 g**	**34.2 oz**	**100.0%**	**60.4 g**
Dried porcini powder	30 g	1.1 oz	3.1%	1.9 g
Dried morel powder	30 g	1.1 oz	3.1%	1.9 g
Grapeseed oil	62 g	2.2 oz	6.4%	3.9 g
Pumpkin seed oil	18 g	0.6 oz	1.9%	1.1 g
Almond flour	400 g	14.1 oz	41.4%	25.0 g
Pumpernickel bread	300 g	10.6 oz	31.0%	18.8 g
Barley malt powder	37 g	1.3 oz	3.8%	2.3 g
Caramel color	50 g	1.8 oz	5.2%	3.1 g
Salt	To taste	n/a	n/a	n/a
Tapioca maltodextrin	40 g	1.4 oz	4.1%	2.5 g

EQUIPMENT		
Baking sheet	Measuring spoons	Saucepan
Bamboo skewers	Oven	Spice grinder
Fine sieve	Parchment paper	Whisk
Induction burner	Rolling pin	Wooden spoon
Kitchen scale + analytical scale, high precision to 0.001 g	Rubber gloves	
	Rubber spatula	

NOTES

1. A dough sheeter machine can be used to roll down the chocolate and polenta tuiles to obtain an even thickness.

2. Additional amounts of caramel color can be added in smaller amounts for darker-colored "earth."

3. Avoid excess moisture after grinding the isomalt into a fine powder.

4. Cut the polenta into tuiles while still hot and let cool on a flat surface if a flat final product is desired.

5. Variations of the isomalt tuiles can be made with the addition of alternative spices and food coloring.

Method

POLENTA TUILE

1. Combine the pectin and sugar in a small bowl and set aside.

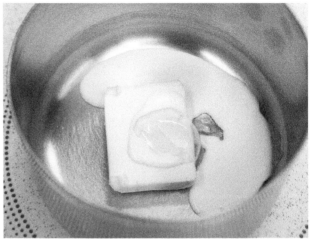

2. Mix together the butter and 6.25 g/ 0.4 oz of the cream in a saucepan and bring to a boil.

3. In a separate bowl, combine the polenta and 6.25 g/0.4 oz of the cream to create a paste.

4. Disperse the pectin mixture and glucose into the boiling butter mixture.

5. Then add the polenta mixture to the boiling butter mixture and cook for 2 minutes, or until proper hydration has occurred.

6. Pour the hot mixture into a baking sheet pan lined with parchment paper or a silicone baking sheet.

7. Place another sheet of parchment paper on top and roll with a rolling pin into a thin sheet.

8. Let it cool in the refrigerator, then peel off the top sheet of parchment paper.

9. Place the sheet pan in the oven and bake at 320°F/160°C on a low fan setting at 5-minute intervals.

10. Rotate the sheet pan in the oven at above mentioned intervals to avoid air bubbles, and bake for a total of 10 minutes.

11. Cut into desired shapes while hot and insert bamboo skewers. At this point the optional pistachio garnish can be sprinkled on, if desired.

12. Let the pieces cool.

13. Store in a dry container until use.

ISOMALT TUILE

1. Place the isomalt in a saucepan and heat to 320°F/160°C, stirring occasionally, and let it melt until dissolved.

2. Add the food coloring and the peppercorns.

3. Quickly pour the hot isomalt mixture onto a silicone mat and let it cool.

4. When the isomalt candy is completely cooled, break it into small pieces.

5. Grind the pieces in a spice grinder to create a fine powder.

6. Place the powder in a fine sieve and sprinkle evenly over a silicone mat.

7. Bake at 320°F/160°C for 3 minutes, until the powder melts and resembles glass.

8. Let it cool and break into pieces of a size that will fit your bamboo skewer.

9. Place a bamboo skewer onto the broken isomalt pieces, using glucose as an adhesive to create a candy lollipop.

10. Store in a dry container until use.

CHOCOLATE TUILE

1. Combine the pectin, sugar, and cocoa powder together in a small bowl and set aside.

2. Place the butter, water, and glucose in a saucepan and heat to 392°F/200°C, until melted but not boiling.

3. Slowly disperse the pectin mixture into the saucepan, one third at a time.

4. When all the ingredients are incorporated, bring the mixture to a boil to 212°F/100°C.

5. Then add the cacao paste to the saucepan and boil for an additional 2 minutes.

6. Pour the hot mixture onto a large sheet of parchment paper on a flat surface.

7. Place another sheet of parchment paper on top and roll with a rolling pin into a thin sheet.

8. Let it cool and cut into desired shapes.

9. Bake the tuiles with the parchment paper at 320°F/160°C for 6 minutes.

10. Let cool and remove both pieces of parchment paper.

11. Bake the chocolate pieces again at the same temperature for an additional 8 minutes.

12. Insert the bamboo skewers while the tuiles are still hot.

13. Let cool and store in a dry container until use.

EDIBLE EARTH

1. Place all the dry ingredients except the maltodextrin in a Robot Coupe and operate until combined.

2. Add the maltodextrin and continue mixing.

3. Slowly pour the oils into the mixture while operating the Robot Coupe.

4. Then add caramel color.

5. Reserve until use in an airtight plastic container or in a vacuum-sealed bag.

Stained Glass

SERVED WITH CUCUMBER SORBET

NUMBER OF PORTIONS	INGREDIENT	TECHNIQUE/METHOD	TEMPERATURE
10	Trehalose	Crystallization	Room Temperature/Cold
	Gelatin	Stable Sorbet	

	Ingredients	Amount (g)	Amount (oz)	%	Amount per portion (g)
Stained Glass	**Total amount**	**666.0 g**	**23.5 oz**	**100.0%**	**66.6 g**
67 g or 2.4 oz per portion size	Water	120 g	4.2 oz	18.0%	12.0 g
	Trehalose	312 g	11.0 oz	46.8%	31.2 g
	Sugar	234 g	8.3 oz	35.1%	23.4 g
	Food coloring (assorted colors)	As needed			
	Spices (toasted and crushed)	As needed			
Cucumber Sorbet	**Total amount**	**787 g**	**27.8 oz**	**100.0%**	**78.7 g**
79 g or 3 oz per portion size	Gelatin powder (160 Bloom)	10 g	0.4 oz	1.3%	1.0 g
	Fresh cucumber juice	500 g	17.6 oz	63.5%	50.0 g
	Water	65 g	2.3 oz	8.3%	6.5 g
	Simple syrup	120 g	4.2 oz	15.2%	12.0 g
	Gin	45 g	1.6 oz	5.7%	4.5 g
	Lime juice	42 g	1.5 oz	5.3%	4.2 g
	Salt	5 g	0.2 oz	0.6%	0.5 g

EQUIPMENT			
	Fine sieve	Measuring spoon	Spice grinder
	Induction burner	Pacojet	Superbag
	Juicer	Rubber gloves	Thermometer
	Kitchen scale + analytical scale, high precision to 0.001 g	Rubber spatula	Whisk
		Saucepan	
	Knife	Silicone mat	

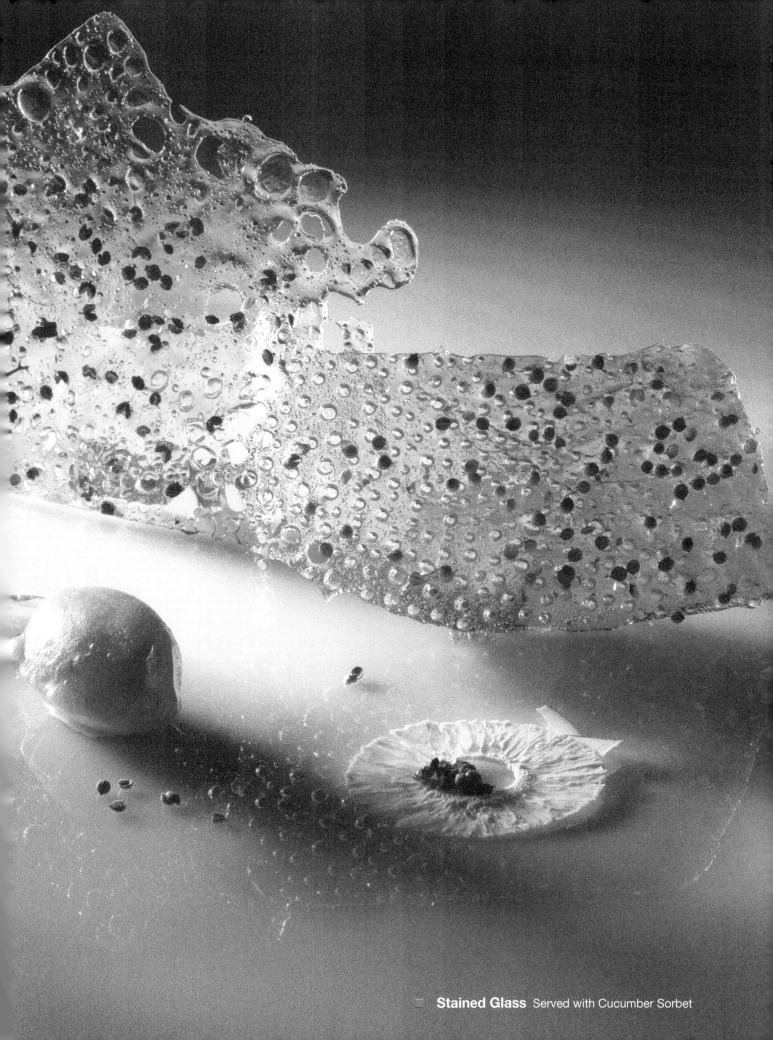

Stained Glass Served with Cucumber Sorbet

1. When heating the trehalose and water, use a wet brush to clean the sides of the pot to avoid crystallization.

2. The formed glass can be used to form spice-infused tuile.

3. The alcohol used to make food coloring can cause crystallization and should be considered when making this recipe.

4. If a Pacojet is not available, LN2 can be used to freeze the cucumber mixture or a regular ice cream machine can also be utilized. Follow until step 5, then pour the cooled mixture into the ice cream machine. Turn and reserve in the freezer until use.

5. When pouring the hot trehalose mixture onto a silicone mat, it is advised to preheat the silicone mat to prevent the sugar from cooling too quickly.

6. The gelatin in the cucumber sorbet is used as a stabilizer.

Method

STAINED GLASS

1. Combine water, trehalose, and sugar in a saucepan and stir until a paste is formed.

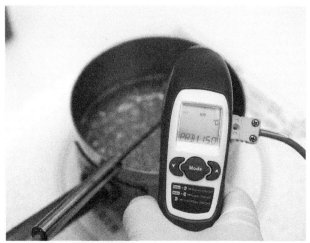

2. Heat the mixture to 239°F/115°C.

3. Add food coloring until desired color is obtained.

4. Continue heating to 283°F/145°C and add a small amount of spices, reserving the remaining amount. If you want to achieve a clear colored glass effect, omit the spices in this step.

5. At 302°F/150°C, quickly pour the syrup onto a silicone mat and spread evenly to form a thin film.

6. Once completely cooled, break the candy into small pieces.

7. Grind the pieces in a spice grinder to create a fine powder.

8. Place the powder in a fine sieve and sprinkle evenly over a silicone mat.

9. Bake at 320°F/160°C for 3 minutes until the powder melts and resembles glass.

10. Sprinkle the remaining spices over the syrup and let cool until set.

11. Break into desired sized pieces.

CUCUMBER SORBET

1. Bloom gelatin in cucumber juice and set aside.

2. Combine water, simple syrup, gin, lime juice, and salt in a saucepan and bring to a boil at 210°F/99°C.

3. Once at temperature, remove the saucepan from the heat and whisk in the gelatin-cucumber mixture.

4. Pass the mixture through a Superbag or a fine sieve.

5. Cool the mixture in an ice bath.

6. Pour the cooled mixture into a Pacojet canister and place it in the freezer, allowing the canister to freeze until solid.

7. Insert the frozen canister into the Pacojet and operate to create the sorbet.

8. Serve immediately or keep in the freezer until use.

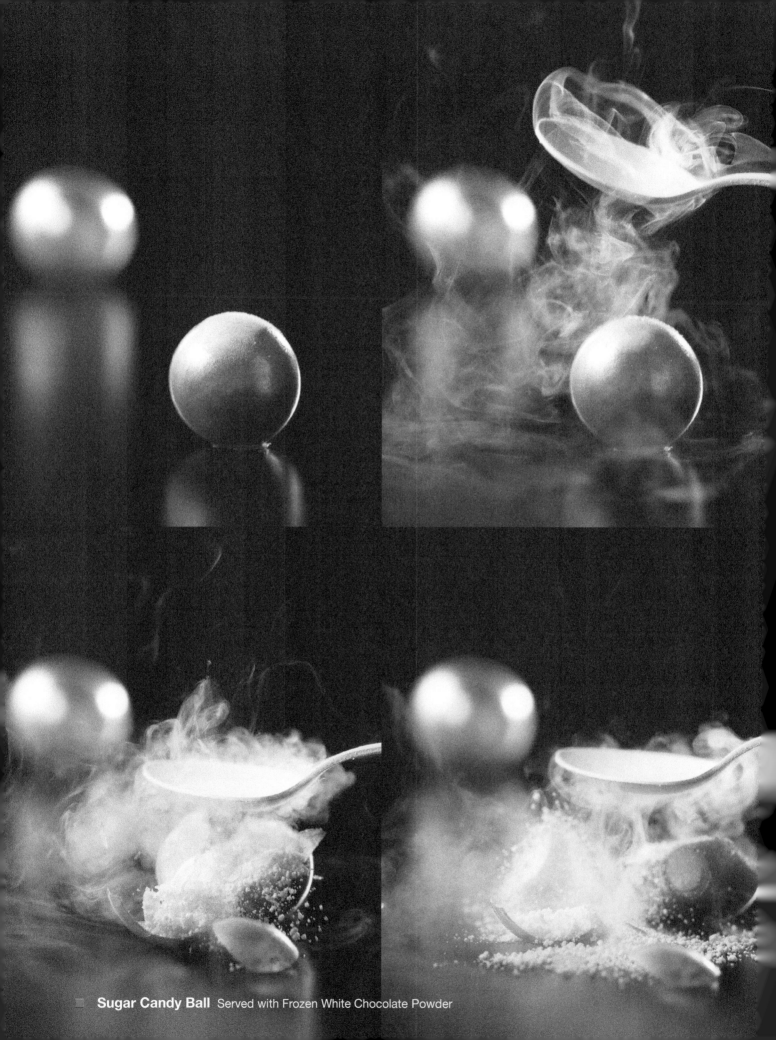

Sugar Candy Ball Served with Frozen White Chocolate Powder

Sugar Candy Ball

SERVED WITH FROZEN WHITE CHOCOLATE POWDER

NUMBER OF PORTIONS	INGREDIENT	TECHNIQUE/METHOD	TEMPERATURE
24	Isomalt	Candy	Cold
	Liquid Nitrogen	Freezing Powder	

	Ingredients	Amount (g)	Amount (oz)	%	Amount per portion (g)
Sugar Candy Ball 46 g or 1.6 oz per portion size	**Total amount**	**1100.0 g**	**38.8 oz**	**100.0%**	**45.8 g**
	Isomalt	1000 g	35.3 oz	90.9%	41.7 g
	Water	100 g	3.5 oz	9.1%	4.2 g
	Food coloring	As needed			
Frozen White Chocolate Powder 19 g or 0.7 oz per portion size	**Total amount**	**448.0 g**	**15.8 oz**	**100.0%**	**18.7 g**
	White chocolate	64 g	2.3 oz	14.3%	2.7 g
	Cacao butter	40 g	1.4 oz	8.9%	1.7 g
	Fresh cream (47%)	80 g	2.8 oz	17.9%	3.3 g
	Water	240 g	8.5 oz	53.6%	10.0 g
	Sugar	24 g	0.8 oz	5.4%	1.0 g
	Liquid nitrogen (LN2)	As needed			

EQUIPMENT			
	Air pump	Induction burner	Protective gloves
	Bowls in various sizes	Insulated bowl	Robot Coupe
	Candy lamp	Kitchen scale + analytical scale, high precision to 0.001 g	Rubber gloves
	Dewar flask		Rubber spatula
	Fan	Marble slab	Saucepan
	Gas torch	Measuring spoons	Scissors
	Goggles		Silicone mat

NOTES

1. Pulling and folding hot candy creates air bubbles and results in the change of texture and color.

2. Use of double-layered gloves is recommended when handling hot and pliable isomalt candy.

3. A small fan can be used to help cool the hot candy mixture during the pulling and folding process.

4. It is recommended to work on a marble slab when handling hot sugar to help cool the mixture.

5. Once pulled, isomalt candy can be reheated in the microwave to create more candy balls at a later time.

6. Steps 5 through 7 for the frozen chocolate powder can be repeated if the powder begins to melt.

7. Cool or freeze all cooking utensils and tools when using liquid nitrogen by dousing the tools in LN2 or simply placing them in the freezer in order to prevent the mixture from melting and/or sticking.

Method

SUGAR CANDY BALL

1. Combine the isomalt and water in a saucepan and heat to 302°F/150°C, mixing well.

2. At temperature, add food coloring until the desired hue is achieved.

3. Continue heating to 338°F/170°C, then quickly pour the isomalt candy onto a silicone mat.

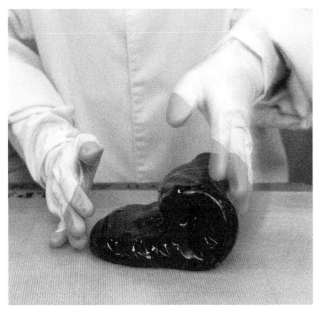

4. Quickly pour the isomalt candy on to the silicone.

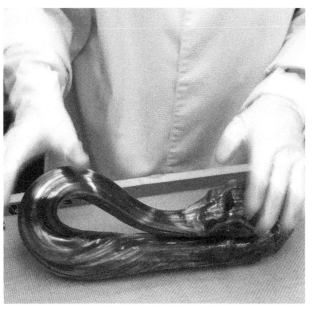

5. Repeat the process of folding and pulling the isomalt candy for about 4 minutes, or until a metallic shine results and the candy temperature reaches about 131°F/55°C.

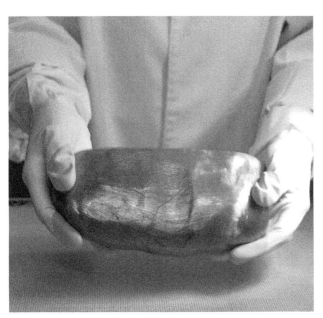

6. Continue pulling until a metallic shine results.

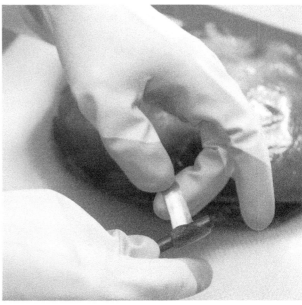

7. While working under a heating lamp, place a small piece of candy (¼ in/1 cm) on the tip of an air pump.

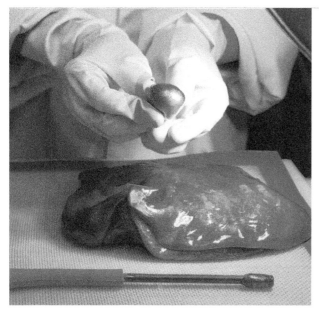

8. Continue working under the heating lamp. Cut approximately 2 ounces of candy.

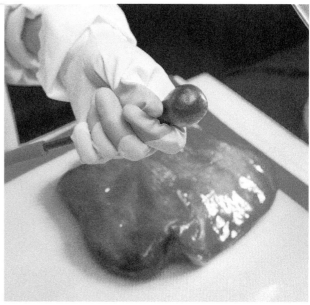

9. Place candy on the tip of the pump, ready to be blown up.

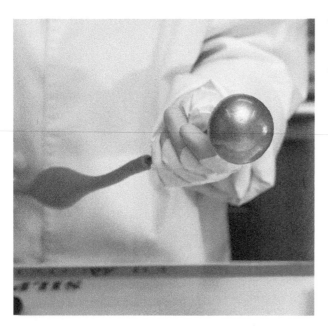

10. Pump air into the candy piece and inflate it until a balloon shape is formed.

11. Heat a knife or the blades of scissors with a blow torch and lightly tap the bottom of the balloon to detach it from the air pump.

12. Keep the candy in an airtight dry container until use.

FROZEN WHITE CHOCOLATE POWDER

1. Place the white chocolate and cacao butter in a bowl and melt over a bain-marie. Set aside.

2. Combine the cream, water, and sugar in a saucepan and heat to 194°F/90°C.

3. Once at temperature, add the chocolate mixture and mix until combined.

4. Let the mixture cool.

5. Pour the cooled mixture into a Pacojet canister and freeze until solid.

6. Insert the frozen canister into the Pacojet and operate.

7. Transfer the semisolid mixture to an insulated bowl and add LN2.

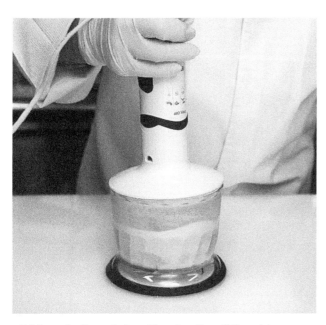

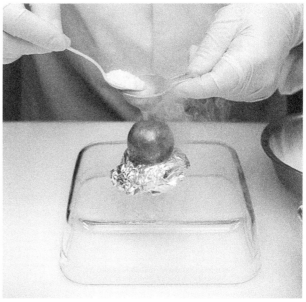

8. Mix well with cooled cooking utensils until the mixture becomes dry.

9. Place the mixture in a Robot Coupe and create a dry powder.

10. Carefully fill the already-made candy ball with the powder using a funnel and a spoon.

11. Cover the opening of the small piece of candy with cream or any other edible sealant such as glucose.

12. Serve immediately.

Composed Dishes

10

RECIPES

Beer Pork and Cotton Candy

COOKED IN THE GASTROVAC

NUMBER OF PORTIONS	INGREDIENT	TECHNIQUE/METHOD	TEMPERATURE
12	Sucrose	Cotton Candy	Hot/Cold
	Locust Bean Gum	Gastrovac	
	Xanthan Gum		

Gastrovac Beer Pork
180 g or 6 oz per portion size

Ingredients	Amount (g)	Amount (oz)	%	Amount per portion (g)
Total amount	**2161.9 g**	**76.2 oz**	**100.0%**	**180.2 g**
Pork loin	600.0 g	21.2 oz	27.8%	50.0 g
Salt	To taste			
Pepper	To taste			
Apple juice	500.0 g	17.6 oz	23.1%	41.7 g
Beer	500.0 g	17.6 oz	23.1%	41.7 g
Vegetable stock	300.0 g	10.6 oz	13.9%	25.0 g
Apple, sliced	250.0 g	8.8 oz	11.6%	20.8 g
Black tea (lapsang souchong)	5.0 g	0.2 oz	0.2%	0.4 g
South African peppercorns	3.0 g	0.1 oz	0.1%	0.3 g
Locust bean gum	2.9 g	0.1 oz	0.1%	0.2 g
Xanthan gum	1.0 g	0.0 oz	0.0%	0.1 g

Cotton Candy
8 g or 0.3 oz per portion size

Ingredients	Amount (g)	Amount (oz)	%	Amount per portion (g)
Total amount	**100.0 g**	**3.5 oz**	**100.0%**	**8.3 g**
Sucrose	100.0 g	3.5 oz	100.0%	8.3 g

For ingredients that have "0.0 oz" as an amount, please refer to the metric measure as the oz quantity is too small to measure.

EQUIPMENT

Bamboo sticks

Cotton candy machine

Cutting board

Gastrovac

Immersion blender

Induction burner

Kitchen scale + analytical scale, high precision to 0.001 g

Knife

Measuring spoon

Rubber gloves

Rubber spatula

Saucepan

Superbag

Tea bag for loose tea

Thermometer

Beer Pork and Cotton Candy Cooked in the Gastrovac

1. A pressure cooker can be used if a Gastrovac is not available; however, the texture and the flavor absorption will be altered.

2. The Gastrovac cooking method will infuse the food item with the liquid contents by absorbing the flavors (similar to a sponge) while maintaining a certain texture.

3. Sous-vide cooking method can also be used instead of the Gastrovac. See Table 7.10, Basic Sous Vide Temperatures (pages 136–139) for appropriate temperatures and cooking times.

4. Locust bean gum has synergy with xanthan gum and is used to thicken sauces in addition to its sweet flavor profile.

5. If you prefer the sauce consistency to be more syrup-like, then reduce it to 8–10 ounces and the add the locust bean gum mixture.

6. To avoid the sucrose particles present when collecting the candied threads, carefully place the sucrose in the center of the cotton candy machine from the start,

7. Colored sucrose is available, or the cotton candy can be flavored after it is prepared by sprinkling dry powders or freeze-dried flavored powders.

8. The flavor and aroma of South African peppercorns are very distinct. If not available, replace with any preferred type of peppercorns.

Method

GASTROVAC BEER PORK

1. Season the pork loin with salt and pepper and sear in a hot saucepan to add color. Set aside.

2. Deglaze the saucepan with beer, apple juice, and vegetable stock by bringing it up to 140°F/60°C.

3. Then place the pork, hot liquid mixture, cleaned and sliced apples, and black tea (in a tea bag) into the Gastrovac.

4. Set the Gastrovac machine to 145°F/62°C and set the timer for 25 minutes (follow the instructions provided by the manufacturer).

5. After 25 minutes, release the pressure of the Gastrovac and open.

6. The pork should be cooked until the internal temperature reaches 145°F/62°C (or 129°F/54°C for a rosé finish).

7. Remove the liquids from the Gastrovac and reduce in a saucepan to 16 oz/150 g.

8. Combine the locust bean gum and xanthan gum in a small bowl.

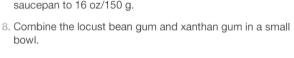

9. Disperse the locust bean gum mixture into the saucepan.

10. Add shear force with an immersion blender or stirrer until the locust bean gum mixture is dissolved.

11. Pass the mixture through a Superbag and reserve until use.

COTTON CANDY

1. Preheat the cotton candy machine by letting it run for approximately 7 minutes.

2. Turn off the machine and pour the sucrose into the dispenser using a small spoon.

3. Restart the machine; the sucrose will begin to melt after approximately 2 minutes.

4. Collect the candied threads using a bamboo stick.

5. Serve immediately.

Caesar Salad Soup

SERVED WITH BACON POWDER AND SOUS VIDE QUAIL EGG

NUMBER OF PORTIONS	INGREDIENT	TECHNIQUE/METHOD	TEMPERATURE
6	Tara Gum	Thickener	Hot/Cold
	Sodium Citrate	Powdered Fat	
	Maltodextrin	Sous Vide	

	Ingredients	Amount (g)	Amount (oz)	%	Amount per portion (g)
Lettuce Pureé	**Total amount**	**472.2 g**	**16.7 oz**	**100 %**	**26.7 g**
79 g or 2.8 oz per portion size	Sodium citrate	5 g	0.2 oz	1.1 %	0.8 g
	Tara gum	3 g	0.1 oz	0.6 %	0.5 g
	Sugar	1 g	0.035oz	0.2 %	0.2 g
	Vegetable stock	300 g	10.6 oz	63.5 %	50.0 g
	Romaine lettuce	160 g	5.6 oz	33.9 %	26.7 g
	Fresh mint leaves	3.2 g	0.1 oz	0.7 %	0.5 g
	Salt	To taste			
Sous Vide Quail Eggs	**Total amount**	**6 pieces**	**6 pieces**	**100.0%**	**1 piece**
1 each per portion size	Quail eggs	6 pieces	6 pieces	100.0%	1 piece
Bacon Powder	**Total amount**	**100.0**	**3.5**	**100.0%**	**16.7**
17 g or 0.6 oz per portion size	Bacon fat	60	2.1	60.0%	10.0
	Tapioca maltodextrin	40	1.4	40.0%	6.7

EQUIPMENT			
	Bowls in various sizes	Knife	Superbag
	Cuisinart/Robot Coupe	Measuring spoons	Thermocirculator
	Cutting board	Rubber gloves	Thermometer
	Kitchen scale + analytical scale, high precision to 0.001 g	Rubber spatula	Thermomix
		Spider	

NOTES

1. If a Thermomix is not available, a heating element such as a gas burner or an induction burner can be used in conjunction with a thermometer and a high-powered blender.

2. Alternatively, a vacuum pack pouch can be used to hydrate the lettuce mixture by cooking it sous vide in an immersion water bath at 113°F/45°C for 35 minutes.

3. A fine sieve or chinois can also be used if a Superbag is not available.

4. The lettuce soup can also be served cold.

5. Any prepared rendered fat can be used to make the powder.

6. Tara gum is a great thickener for soups. Lettuce can be replaced by any other vegetable, such as green peas or corn.

Method

LETTUCE PURÉE

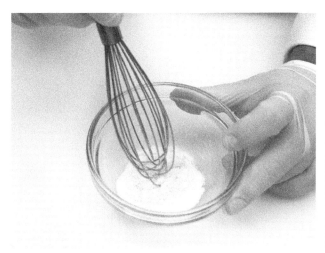

1. Mix the sodium citrate, tara gum, and sugar in a bowl to disperse the powders.

2. Pour the vegetable stock into the Thermomix and sprinkle in the tara gum mixture.

3. Set the Thermomix to 131°F/55°C on the lowest stirring setting for approximately 6 minutes, or until fully hydrated.

4. Add the romaine lettuce and fresh mint to the Thermomix.

5. Bring the mixture to 140°F/60°C at the lowest stirring setting.

6. Once at temperature, increase to speed 3 for 2 minutes and then to speed 8 for an additional 5 minutes, or until a smooth purée is formed.

7. Add salt to taste.

8. Pass the smooth purée through a Superbag.

9. Keep warm for immediate service or allow to cool in an ice bath for later use.

1. Preheat the immersion circulator to 147°F/64°C.

2. Carefully insert the quail eggs into the preheated water bath.

3. Set the timer for 90 minutes.

4. After 90 minutes, remove the quail eggs from the hot bath and place them in a stainless-steel bowl in an ice water bath until fully cooled.

5. Carefully peel the poached eggs and reserve in a plastic container.

BACON POWDER

1. Place the bacon fat and half of the tapioca maltodextrin inside a Robot Coupe or a Cuisinart and pulse until combined and starting to form a paste.

2. Add the remaining tapioca maltodextrin and continue pulsing to create a powder fluffy in texture.

3. Reserve powder in a cool dry place.

Foie Royale

SERVED WITH BEER GEL AND COMPRESSED FRUIT

NUMBER OF PORTIONS	INGREDIENT	TECHNIQUE/METHOD	TEMPERATURE
6	Iota/Kappa Carrageenan	Emulsified Gel	Cold
	Potassium Citrate	Gel	
	Gelatin	Sous Vide	
	Glucose		

	Ingredients	Amount (g)	Amount (oz)	%	Amount per portion (g)
Foie Royale 71 g or 2.5 oz per portion size	**Total amount**	**423.2 g**	**14.9 oz**	**100.0%**	**70.5 g**
	Iota carrageenan	2.2 g	0.1 oz	0.5%	0.4 g
	Gelatin powder (160 Bloom)	1 g	0.035 oz	0.2%	0.2 g
	Foie gras	300 g	10.6 oz	70.9%	50.0 g
	Consommé	60 g	2.1 oz	14.2%	10.0 g
	Bonito broth	60 g	2.1 oz	14.2%	10.0 g
	Salt	To taste			
Beer Gel 50 g or 1.8 oz per serving portion	**Total amount**	**302.3 g**	**10.7 oz**	**100.0%**	**50.4 g**
	Potassium citrate	0.25 g	0.0 oz	0.1%	0.0 g
	Kappa carrageenan	2.0 g	0.1 oz	0.7%	0.3 g
	Sugar	50.0 g	1.8 oz	16.5%	8.3 g
	Glucose	50.0 g	1.8 oz	16.5%	8.3 g
	Beer	200.0 g	7.1 oz	66.2%	33.3 g
Compressed Fruit 97 g or 3.4 oz per serving portion	**Total amount**	**580.0 g**	**20.5 oz**	**100.0%**	**96.7 g**
	Plums (2 pieces)	130 g	4.6 oz	22.4%	21.7 g
	Cantaloupe	250 g	8.8 oz	43.1%	41.7 g
	Double syrup	200 g	7.1 oz	34.5%	33.3 g

For ingredients that have "0.0 oz" as an amount, please refer to the metric measure as the oz quantity is too small to measure.

EQUIPMENT			
	Chinois	Measuring spoon	Thermometer
	Cutting board	Rubber gloves	Thermomix
	Kitchen scale + analytical scale, high precision to 0.001 g	Rubber spatula	Tweezers
		Silicone molds	Vacuum pack machine
	Knife	Superbag	Vacuum pack pouches

■ **Foie Royale** Served with Beer Gel and Compressed Fruit

NOTES

1. If a Thermomix is not available, a heating element such as a gas burner or an induction burner can be used in conjunction with a thermometer and an immersion blender.

2. A fine sieve or chinois can also be used if a Superbag is not available.

3. Angler fish liver or other high fat content livers can also be used for this recipe

4. Dark or lager beers can be used as an alternative in the beer gel recipe.

5. Iota carrageenan will add creaminess and gel softness to the royale gel.

6. Gelatin can be added for a royale gel with a more brittle consistency.

7. Kappa carrageenan will produce opaque gels but will become transparent with the addition of sugar.

Method

FOIE ROYALE

1. Mix the iota carrageenan and gelatin powder together in a bowl.

2. Combine the foie gras consommé and bonito broth in the Thermomix.

3. Then add the iota carrageenan mixture to the Thermomix with salt to taste.

4. Set the Thermomix to 194°F/90°C at the lowest stirring setting.

5. Once at temperature, blend at high speed for 1 to 2 minutes or until emulsified.

6. Strain with a Superbag or a chinois.

7. Pour into a mold of a desired shape from which once it sets you can unmold and hand cut the shape you prefer (for example, a 2.5-oz silicone mold or a 500-g metal square cake mold).

8. Cool to set in the refrigerator.

BEER GEL

1. Mix the potassium citrate, kappa carrageenan, and sugar together. Set aside.

2. Pour the glucose and beer into the Thermomix.

3. Add the kappa carrageenan mixture to the Thermomix to disperse the powders for proper hydration to occur.

4. Set the Thermomix to 194°F/90°C and on the lowest stirring setting.

5. Once at temperature, set the Thermomix to speed 3 for 30 seconds and then to speed 8 for another minute.

6. Strain using a Superbag.

7. Remove any excess foam formed on the surface with the help of a spoon or apply heat with the blow torch until the foam vanishes. Pour the beer mixture into a silicone mold.

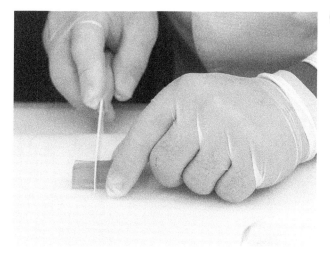

COMPRESSED FRUIT

1. Clean and portion fruit into desired shapes.

2. Place the cut fruit in a vacuum pack pouch and add the syrup.

3. Vacuum seal the pouch and allow the fruit to compress for 30 minutes.

8. Cool in the refrigerator to set. Portion as needed.

■ **Fried Béarnaise** Served with Sous Vide Beef Steak and Soufflé Potato

Fried Béarnaise

SERVED WITH SOUS VIDE BEEF STEAK AND SOUFFLÉ POTATO

NUMBER OF PORTIONS	INGREDIENT	TECHNIQUE/METHOD	TEMPERATURE
16	Low Acyl Gellan	Emulsified Heat-Stable Gel	Hot
	Gelatin	Sous Vide	
	Sodium hexametaphosphate (SHMP)		
	Citric Acid		
	Modified Starch/Ultra-Sperse 3		

	Ingredients	Amount (g)	Amount (oz)	%	Amount per portion (g)
Fried Béarnaise	**Total amount**	**986.1 g**	**34.8 oz**	**100.0%**	**61.6 g**
62 g or 2.2 oz per portion size:	Gelatin sheets (160 Bloom)	60 g	2.1 oz	6.1%	3.8 g
5 cubes per portion	Unsalted butter	640 g	22.6 oz	64.9%	40.0 g
	Low acyl gellan	3.5 g	0.1 oz	0.4%	0.2 g
	Sodium hexametaphosphate (SHMP)	2 g	0.1 oz	0.2%	0.1 g
	Citric acid	0.6 g	0.0 oz	0.1%	0.0 g
	Water	170 g	6.0 oz	17.2%	10.6 g
	Egg yolks	100 g	3.5 oz	10.1%	6.3 g
	Ultra-Sperse 3	10 g	0.4 oz	1.0%	0.6 g
	Lemon juice	To taste			
	Salt	To taste			
Béarnaise Reduction	**Total amount**	**110.5 g**	**5.0 oz**	**100.0%**	**6.9 g**
7 g or 0.2 oz per portion size	Shallots, chopped (2 pieces)	30.0 g	1.1 oz	27.1%	1.9 g
	Tarragon	0.5 g	0.0 oz	0.5%	0.0 g
	White wine	30.0 g	1.1 oz	27.1%	1.9 g
	Water	80.0 g	2.8 oz	72.4%	5.0 g
Breading	**Total amount**	**400.0 g**	**14.1 oz**	**100.0%**	**25.0 g**
25 g or 0.9 oz per portion size	All-purpose flour	100.0 g	3.5 oz	25.0%	6.3 g
	Eggs (beaten)	100.0 g	3.5 oz	25.0%	6.3 g
	Bread crumbs	200.0 g	7.1 oz	50.0%	12.5 g
Sous Vide Beef Steak	**Total amount**	**3052.0 g**	**107.6 oz**	**100.0%**	**190.8 g**
191 g or 6.7 oz per portion size	Beef filet	2600 g	91.7 oz	85.2%	162.5 g
	Vegetable stock	452 g	15.9 oz	14.8%	28.3 g
Soufflé Potato	**Total amount**	**1000.0 g**	**105.8 oz**	**100.0%**	**62.5 g**
62 g or 2.2 oz per portion size	Potato	1000 g	35.3 oz	100.0%	62.5 g
	Frying oil	2000 g	70.5 oz	200.0%	125.0 g

For ingredients that have "0.0 oz" as an amount, please refer to the metric measure as the oz quantity is too small to measure.

EQUIPMENT			
	Adhesive tape	Mandolin slicer	Spider
	Bowls and containers in various sizes	Measuring spoon	Thermometer
		Probe thermometer	Vacuum pack machine
	Immersion blender	Rubber gloves	Vacuum pack pouches
	Immersion circulator	Rubber spatula	Whisk
	Induction burner	Saucepan	
	Kitchen scale + analytical scale, high precision to 0.001 g	Spoon	

NOTES

1. The butter must be warmed when added to the gellan solution in order for proper emulsification to occur.

2. The Ultra Sperse-3 can be substituted with Ultra-Sperse M.

3. Stir the oil while frying the potatoes for even cooking to occur.

4. The béarnaise can be frozen and thawed before frying to extend shelf life.

5. Any high-powered blender can be substituted for the immersion blender.

6. Portioning the béarnaise butter can be done using cake-cutting rulers or metal bars over a silicone sheet to create the desired shape or silicone molds of 2 oz each.

Method

FRIED BÉARNAISE

1. Soften the gelatin sheets in cold water.

2. Melt the butter and add the gelatin; keep warm and reserve.

3. Disperse the low acyl gellan, sodium hexametaphosphate, and citric acid in cold water and place in a saucepan.

4. Bring the liquid to a boil, strain with a Superbag into a container, and chill in the refrigerator for 10 to 15 minutes or until it sets.

5. In a separate saucepan, bring the white wine, water, shallots, and tarragon to a temperature of 194°F/90°C in order to create an infusion; do not allow the mixture to boil.

6. Strain the mixture using a Superbag or chinois and let it cool.

7. Place the Ultra-Sperse in a bowl and slowly add the cooled white wine–infused solution while whisking to create a soft paste.

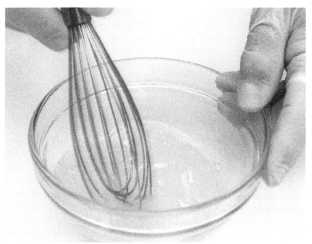

8. Continue to whisk to create a soft paste.

9. Combine the low acyl gellan solution and eggs in a deep container.

10. Add shear force with an immersion blender.

11. Add the Ultra-Sperse paste and continue to add shear force until a smoother paste is formed.

12. Slowly pour the warmed butter solution into the egg mixture.

13. Continue blending until a creamy emulsion results.

14. Season with salt and lemon juice to taste.

15. Pour the solution into a mold or container of the desired shape. (It can also be portioned by hand.)

16. Cool in the refrigerator for 2 to 3 hours, or until set.

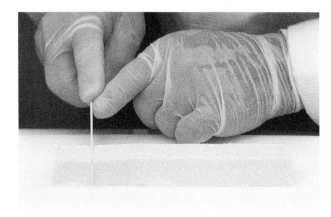

17. Set up standard breading procedures and bread the unmolded or portion cut béarnaise.

18. Deep-fry the béarnaise at 356°F/180°C for about 1 minute.

19. Serve immediately.

SOUS VIDE BEEF STEAK

1. Cut and prepare the beef filet, and place in a vacuum pack pouch, then add vegetable stock and proceed to vacuum seal.

2. Cook the beef sous vide at 136°F/58°C for 45 minutes.

3. Sear on a grill or in a pan for color.

SOUFFLÉ POTATO

1. Cut potatoes and slice thinly (0.1 in/0.4 cm) before trimming the slices into octagonal shapes.

2. Heat the first half of the frying oil to 212°F/100°C and add the potatoes. Cook for 2 to 3 minutes. The potatoes should be soft, but removed from the oil before they get any color or start puffing.

3. Heat the second half of the frying oil to 320°F/160°C and fry the potatoes again, carefully coating with oil on both sides until puffed and evenly browned this time.

■ **Hot Lobster Tokoroten** Served with Sous Vide Lobster, Truffle Oil Encapsulation, and Pernod Air (Optional)

Hot Lobster Tokoroten

SERVED WITH SOUS VIDE LOBSTER, TRUFFLE OIL ENCAPSULATION, AND PERNOD AIR (OPTIONAL)

NUMBER OF PORTIONS	INGREDIENT	TECHNIQUE/METHOD	TEMPERATURE
6	Kappa Carrageenan	Gel	Hot/Cold
	Locust Bean Gum	Clarification by Centrifuge	
	Potassium Citrate	Encapsulation	
	Calcium Chloride	Aeration	
	Isomalt		

	Ingredients	Amount (g)	Amount (oz)	%	Amount per portion (g)
Tokoroten 100 g or 3.5 oz per portion size	**Total amount**	**607 g**	**21.4 oz**	**100.0%**	**101.2 g**
	Lobster stock	500 g	17.6 oz	98.6%	83.3 g
	Calcium chloride	0.19 g	0.0 oz	0.0%	0.0 g
	Locust bean gum	2.5 g	0.1 oz	0.5%	0.4 g
	Kappa carrageenan	2.5 g	0.1 oz	0.5%	0.4 g
	Potassium citrate	1.8 g	0.1 oz	0.4%	0.3 g
	Low acyl gellan	0.5 g			0.1 g
	Water	100 g	3.0 oz	17%	14.0 g
Sous Vide Lobster 95 g or 3.4 oz per portion size	**Total amount**	**570.0 g**	**20.1 oz**	**100.0%**	**95.0 g**
	Lobster tail	320 g	11.3 oz	56.1%	53.3 g
	Butter	250 g	8.8 oz	43.9%	41.7 g
Truffle Oil Encapsulation 196 g or 7 oz per portion size	**Total amount**	**1175.0 g**	**41.4 oz**	**100.0%**	**195.8 g**
	Isomalt	1000 g	35.3 oz	85.1%	166.7 g
	Truffle oil	175 g	6.2 oz	14.9%	29.2 g
Pernod Air (Optional) 43 g or 1.4 oz per portion size	**Total amount**	**431.0 g**	**15.2 oz**	**100.0%**	**71.8 g**
	Milk	300 g	10.6 oz	69.6%	50.0 g
	Pernod liqueur	131 g	4.6 oz	43.7%	21.8 g
	Salt	To taste			

For ingredients that have "0.0 oz" as an amount, please refer to the metric measure as the oz quantity is too small to measure.

Adhesive tape	Induction burner	Small circular metal cutter
Bowls of various sizes	Kitchen scale + analytical scale, high precision to 0.001 g	Superbag
Centrifuge machine		Syringe
Digital thermometer	Measuring spoon	Thermomix
Funnel	Rubber gloves	Tokoroten cutter
Half-sphere silicone molds	Rubber spatula	Vacuum pack machine
Immersion blender	Saucepan	Vacuum pack pouches
Immersion circulator		

NOTES

1. If a Thermomix is not available, a heating element such as a gas burner or an induction burner can be used in conjunction with a thermometer and an immersion blender.

2. Equal amounts of fluid must be placed within the centrifuge canisters in order for the machine to operate properly. Water may be used to fill the canister to equalize the weight distribution. Refer to manufacturer's machine manual for specification usage.

3. Wear rubber gloves when handling food hydrocolloids and during the cooking process.

4. Alternatives for the tokoroten cutter include using a pasta cutter, cutting by hand with a knife, or using a pasta guitar machine.

5. The tokoroten can be served at temperatures of up to 140°F/60°C.

6. The texture of the tokoroten will be firm and brittle due to kappa carrageenan's gelling properties.

7. Locust bean gum will add clarity to the gel and will synergize with the kappa carrageenan to form the gel.

8. A fine sieve or chinois can be used if a Superbag is not available.

9. A coffee filter can be used to strain the lobster consommé.

Method

CLARIFYING LOBSTER STOCK USING A CENTRIFUGE

1. Pour 250 g of lobster stock into each of two plastic centrifuge containers.

2. Place the containers in the centrifuge in opposing positions.

3. Set the speed to 3,500 rpm and let the centrifuge operate for 2 hours.

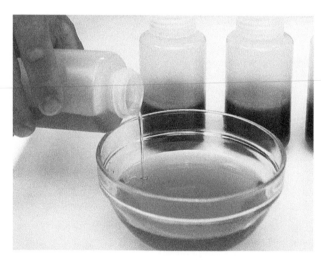

4. Take the containers out of the centrifuge and strain the separated fluid with a paper towel or coffee filter.

1. Add 1 tablespoon of water (from the 100 g of water) to the calcium chloride and set aside.

2. Mix dry powders of locust bean gum, kappa carrageenan, and potassium citrate and disperse well in a separate bowl.

3. In another bowl, disperse the acyl gellan in water and mix well.

4. Place the cold lobster stock in the Thermomix. Disperse the powder mixture from step 2.

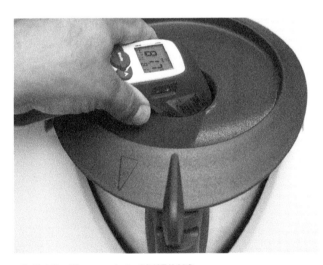

5. Set the Thermomix to 194°F/90°C.

6. Let the powder hydrate in the Thermomix at speed 5 for 30 seconds.

7. Once at temperature, turn down the speed to the low stirring setting, add the gellan solution from step 3, and continue mixing for about 12 minutes.

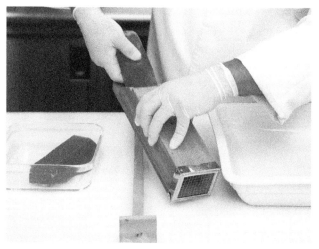

8. Then set the Thermomix to speed 3 for 30 seconds and add the calcium chloride mixture from step 1.

9. Increase the Thermomix to speed 8 for an additional 30 seconds.

10. Strain the mixture using a Superbag or a chinois.

11. Let the solution cool in a square mold similar in size to the tokoroten cutter.

12. Once set, cut the gel using a tokoroten cutter into square noodle-like shapes.

SOUS VIDE LOBSTER

1. Place the lobster tail and melted butter in a vacuum pack pouch and vacuum seal.

2. Preheat the immersion circulator water bath temperature to 135°F/59.5°C and cook the lobster until the internal temperature reaches 127°F/53°C for a minimum of 15 minutes.

TRUFFLE OIL ENCAPSULATION

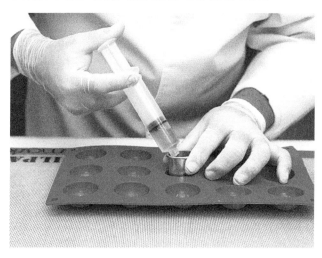
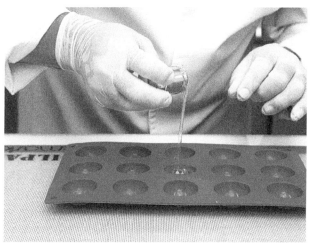

1. Place the isomalt in a saucepan and heat to 330°F/166°C, stirring occasionally.

2. Once the isomalt is fully dissolved, remove from the heat and let it cool to 203°F/95°C to 212°F/100C.

3. Dip a metal ring into the isomalt and place it in a silicone mold.

4. Fill a syringe with truffle oil and pour about 15 cc inside the metal ring within the mold.

5. Slowly lift the metal ring to cover the truffle oil with the melted isomalt.

6. Trim the excess isomalt with scissors.

PERNOD AIR

1. Warm the milk in a saucepan over low heat.

2. Add the Pernod and salt to taste.

3. Create air using an immersion blender.

7. Remove the truffle encapsulation from the silicone mold. Truffle oil encapsulation should be served immediately.

Hot Truffle Gel

SERVED WITH SOUS VIDE SEA BASS AND HOT CORN FOAM

NUMBER OF PORTIONS	INGREDIENT	TECHNIQUE/METHOD	TEMPERATURE
8	Methylcellulose	Hot Gel	Hot
		Sous vide	

	Ingredients	Amount (g)	Amount (oz)	%	Amount per portion (g)
Hot Truffle Gel	**Total amount**	**460.2 g**	**16.2 oz**	**100.0%**	**57.5 g**
57 g or 2 oz per portion size	Methylcellulose	5.7 g	0.2 oz	1.2%	0.7 g
	Gelatin powder (160 Bloom)	4.5 g	0.2 oz	1.0%	0.6 g
	Truffle water	225 g	7.9 oz	48.9%	28.1 g
	Hijiki paste	225 g	7.9 oz	48.9%	28.1 g
	Salt	To taste			
Sous Vide Sea Bass	**Total amount**	**1380 g**	**48.7 oz**	**100.0**	**172.5 g**
172 g or 6 oz per portion size	Sea bass	1360 g	48.0 oz	98.6%	170.0 g
	Salt	To taste			
	Pepper	To taste			
	Vegetable stock	20 g	0.7 oz	1.4%	2.5 g
Hot Corn Foam	**Total amount**	**499.8 g**	**17.6 oz**	**100.0%**	**62.5 g**
62 g or 2 oz per portion size	Tara gum	1.0 g	0.0 oz	0.2%	0.1 g
	Xanthan gum	1.4 g	0.0 oz	0.3%	0.2 g
	Shucked corn	260.0 g	9.2 oz	52.0%	32.5 g
	Vegetable stock	115.0 g	4.1 oz	23.0%	14.4 g
	Water	115.0 g	4.1 oz	23.0%	14.4 g
	Maple syrup	4.0 g	0.1 oz	0.8%	0.5 g
	Salt	3.0 g	0.1 oz	0.6%	0.4 g
	Turmeric	0.4 g	0.0 oz	0.1%	0.1 g

For ingredients that have "0.0 oz" as an amount, please refer to the metric measure as the oz quantity is too small to measure.

Adhesive tape	Rubber spatula	Thermometer
Convection oven	Ruler	Thermomix
Immersion circulator	Silicone mat	Tray
Kitchen scale + analytical scale, high precision to 0.001 g	Siphon	Vacuum pack machine
	Spoon	Vacuum pack pouches
Measuring spoons	Strainer	
Probe thermometer	Superbag	

1. If a Thermomix is not available, a heating element such as a gas burner or an induction burner can be used in conjunction with a thermometer and an immersion blender.

2. A fine sieve or a chinois can also be used if a Superbag is not available.

3. Methylcellulose can create thermo-reversible gel (i.e., a gel in hotter temperatures that will melt when cooled).

4. For this recipe, methylcellulose does not melt at low temperature since it has been dehydrated.

5. Hijiki paste can be replaced by any other type of paste, such as spinach, tomato, or bell pepper.

6. It is important to keep in the gel in an airtight container after it has been dehydrated in the oven.

7. A dehydrator can be used alternatively to dehydrate the gel at a temperature of 176°F/80°C.

Method

HOT TRUFFLE GEL

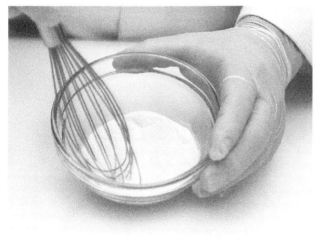

1. Combine the methylcellulose and gelatin powder together and mix well to disperse the powders.

2. Place the truffle water and hijiki paste in the Thermomix with salt to taste.

3. Sprinkle the methylcellulose mixture into the cold truffle and hijiki mixture.

4. Set the Thermomix to 194°F/90°C at the lowest stirring setting.

■ **Hot Truffle Gel** Served with Sous Vide Sea Bass and Hot Corn Foam

5. Once at temperature, blend at speed 3 for 30 seconds and then at speed 8 for an additional 30 seconds until a purée results.

6. Cool the mixture over an ice water bath.

7. Place in a vacuum pack pouch, vacuum seal the mixture, and let it rest for at least 6 hours in the refrigerator.

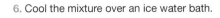
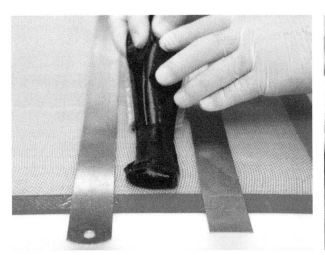

8. Spread a thin amount (approximately 1 mm thick) of the rested paste onto a silicone mat.

9. Preheat the oven to 113°F/45°C and let the gel hydrate until dry and pliable to the touch, about 30 to 45 minutes.

10. Reserve in a cool dry place until use.

SOUS VIDE SEA BASS

1. Set the immersion circulator water bath temperature to 122°F/50C.

2. Season the sea bass with salt and pepper, and place a slice of dehydrated truffle and hijiki sheet on the fish.

3. Place the fish in a vacuum pack pouch, add the vegetable stock, and vacuum seal the bag.

4. Cook the fish sous vide for 16 minutes at 122°F/50C.

5. Remove the fish from the plastic bag and drain the excess stock.

6. Serve immediately.

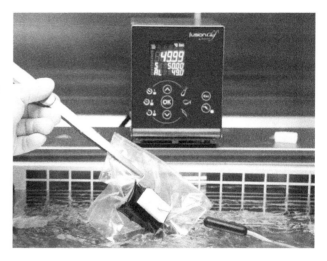

HOT CORN FOAM

1. Combine the tara gum and xanthan gum in a bowl; mix well to disperse the powders.

2. Combine the corn, stock, water, maple syrup, salt, and turmeric in the Thermomix.

3. Sprinkle the tara gum–xanthan gum mixture into the Thermomix to hydrate the powders.

4. Set the Thermomix to 125°F/52°C and on the lowest stirring setting.

5. Once preheated, blend on speed 3 for 1 minute and then increase to speed 8 for about 3 minutes, until a smooth purée results.

6. Pass the mixture through a Superbag or chinois.

7. Pour the purée into a siphon and charge with NO 2.

8. Reserve in a warm water bath at approximately 113°F/45°C until use.

Puffed Chicken Skin

SERVED WITH RED WINE SAUCE AND SOUS VIDE CHICKEN

NUMBER OF PORTIONS	INGREDIENT	TECHNIQUE/METHOD	TEMPERATURE
6	Transglutaminase	Adhesion	Hot
	Locust Bean Gum	Thickener	
		Sous Vide	

	Ingredients	Amount (g)	Amount (oz)	%	Amount per portion (g)
Puffed Chicken Skin	**Total amount**	**504.0 g**	**10.7 oz**	**100.0%**	**84.0 g**
84 g or 3 oz per portion size	Chicken skin	500 g	10.6 oz	99.2%	83.3 g
	Transglutaminase (Activa GS)	4 g	0.1 oz	0.8%	0.7 g
Red Wine Sauce	**Total amount**	**466.0 g**	**16.5 oz**	**100.0%**	**77.7 g**
78 g or 2.7 oz per portion size	Red wine	200 g	7.1 oz	42.9%	33.3 g
	Shallots	8 g	0.3 oz	1.7%	1.3 g
	Veal stock	200 g	7.1 oz	42.9%	33.3 g
	Semisweet chocolate	50 g	1.8 oz	10.7%	8.3 g
	Salt	To taste			
	Locust bean gum	8 g	0.3 oz	1.7%	1.3 g
Sous Vide Chicken	**Total amount**	**500.0 g**	**17.6 oz**	**100.0%**	**83.3 g**
83 g or 3 oz per portion size	Chicken breast (roulade)	500 g	17.6 oz	100.0%	83.3 g
Smoked Flavor	**Total amount**	**5.0 g**	**0.2 oz**	**100.0%**	**0.8 g**
0.8 g or 0.03 oz per portion size	Wood chips	5 g	0.2 oz	100.0%	0.8 g

EQUIPMENT	Bowls in various sizes	Knife	Smoke gun and smoke chips
	Brush	Lighter	
	Cutting board	Measuring spoons	Spider
	Digital thermometer (oil)	Metal spatula	Superbag
	Glass plate cover (bell/cloche)	Paper towels	Thermomix
	Immersion circulator	Rubber gloves	Tweezers
	Induction burner	Rubber spatula	Vacuum pack machine
	Kitchen scale + analytical scale, high precision to 0.001 g	Saucepan	Vacuum pack pouches

NOTES

1. If a Thermomix is not available, a heating element such as a gas burner or an induction burner can be used in conjunction with an immersion blender.

2. The chicken skin can be substituted with fish skin or guinea hen skin.

3. Activa GS is recommended in a slurry created with a formula weight of 0.75 (1.0%).

4. Activa GS is directly applied in this recipe due to the moist nature of the chicken skin.

5. The chicken roulade can be wrapped with cabbage, pancetta, or any other desired ingredient.

6. Xanthan gum or lambda carrageenan can be substituted for locust bean gum in the red wine sauce.

7. Refer to the manufacturer's instruction manual for specific use of the smoke gun.

Method

PUFFED CHICKEN SKIN

1. Trim as much fat off the skin as possible, place the skin in a vacuum pack pouch, and vacuum seal.

2. Cook the chicken skin sous vide at 185°F/85°C for 3 hours and let cool in an ice water bath.

3. Cut the cooked chicken skin into rectangular shapes 4 inches/10 cm by 1 inch/3 cm (continued on page 260).

Puffed Chicken Skin Served with Red Wine Sauce and Sous Vide Chicken

4. Apply Activa GS.

5. Brush Activa GS on the edges of the skin.

6. Fold into halves and press.

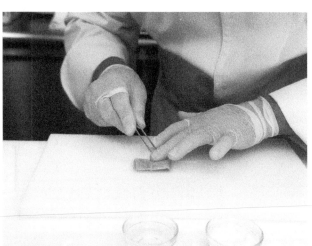

7. Secure and seal all edges.

8. Place the chicken skin rectangles in a vacuum pack pouch and vacuum seal.

9. Refrigerate for 4 hours or overnight.

10. Fry the rectangular chicken skins in oil at 356°F/180° until puffed and crispy.

11. Serve immediately.

RED WINE SAUCE

1. Combine the red wine and shallots in a saucepan, place it on an induction burner over medium heat, and reduce to 1 oz/30 g.

2. Place the veal stock, chocolate, red wine reduction, and salt into the Thermomix.

3. Set the Thermomix to 194°F/90°C on the lowest stirring setting.

4. Once at temperature, add the locust bean gum and increase the speed to 3 for 1 minute, then to speed 8 for an additional 3 minutes.

5. Strain using a Superbag.

6. Keep warm until use.

SOUS VIDE CHICKEN

1. Season chicken breast and place in a vacuum pack pouch and vacuum seal.

2. Cook the chicken sous vide at 149°F/65°C for 30 minutes.

3. If not serving immediately, cool in an ice water bath and reserve until use.

SMOKED FLAVOR

1. Prepare the smoke gun by placing wood chips of preferred flavor in the dispenser.

2. Turn on the smoke gun and carefully light the wood chips.

3. Direct the hose attachment toward the plate and enclose the smoke by using a plate cover.

4. Serve immediately.

Ras El Hanout Essence Gelatin

SERVED WITH WAKAME GRANITÉ

NUMBER OF PORTIONS	INGREDIENT	TECHNIQUE/METHOD	TEMPERATURE
10	Gelatin	Distillation	Cold
	Liquid Nitrogen	Gel	
		Freezing (Granité)	

	Ingredients	Amount (g)	Amount (oz)	%	Amount per potion (g)
Ras El Hanout Essence 91 g or 3 oz per portion size	**Total amount**	**906.0 g**	**31.9 oz**	**100.0%**	**90.6 g**
	Yuzu peel	1 g	0.0 oz	0.1%	0.1 g
	Orange peel	1 g	0.0 oz	0.1%	0.1 g
	Ginger	40 g	1.4 oz	4.4%	4.0 g
	Turmeric	30 g	1.1 oz	3.3%	3.0 g
	Black peppercorns	25 g	0.9 oz	2.8%	2.5 g
	Coriander	15 g	0.5 oz	1.7%	1.5 g
	Cinnamon sticks	4 g	0.1 oz	0.4%	0.4 g
	Star anise (toasted)	5 g	0.2 oz	0.6%	0.5 g
	Cloves	3 g	0.1 oz	0.3%	0.3 g
	Nutmeg	3 g	0.1 oz	0.3%	0.3 g
	Dried chiles	4 g	0.1 oz	0.4%	0.4 g
	Edible flowers	175 g	6.2 oz	19.3%	17.5 g
	Dry gin	400 g	14.1 oz	44.2%	40.0 g
	Orange juice	200 g	7.1 oz	22.1%	20.0 g
Ras El Hanout Essence Gelatin 23 g or 0.8 oz per portion size	**Total amount**	**234.0 g**	**53.8 oz**	**100.0%**	**23.4 g**
	Gelatin sheets (185 Bloom)	10 g	0.4 oz	4.3%	1.0 g
	Water	100 g	3.5 oz	42.7%	10.0 g
	Ras el hanout essence	60 g	2.1 oz	25.6%	6.0 g
	Double syrup	40 g	1.4 oz	17.1%	4.0 g
	Pitted cherries	24 g	0.8 oz	10.3%	2.4 g
Wakame Granité 100 g or 3.5 oz per portion size	**Total amount**	**1003.5 g**	**35.4 oz**	**100.0%**	**100.4 g**
	Dry wakame	6.5 g	0.2 oz	0.6%	0.7 g
	Spinach	50 g	1.8 oz	5.0%	5.0 g
	Kombu stock	260 g	9.2 oz	25.9%	26.0 g
	Sugar	20 g	0.7 oz	2.0%	2.0 g
	Salt	2 g	0.1 oz	0.2%	0.2 g
	Water	665 g	23.5 oz	66.3%	66.5 g

For ingredients that have "0.0 oz" as an amount, please refer to the metric measure as the oz quantity is too small to measure.

Cherry pitter	Knife	Sheet trays
Cutting board	Measuring spoon	Silicone mold
Dewar flask	Pacojet	Spider
Drop gun	Protective gloves	Spoon
Goggles	Robot Coupe	Strainer
Induction burner	Rotary evaporator/distiller	
Insulated bowl	Rubber spatula	
Kitchen scale + analytical scale, high precision to 0.001 g	Saucepan	

NOTES

1. If a distiller is not available, place all the ingredients in a vacuum pack pouch, vacuum seal, and cook sous vide in an immersion circulator at 113°F/45°C for 45 minutes.

2. If an immersion circulator is not available, place all ingredients in a container, add hot water at 194°F/90°C, and let infuse in the hot water for about an hour and a half.

3. The above two methods will produce a colored liquid versus a transparent liquid created by the distiller.

4. If a Thermomix is not available, a heating element such as a gas burner or an induction burner can be used in conjunction with a thermometer and an immersion blender.

5. Avoid using kiwi and pineapple in gelatin due to enzymic properties that inhibit gel formation.

6. Avoid boiling or freezing gelatin, or it will lose its smooth texture and result in a loss of gelling.

Method

RAS EL HANOUT ESSENCE

1. Toast all the spices and the chiles in a pan over medium heat until fragrant.

2. Place the toasted spices and chiles into the flask of the rotary evaporator/distiller with the edible flowers, gin, and orange juice. Attach the flask to the distiller. For a photo of the distiller, see page 32.

3. Set the pressure to 90 hPa with a hot water bath temperature of 125°F/52°C, and select rotation speed 5 with the water cooler set to 47°F/8.5°C.

4. Run the distiller for about 1 hour.

5. Reserve the collected distilled liquid for the gel.

6. Discard the used spices and flowers.

RAS EL HANOUT ESSENCE GELATIN

1. Soak the gelatin in ice water and set aside.

2. Place the distilled liquid in a saucepan and cook off the alcohol (i.e., flambé).

3. Then add the syrup and water to the saucepan with the essence and bring it to a boil.

4. Remove the saucepan from the heat and add the gelatin.

5. Place pitted cherries in the silicone molds.

6. Pour the gelatin solution into a drop gun and dispense appropriate amounts into the silicone molds containing the pitted cherries.

7. Refrigerate until set.

WAKAME GRANITÉ

1. Soak the wakame in chilled water for about 30 minutes.

2. Blanch the spinach leaves in boiling water for 30 seconds and drain well.

3. Place all the ingredients in the Thermomix.

4. Set the Thermomix to 125°F/50°C on the lowest stirring setting.

5. Once at temperature, increase to speed 3 for 30 seconds and then to speed 8 for an additional 1 to 2 minutes.

6. Pour the mixture into a Pacojet canister and let it cool.

7. Freeze the cooled Pacojet canister.

8. Insert the canister in the Pacojet and operate to create the granité.

9. Transfer the granité mixture to an insulated bowl and add LN2.

10. With the help of a spider remove the frozen granité mixture, place it in a Robot Coupe, and pulse to create the powder.

Sweets

11

RECIPES

Ants on a Log

SERVED WITH NUTELLA POWDER

NUMBER OF PORTIONS	INGREDIENT	TECHNIQUE/METHOD	TEMPERATURE
21	Modified Starch (Pure-Cote)	Film	Room Temperature
	Fructose	Powdered Fat	
	Ascorbic Acid		
	Tapioca Maltodextrin (N-Zorbit)		

	Ingredients	Amount (g)	Amount (oz)	%	Amount per portion (g)
Celery Film	**Total amount**	**595 g**	**21 oz**	**100.0%**	**28.3 g**
28 g or 1 oz per portion size	Juiced celery	450 g	15.9 oz	75.6%	21.4 g
	Juiced parsley	50 g	1.8 oz	8.4%	2.4 g
	Fructose	14 g	0.5 oz	2.4%	0.7 g
	Ascorbic acid	4 g	0.1 oz	0.7%	0.2 g
	Salt	4 g	0.1 oz	0.7%	0.2 g
	Fennel seeds	2 g	0.1 oz	0.3%	0.1 g
	Pure-Cote	71 g	2.5 oz	11.9%	3.4 g
Nutella Powder	**Total amount**	**100 g**	**3.5 oz**	**100.0%**	**4.8 g**
5 g or 0.2 oz per portion size	Nutella	60 g	2.1 oz	60.0%	2.9 g
	Tapioca maltodextrin N-Zorbit	40 g	1.4 oz	40.0%	1.9 g
Compressed Celery	**Total amount**	**141 g**	**5.0 oz**	**100.0%**	**6.7 g**
5 g or 0.2 oz per portion size	Celery	80 g	2.8 oz	56.7%	3.8 g
	Grenadine	30 g	1.1 oz	21.3%	1.4 g
	Simple syrup	30 g	1.1 oz	21.3%	1.4 g
	Saffron	1 g	0.0 oz	0.7%	0.0 g

For ingredients that have "0.0 oz" as an amount, please refer to the metric measure as the oz quantity is too small to measure.

EQUIPMENT			
	Acetate sheets	Robot Coupe	Thermomix
	Bowls in various sizes	Rubber gloves	Vacuum pack machine
	Dehydrator	Rubber spatula	Vacuum pack pouches
	Juicer	Squeeze bottle	
	Kitchen scale + analytical scale, high precision to 0.001 g	Superbag	
		Thermometer	

Ants on a Log Served with Nutella powder

1. If a Thermomix is not available, a heating element such as a gas burner or an induction burner can be used in conjunction with a thermometer and an immersion blender.

2. A fine sieve or chinois can also be used if a Superbag is not available.

3. If a dehydrator is not available, let the celery gel set at room temperature for 15 to 18 hours or until dry, or place in a warm oven set at 131°F/55°C until dry.

4. The acetate sheet can be replaced by a silicone pad.

5. Celery juice can be replaced by any juice, such as rhubarb or pineapple.

6. An alternative to acetate sheets is to place the celery gel on plastic sheets from flat chocolate or cookie packages. These sometimes work well as they come with small dents and shapes.

7. Tapioca maltodextrin has a unique characteristic that changes fat into a powdery texture. Any paste with a high fat content, such as peanut butter, can also be substituted.

Method

CELERY FILM

1. Peel and juice the raw celery and parsley.

2. Strain the mixture through a Superbag, then place in the Thermomix.

3. Mix together the fructose, ascorbic acid, and salt in a separate bowl.

4. Add the fructose mixture with the fennel seeds to the Thermomix.

5. Set the Thermomix to 212°F/100°C and to the lowest stirring setting.

6. Once at temperature, add the Pure-Cote to the juice mixture and blend for 7 minutes on speed 3, then increase to high speed for an additional 1 minute for proper hydration to occur.

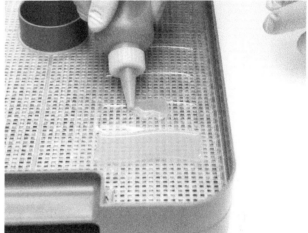

7. Strain through a Superbag.

8. Cool the mixture down to 59°F/15°C.

9. Pour the mixture into a plastic squeeze bottle.

10. Squeeze out the mixture onto a prepared sheet of acetate at 0.5 mm thickness.

11. Place the acetate sheet in a dehydrator at 125°F/51.7°C and let it set for 12 hours, or until dry.

12. Carefully peel off the acetate sheet from the dried film.

NUTELLA POWDER

1. Place the Nutella and half of the amount of tapioca malto-dextrin into a Robot Coupe and pulse until combined and starting to form a paste.

2. Add the remaining tapioca maltodextrin and continue pulsing to create a powder with a fluffy texture.

3. Store the powder in a plastic container with a lid in a cool and dry place for up to 3 days.

COMPRESSED CELERY

1. Peel and wash the celery.

2. Place the celery and grenadine in a vacuum pack pouch and vacuum seal.

3. Let it sit for 30 minutes to 1 hour.

4. Pour the simple syrup into a saucepan over medium heat, and bring to 194°F/90°C. Add the saffron.

5. Once at temperature, remove the saucepan from the heat and let the saffron infuse and cool to room temperature.

6. Repeat step 2 with the saffron syrup and vacuum seal.

Frozen Macarons

SERVED WITH LEMON CREAM

NUMBER OF PORTIONS	INGREDIENT	TECHNIQUE/METHOD	TEMPERATURE
15	Gelatin	Freezing	Cold
	Xanthan Gum	Anti-Griddle	
		Sous Vide	

	Ingredients	Amount (g)	Amount (oz)	%	Amount per portion (g)
Frozen Macarons 68 g or 2.4 oz per portion size	**Total amount**	**1023.0**	**36.1 oz**	**100.0%**	**68.2 g**
	Gelatin	20.0	0.7 oz	2.0%	1.3 g
	Sugar	200.0	7.1 oz	19.6%	13.3 g
	Xanthan gum	3.0	0.1 oz	0.3%	0.2 g
	Mango purée	350.0	12.3 oz	34.2%	23.3 g
	Pineapple purée	150.0	5.3 oz	14.7%	10.0 g
	Passion fruit purée	75.0	2.6 oz	7.3%	5.0 g
	Lime purée	25.0	0.9 oz	2.4%	1.7 g
	Water	200.0	7.1 oz	19.6%	13.3 g
Lemon Paste 15 g or 0.5 oz per portion size	**Total amount**	**230.0 g**	**29.3 oz**	**100.0%**	**15.3 g**
	Lemon	150.0 g	5.3 oz	65.2%	10.0 g
	Sugar	80.0 g	2.8 oz	34.8%	5.3 g
Lemon Cream 20 g or 0.7 oz per portion size	**Total amount**	**300.0 g**	**10.6 oz**	**100.0%**	**20.0 g**
	Fresh cream (47%)	150.0 g	5.3 oz	50.0%	10.0 g
	Lemon Paste	150.0 g	5.3 oz	50.0%	10.0 g

Anti-griddle	Kitchen scale + analytical scale, high precision to 0.001	Robot Coupe
Bowls in various sizes		Saucepan
Cutting board	Knife	Strainer
Espuma canister	Measuring spoons	Vacuum pack machine
Espuma chargers	Metal spatula (small)	Vacuum pack pouches
Funnel	Rubber gloves	
Induction burner	Rubber spatula	

NOTES

1. Use cream chargers for espuma (NO2) or espuma advance (available in Japan).

2. Diced fruit can be added to the macaron disks approximately 2 minutes into the anti-griddle freezing time or before flipping the disks over.

3. To produce macaron disks faster, the batter can be placed on the anti-griddle for 5 minutes. Then drop the disks into an insulated bowl containing LN2 for about 1 minute or until fully frozen.

4. The lemon cream can be replaced with any other flavors (e.g., basil cream, chocolate cream, cassis cream, hazelnut cream, etc.).

5. If a Thermomix is available, all the steps to make the mixture for macarons can be done in it.

Method

FROZEN MACARONS

1. Soak the gelatin in a small amount of water and set aside.

2. Mix the sugar and xanthan gum together in a small bowl to disperse.

3. Combine all the fruit purées and water in a saucepan and boil to 194°F/90°C.

4. Once at temperature, add the xanthan gum and sugar and continue boiling for 2 additional minutes.

5. Remove the saucepan from the heat and add the softened gelatin, mixing until dissolved.

6. Pass the mixture through a Superbag or a medium-size strainer and let it rest for 2 to 4 hours in the refrigerator.

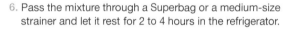

7. Turn on the anti-griddle and allow it to reach freezing temperatures.

8. Mix the chilled gel with a spoon or whisk until it becomes soft and pourable.

9. Pour the mixture into a siphon and charge with NO2.

10. Shake the canister well. Using a round tip dispenser, spray foam onto the frozen anti-griddle, creating disks 1 inch/2 to 3 cm in diameter.

11. Let the disks set and freeze for about 10 to 12 minutes, then, using a spatula, flip them over.

12. Place lemon cream on the frozen side of the disk and sandwich the two pieces together.

13. Serve immediately.

LEMON PASTE

1. Place the lemon in a vacuum pack pouch and vacuum seal.

2. Cook the lemon sous vide at 107°F/42°C for 55 minutes.

3. Seed the boiled lemon while still warm, and cut into small dice.

4. Place the diced lemon in the Robot Coupe and combine it with the sugar.

5. Pulse mixture until combined.

6. Let cool and reserve.

LEMON CREAM

1. Whip the cream using a whisk or an electric mixer until soft peaks form.

2. Fold in about 3.5 oz/100 g of Lemon Paste into the cream until combined.

3. Reserve for macaron assembly.

Jaleas

STRAWBERRY-BALSAMIC, LOBSTER-TARRAGON, AND TOMATO-SAFFRON

NUMBER OF PORTIONS	INGREDIENT	TECHNIQUE/METHOD	TEMPERATURE
16	Pectin	Gel	Room Temperature
	Trehalose		
	Trimoline		
	Glucose		
	Citric Acid		
	Sodium Hexametaphosphate (SHMP)		

Strawberry-Balsamic Jaleas

29 g or 1 oz per portion size

Ingredients	Amount (g)	Amount (oz)	%	Amount per portion (g)
Total amount	**468.0 g**	**16.5 oz**	**100.0%**	**29.3 g**
Citric acid	2.5 g	0.1 oz	0.5%	0.2 g
Water	4 g	0.1 oz	0.9%	0.3 g
Sugar	80 g	2.8 oz	17.1%	5.0 g
Pectin (HM) (see note)	6.5 g	0.2 oz	1.4%	0.4 g
Trehalose	50 g	1.8 oz	10.7%	3.1 g
Clarified strawberry purée	250 g	8.8 oz	53.4%	15.6 g
Balsamic reduction	45 g	1.6 oz	9.6%	2.8 g
Trimoline	30 g	1.1 oz	6.4%	1.9 g
Sugar for garnish	As needed			

Lobster Tarragon Jaleas

34 g or 1 oz per portion size

Ingredients	Amount (g)	Amount (oz)	%	Amount per portion (g)
Total amount	**549.6 g**	**19.4 oz**	**100.0**	**34.4 g**
Citric acid	4 g	0.1 oz	0.7%	0.3 g
Water	4 g	0.1 oz	0.7%	0.3 g
Sugar	250 g	8.8 oz	45.5%	15.6 g
Glucose	25 g	0.9 oz	4.5%	1.6 g
Pectin (HM) (see note)	10 g	0.4 oz	1.8%	0.6 g
Sodium hexametaphosphate (SHMP)	0.6 g	0.0 oz	0.1%	0.0 g
Clarified lobster stock	250 g	8.8 oz	45.5%	15.6 g
Tarragon (chopped)	6 g	0.2 oz	1.1%	0.4 g
Sugar for garnish	As needed			

Tomato-Saffron Jaleas

29 g or 1 oz per portion size

Ingredients	Amount (g)	Amount (oz)	%	Amount per portion (g)
Total amount	**468.2 g**	**16.5 oz**	**100.0%**	**29.3 g**
Citric acid	4 g	0.1 oz	0.9%	0.3 g
Water	4 g	0.1 oz	0.9%	0.3 g
Tomato water	250 g	8.8 oz	53.4%	15.6 g
Saffron	0.2 g	0.0 oz	0.0%	0.0 g
Sugar	175 g	6.2 oz	37.4%	10.9 g
Pectin (HM) (see note)	10 g	0.4 oz	2.1%	0.6 g
Glucose	25 g	0.9 oz	5.3%	1.6 g
Sugar for garnish	As needed			

For ingredients that have "0.0 oz" as an amount, please refer to the metric measure as the oz quantity is too small to measure.

■ **Jaleas** Strawberry-Balsamic, Lobster-Tarragon, and Tomato-Saffron

EQUIPMENT	Bowls in various sizes	Knife	Silicone mat
	Cheesecloth	Measuring spoons	Saucepan
	Cutting board	Mold borders	Thermometer
	Induction burner	Refractor	Whisk
	Kitchen scale + analytical scale, high precision to 0.001 g	Rubber spatula	

NOTES

1. Different clarification techniques can be used. Examples include centrifuging, freezing, and thawing by slowly passing through a cheesecloth—or a traditional method of using egg whites can be used to prepare consommé and flavored waters.

2. Avoid using purchased consommé or flavored waters containing any gelatins. The addition of gelatin to the liquid will cause the gel to be cloudy and opaque.

3. Using a whisk for an extended amount of time after the addition of pectin may cause unwanted bubbles to be present in the final product.

4. There are various types of available pectin, and this recipe calls for HM (high-ester) due to its gelling properties in acidic and high-sugar-content mediums.

Method

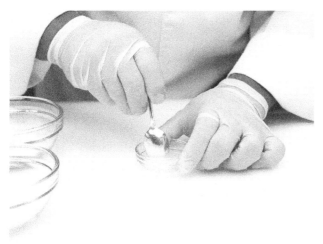

1. Dissolve the citric acid in 4 g of hot water in a bowl and set aside.

2. Separate the sugar into two bowls and disperse the pectin with one half of the sugar.

3. Then combine the trehalose with the other half of the sugar and reserve.

4. Combine the strawberry purée and balsamic reduction in a saucepan and bring it to 194°F/90°C.

5. Once at temperature, add the trimoline to the strawberry purée mixture and stir until dissolved.

6. Then add the trehalose-sugar mixture and stir until combined, followed by the pectin-sugar mixture.

7. Heat the syrup to 73°Brix on the refractor reading at about 230°F/110°C.

8. Once at temperature, quickly combine the citric acid with the hot pectin syrup and stir until combined.

9. Carefully pour the hot syrup onto a silicone mat with mold borders securely placed to prevent leakage.

10. Let the syrup set and cool to room temperature.

11. Store in the refrigerator once cooled.

12. Bring to room temperature, cut into desired shape, and lightly coat with sugar before serving.

LOBSTER-TARRAGON JALEAS

1. Dissolve the citric acid in 4 g of hot water in a bowl and set aside.

2. Separate the sugar into two bowls and combine the glucose with one half of the sugar.

3. Then combine the pectin and SHMP with the other half of the sugar and reserve.

4. Pour the prepared clarified lobster stock into a saucepan and heat to 194°F/90°C.

5. First add the glucose mixture to the saucepan and stir until dissolved, followed by the pectin mixture.

6. Heat the syrup to 73°Brix on the refractor reading at about 230°F/110°C.

7. Once at temperature, add the tarragon and the citric acid solution to the saucepan and stir until combined.

8. Carefully pour the hot syrup onto a silicone mat with mold borders securely placed to prevent leakage.

9. Let the syrup set and cool to room temperature.

10. Store in the refrigerator.

11. Bring to room temperature, cut into desired shapes, and lightly coat with sugar before serving.

TOMATO-SAFFRON JALEAS

1. Dissolve the citric acid in 4 g of hot water in a bowl and set aside.

2. Heat 50 g of the tomato water at 194°F/90°C and bloom the saffron until the flavor is extracted; strain and reserve the liquid.

3. Separate the sugar into two bowls and combine the glucose with one half of the sugar.

4. Then combine the pectin with the other half of the sugar and reserve.

5. Combine the prepared clarified tomato water and the infused saffron water in a saucepan and bring it to 194°F/90°C.

6. First add the glucose mixture to the saucepan and stir until dissolved, followed by the pectin mixture.

7. Heat the syrup to 73°Brix on the refractor reading at about 230°F/110°C.

8. Once at temperature, add the citric acid solution to the saucepan and stir until combined.

9. Carefully pour the hot syrup onto a silicone mat with mold borders securely placed to prevent leakage.

10. Let the syrup set and cool to room temperature.

11. Store in the refrigerator.

12. Bring to room temperature, cut into desired shapes, and lightly coat with sugar before serving.

Kuromame Bean Ice Cream

NUMBER OF PORTIONS	INGREDIENT	TECHNIQUE/METHOD	TEMPERATURE
8	Guar Gum	Thickener	Cold
	Trimoline	Freeze	
	Liquid Nitrogen		

Kuromame Bean Ice Cream

123 g or 4 oz per portion size

Ingredients	Amount (g)	Amount (oz)	%	Amount per portion (g)
Total amount	**987.0 g**	**34.8 oz**	**100.0%**	**123.4 g**
Heavy cream (45%)	400.0 g	14.1 oz	40.5%	50.0 g
Milk	400.0 g	14.1 oz	40.5%	50.0 g
Vanilla bean (halved and split lengthwise)	1 piece	1 piece	100.0%	123.4 g
Trimoline	75.0 g	2.6 oz	7.6%	9.4 g
Evaporated cane sugar	75.0 g	2.6 oz	7.6%	9.4 g
Guar gum	2.0 g	0.1 oz	0.2%	0.3 g
Liquid nitrogen (LN2)	As needed			
Hazelnut purée	10.0 g	0.4 oz	1.0%	1.3 g
Kuromame (black beans in syrup)	15.0 g	0.5 oz	1.5%	1.9 g
Rum	10.0 g	0.4 oz	1.0%	1.3 g

EQUIPMENT			
	Coffee/tea thermo pot	Kitchen scale + analytical scale, high precision to 0.001 g	Rubber spatula
	Dewar flask		Saucepan
	Electrical stirrer	Measuring spoons	Superbag
	Goggles	Protective gloves	Thermometer
	Induction burner	Rubber gloves	Whisk
	Insulated bowl		

NOTES

1. Kuromame are often sold in canned form and can be found in Asian grocery stores.

2. A KitchenAid with a whisk attachment can be used when adding LN2 to the anglaise.

3. Cane sugar can be substituted for granulated sugar.

4. Wear protective gloves and goggles when handling LN2.

5. Let all LN2 vapors evaporate before tasting or the item will stick to the inside of the mouth and can possibly cause injury.

6. Guar gum is used as an egg replacement in this ice cream base; and any flavor of ice cream (e.g., chocolate chip cookie, pistachio) can also be used.

7. Lambda carrageenan or locust bean gum can also be used to produce the ice cream.

Method

KUROMAME BEAN ICE CREAM

1. Place the cream, milk, and vanilla bean in a saucepan and heat to 194°F/90°C.

2. Add the trimoline to the hot cream mixture and stir until dissolved.

3. Combine the sugar and guar gum in a small bowl and disperse in the hot trimoline mixture.

4. Remove the vanilla bean halves from the saucepan and stir the trimoline mixture using a stirrer (at 250 rpm) or an immersion blender for 2 minutes for proper hydration to occur.

5. Strain the mixture using a Superbag.

6. Cool the hot anglaise over an ice water bath.

7. Carefully pour LN2 from a Dewar flask into a coffee/tea thermo pot and set aside.

8. Mix the hazelnut purée, kuromame beans (strained), and rum into the anglaise.

9. Pour the anglaise into an insulated bowl.

10. Pour LN2 into the anglaise.

11. Quickly whisk until frozen.

12. Let the LN2 evaporate and serve immediately.

■ **Yuzu Marshmallow** Served with Freeze-dried Beet Powder

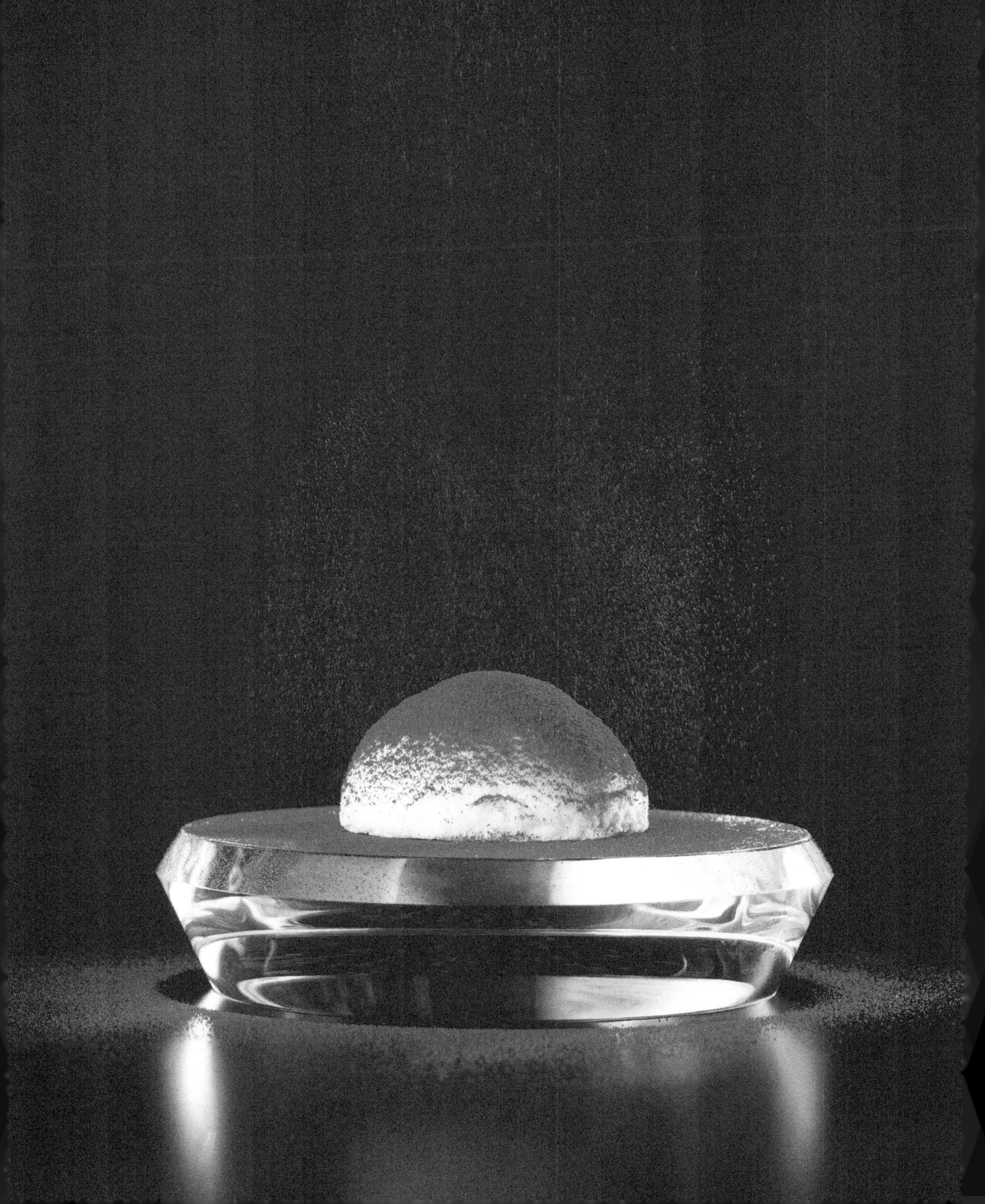

Yuzu Marshmallow

SERVED WITH FREEZE-DRIED BEET POWDER

NUMBER OF PORTIONS	INGREDIENT	TECHNIQUE/METHOD	TEMPERATURE
22	Arabic Gum	Emulsion/Thickener	Room Temperature
	Trimoline	Freeze-Drying	
	Gelatin		

	Ingredients	Amount (g)	Amount (oz)	%	Amount per portion (g)
Yuzu Marshmallow	**Total amount**	**1560.0 g**	**55.0 oz**	**100.0%**	**70.9 g**
71 g or 2.5 oz per portion size	Sugar	250 g	8.8 oz	16.0%	11.4 g
	Concentrated yuzu juice	10 g	0.4 oz	0.6%	0.5 g
	Water	170 g	6.0 oz	10.9%	7.7 g
	Arabic gum	125 g	4.4 oz	8.0%	5.7 g
	Gelatin sheets (185 Bloom)	20 g	0.7 oz	1.3%	0.9 g
	Ice water (to bloom gelatin)	400 g	14.1 oz	25.6%	18.2 g
	Trimoline	85 g	3.0 oz	5.4%	3.9 g
	Powdered sugar (sifted)	500 g	17.6 oz	32.1%	22.7 g
Garnish	**Total amount**	**5.0 g**	**0.2 oz**	**100.0%**	**0.2 g**
0.2 g or 0.001 oz per portion size	Freeze-dried beet powder	5 g	0.2 oz	100.0%	0.2 g

EQUIPMENT			
	Induction burner	Rubber gloves	Spoon
	KitchenAid mixer	Rubber spatula	Stainless-steel bowls
	Kitchen scale + analytical scale, high precision to 0.001 g	Saucepan	Thermometer
		Sifter	Thermomix
	Measuring spoon	Silicone mold	

1. If a Thermomix is not available, a heating element such as a gas burner or an induction burner can be used in conjunction with a thermometer and an immersion blender.

2. Alternative flavoring (including savory flavors) can be used instead of yuzu juice.

3. Appropriate temperature must be reached throughout the cooking process.

4. The trimoline and gelatin mixture must be well whisked to maintain texture. The preparation will resemble the process of making Italian meringue.

5. Freeze-dried powders are commercially available, or refer to Chapter 7 for the specifics of freeze-drying.

6. The marshmallows can be made in advance, but store in an airtight container to keep them from drying out.

7. Dehydrated powders can also be used as a substitute for freeze-dried powders.

Method

YUZU MARSHMALLOW

1. Place sugar, yuzu juice, and water into the Thermomix and set the temperature to 212°F/100°C on the lowest stirring setting.

2. Add yuzu juice.

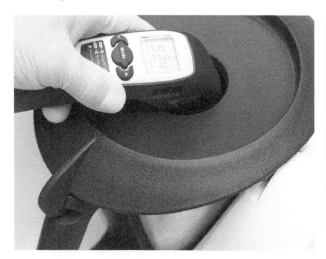

3. Set the temperature.

4. Once at temperature, add the gum arabic and increase the setting to speed 3 for 30 seconds and then to speed 8 for an additional minute.

5. Meanwhile, soak the gelatin in water.

6. Place the trimoline and presoaked gelatin in a bowl over a hot bain-marie and bring the mixture to 145°F/60°C, or until the contents have melted.

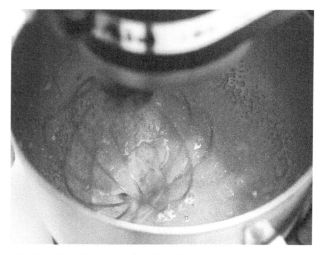

7. Pour the gelatin and trimoline mixture into a KitchenAid and add the whisk attachment.

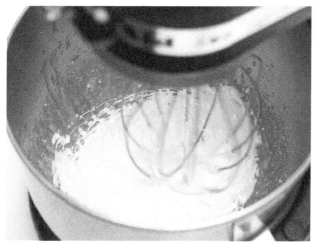

8. Whisk the mixture on medium to high speed for 10 to 15 minutes, or until medium-stiff peaks form.

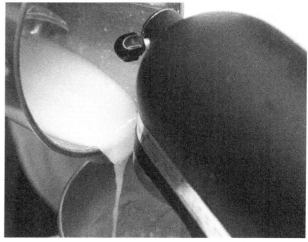

9. Slowly pour the sugar and gum arabic mixture into the trimoline mixture.

10. Continue whisking on medium-high speed for 20 to 25 minutes, or until stiff ribbons form.

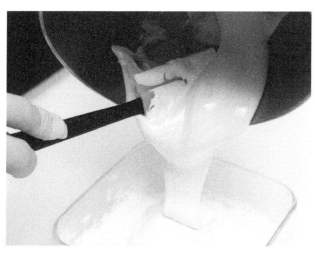

13. Cover with powdered sugar and plastic film. Gently press down on the mixture with your hands to avoid air pockets.

14. Let the marshmallow rest at room temperature for about 24 hours, or until they are dry.

15. Keep in an airtight container covered with ample amounts of powdered sugar.

16. Pour the freeze dried/dehydrated beet powder in a fine sieve and sprinkle over the marshmallow. Serve immediately.

11. Heavily cover a silicone mold with powdered sugar.

12. Pour the marshmallow mixture into the mold.

APPENDIX

1 pound = 16 ounces

16 ounces = 437.5 grams

1 ounce = 28.35 grams

1 kilogram = 35.27 ounces = 2.2 pounds

You can convert them using these formulas:

Ounces = Number of grams ÷ 28.35

Grams = Number of ounces × 28.35

Grams to Ounces						Ounces to Grams					
g	oz	g	oz	g	oz	Oz	g	oz	g	oz	g
0.01	0.0004	18	0.635	46	1.62	0.01	0.28	18	510.3	46	1304
0.05	0.0018	19	0.670	47	1.66	0.05	1.42	19	538.7	47	1332
0.1	0.004	20	0.705	48	1.69	0.1	2.84	20	567.0	48	1361
0.2	0.007	21	0.741	49	1.73	0.2	5.67	21	595.4	49	1389
0.3	0.011	22	0.776	50	1.76	0.3	8.51	22	623.7	50	1418
0.4	0.014	23	0.811	55	1.94	0.4	11.34	23	652.1	55	1559
0.5	0.018	24	0.847	60	2.12	0.5	14.18	24	680.4	60	1701
0.6	0.021	25	0.882	70	2.47	0.6	17.01	25	708.8	70	1985
0.7	0.025	26	0.917	80	2.82	0.7	19.85	26	737.1	80	2268
0.8	0.028	27	0.952	90	3.17	0.8	22.68	27	765.5	90	2552
0.9	0.032	28	0.988	100	3.53	0.9	25.52	28	793.8	100	2835
1	0.035	29	1.02	150	5.29	1	28.35	29	822.2	150	4253
2	0.071	30	1.06	200	7.05	2	56.70	30	850.5	200	5670
3	0.106	31	1.09	250	8.82	3	85.05	31	878.9	250	7088
4	0.141	32	1.13	300	10.58	4	113.4	32	907.2	300	8505
5	0.176	33	1.16	400	14.11	5	141.8	33	935.6	400	11340
6	0.212	34	1.20	500	17.64	6	170.1	34	963.9	500	14175
7	0.247	35	1.23	600	21.16	7	198.5	35	992.3	600	17010
8	0.282	36	1.27	700	24.69	8	226.8	36	1021	700	19845
9	0.317	37	1.31	800	28.22	9	255.2	37	1049	800	22680
10	0.353	38	1.34	900	31.75	10	283.5	38	1077	900	25515
11	0.388	39	1.38	1000	35.27	11	311.9	39	1106	1000	28350
12	0.423	40	1.41	1100	38.80071	12	340.2	40	1134	1100	31185
13	0.459	41	1.45	1200	42.32804	13	368.6	41	1162	1200	34020
14	0.494	42	1.48	1300	45.85538	14	396.9	42	1191	1300	36855
15	0.529	43	1.52	1400	49.38272	15	425.3	43	1219	1400	39690
16	0.564	44	1.55	1500	52.91005	16	453.6	44	1247	1500	42525
17	0.600	45	1.59	1600	56.43739	17	482.0	45	1276	1600	45360

MEASUREMENT CONVERSION OF COMMONLY USED INGREDIENTS

	1 teaspoon		1 tablespoon		½ cup		1 cup	
U.S.			3 teaspoons		8 tablespoons		16 tablespoons	
Metric	5 ml		15 ml		120 ml		240 ml	
Imperial	⅖ fl oz		½ fl oz		4 fl oz		8 fl oz	
					⅕ pint		⅖ pint	
Liquids	g		g		g		g	
Water	5.0		15.0		120.0		240.0	
Milk (dairy/soy)	5.0		15.0		120.0		240.0	
Cream (fresh)	4.8		14.4		115.2		230.4	
Oil	3.9		11.7		93.6		187.2	
Soy sauce	5.3		15.9		127.2		254.4	
Ketchup	5.9		17.7		141.6		283.2	
Agave syrup	7.2		21.6		172.8		345.6	
Maple syrup	1.5		4.4		34.8		69.6	
Honey	7.2		21.6		172.8		345.6	
Barley malt	8.3		24.9		199.2		398.4	
Vinegar	4.3		12.9		103.2		206.4	
Wine	4.4		13.2		105.6		211.2	
Vodka	4.0		12.0		96.0		192.0	
Powders and Solids	g	oz	g	oz	g	oz	g	oz
Fructose	4.1	0.14	12.3	0.43	98.4	3.47	196.8	6.94
Glucose	7.2	0.25	21.6	0.76	172.8	6.10	345.6	12.19
Isomalt	4.7	0.17	14.1	0.50	112.8	3.98	225.6	7.96
Wheat flour	3.3	0.12	9.9	0.35	79.2	2.79	158.4	5.59
Almond flour	2.8	0.10	8.4	0.30	67.2	2.37	134.4	4.74
Durum flour	3.1	0.11	9.3	0.33	74.4	2.62	148.8	5.25
Gluten flour	0.2	0.01	0.6	0.02	4.8	0.17	9.6	0.34
Rice flour	2.4	0.08	7.2	0.25	57.6	2.03	115.2	4.06
Tapioca flour	3.5	0.12	10.5	0.37	84	2.96	168	5.93
Cornstarch	0.2	0.01	0.6	0.02	4.8	0.17	9.6	0.34
Sea salt	3.7	0.13	11.1	0.39	88.8	3.13	177.6	6.26
Fine sea salt	6.2	0.22	18.6	0.66	148.8	5.25	297.6	10.50
Black salt	3.3	0.12	9.9	0.35	79.2	2.79	158.4	5.59
Kosher salt	5.8	0.20	17.4	0.61	139.2	4.91	278.4	9.82
Cocoa powder	2.8	0.10	8.4	0.30	67.2	2.37	134.4	4.74

(continued)

Black pepper (ground)	1.6	0.06	4.8	0.17	38.4	1.35	76.8	2.71
Red chili powder	2.5	0.09	7.5	0.26	60	2.12	120	4.23
Cayenne powder	2	0.07	6	0.21	48	1.69	96	3.39
Fennel seed powder	2.2	0.08	6.6	0.23	52.8	1.86	105.6	3.72
Oregano (dry)	0.8	0.03	2.4	0.08	19.2	0.68	38.4	1.35
Rosemary (dry)	1	0.04	3	0.11	24	0.85	48	1.69
Savory (dry)	1	0.04	3	0.11	24	0.85	48	1.69
Clove powder	2.3	0.08	6.9	0.24	55.2	1.95	110.4	3.89
Ginger powder	1.8	0.06	5.4	0.19	43.2	1.52	86.4	3.05
Saffron threads	1	0.04	3	0.11	24	0.85	48	1.69
Nutmeg powder	2.2	0.08	6.6	0.23	52.8	1.86	105.6	3.72
Tamarind powder	2.3	0.08	6.9	0.24	55.2	1.95	110.4	3.89
Turmeric	2.5	0.09	7.5	0.26	60	2.12	120	4.23
Whole dry mustard seed	3.7	0.13	11.1	0.39	88.8	3.13	177.6	6.26
Poppy seed	2.8	0.10	8.4	0.30	67.2	2.37	134.4	4.74
Caraway seed	2.6	0.09	7.8	0.28	62.4	2.20	124.8	4.40
Sesame seeds	2.7	0.10	8.1	0.29	64.8	2.29	129.6	4.57
Butter	4.7	0.17	14.1	0.50	112.8	3.98	225.6	7.96
Raw Materials	**g**	**oz**	**g**	**oz**	**g**	**oz**	**g**	**oz**
Minced basil (fresh)	1	0.04	3	0.11	24	0.85	48	1.69
Minced lemongrass	2.3	0.08	6.9	0.24	55.2	1.95	110.4	3.89
Garlic	5.7	0.20	17.1	0.60	136.8	4.83	273.6	9.65
Cilantro	2.5	0.09	7.5	0.26	60	2.12	120	4.23
Lemon zest	3.2	0.11	9.6	0.34	76.8	2.71	153.6	5.42
Mint (fresh)	1	0.04	3	0.11	24	0.85	48	1.69
Parsley (fresh)	2.5	0.09	7.5	0.26	60	2.12	120	4.23
Lavender	0.7	0.02	2.1	0.07	16.8	0.59	33.6	1.19
Tarragon	1.7	0.06	5.1	0.18	40.8	1.44	81.6	2.88
Egg yolk	4.2	0.15	12.6	0.44	100.8	3.56	201.6	7.11
Egg white	4.5	0.16	13.5	0.48	108	3.81	216	7.62
Egg, whole	5.8	0.20	17.4	0.61	139.2	4.91	278.4	9.82
Cream cheese	4.4	0.1552	13.2	0.46561	105.6	3.72487	211.2	7.45
Mascarpone	4.7	0.16578	14.1	0.49735	112.8	3.97884	225.6	7.96
Ground fish	4.8	0.16931	14.4	0.50794	115.2	4.06349	230.4	8.13
Ground shrimp	4.7	0.16578	14.1	0.49735	112.8	3.97884	225.6	7.96

LENGTH CONVERSION CHART

1 inch = 2.54 centimeters

1 foot = 12 inches

1 centimeter = 10 milimeter

1 meter = 1000 milimeters

You can convert them using this formula:

Inches = X/2.54

Centimeters = X × 2.54

Inches to cm				cm to Inches			
inch	cm	inch	cm	cm	inch	cm	inch
⅛	0.32	21	53.34	0.1	0.04	21	8.27
¼	0.64	22	55.88	0.2	0.08	22	8.66
⅜	0.95	23	58.42	0.3	0.12	23	9.06
½	1.27	24	60.96	0.4	0.16	24	9.45
¾	1.91	25	63.50	0.5	0.20	25	9.84
1	2.54	26	66.04	1	0.39	26	10.24
2	5.08	27	68.58	2	0.79	27	10.63
3	7.62	28	71.12	3	1.18	28	11.02
4	10.16	29	73.66	4	1.57	29	11.42
5	12.70	30	76.20	5	1.97	30	11.81
6	15.24	31	78.74	6	2.36	31	12.20
7	17.78	32	81.28	7	2.76	32	12.60
8	20.32	33	83.82	8	3.15	33	12.99
9	22.86	34	86.36	9	3.54	34	13.39
10	25.40	35	88.90	10	3.94	35	13.78
11	27.94	36	91.44	11	4.33	36	14.17
12	30.48	37	93.98	12	4.72	37	14.57
13	33.02	38	96.52	13	5.12	38	14.96
14	35.56	39	99.06	14	5.51	39	15.35
15	38.10	40	101.60	15	5.91	40	15.75
16	40.64	41	104.14	16	6.30	41	16.14
17	43.18	42	106.68	17	6.69	42	16.54
18	45.72	43	109.22	18	7.09	43	16.93
19	48.26	44	111.76	19	7.48	44	17.32
20	50.80	45	114.30	20	7.87	45	17.72

In the Celsius scale, water freezes at 0° Celsius and boils at 100° Celsius.

In the Fahrenheit scale, water freezes at 32° Fahrenheit and boils at 212° Fahrenheit.

You can convert them using this formula:

Celsius = (X − 32) × 180/100 = (X − 32) × 9/5

Fahrenheit = 180/100X + 32 = 9/5X + 32

Liquid nitrogen boiling point: -196 °C / −321°F

Celsius to Fahrenheit							
°C	°F	°C	°F	°C	°F	°C	°F
−196	−320.8						
−150	−238						
−100	−148						
−50	−58						
−5	23						
0	32	100	212	200	392	300	572
5	41	105	221	205	401	305	581
10	50	110	230	210	410	310	590
15	59	115	239	215	419	315	599
20	68	120	248	220	428	320	608
25	77	125	257	225	437	325	617
30	86	130	266	230	446	330	626
35	95	135	275	235	455	335	635
40	104	140	284	240	464	340	644
45	113	145	293	245	473	345	653
50	122	150	302	250	482	350	662
55	131	155	311	255	491	355	671
60	140	160	320	260	500	360	680
65	149	165	329	265	509	365	689
70	158	170	338	270	518	370	698
75	167	175	347	275	527	375	707
80	176	180	356	280	536	380	716
85	185	185	365	285	545	385	725
90	194	190	374	290	554	390	734
95	203	195	383	295	563	395	743

			Fahrenheit to Celsius				
°F	°C	°F	°C	°F	°C	°F	°C
−321	−196.11						
−150	−101.11						
−100	−73.33						
−50	−45.56						
−5	−20.56						
0	−17.78	100	37.78	200	93.33	300	148.89
5	−15.00	105	40.56	205	96.11	305	151.67
10	−12.22	110	43.33	210	98.89	310	154.44
15	−9.44	115	46.11	215	101.67	315	157.22
20	−6.67	120	48.89	220	104.44	320	160.00
25	−3.89	125	51.67	225	107.22	325	162.78
30	−1.11	130	54.44	230	110.00	330	165.56
35	1.67	135	57.22	235	112.78	335	168.33
40	4.44	140	60.00	240	115.56	340	171.11
45	7.22	145	62.78	245	118.33	345	173.89
50	10.00	150	65.56	250	121.11	350	176.67
55	12.78	155	68.33	255	123.89	355	179.44
60	15.56	160	71.11	260	126.67	360	182.22
65	18.33	165	73.89	265	129.44	365	185.00
70	21.11	170	76.67	270	132.22	370	187.78
75	23.89	175	79.44	275	135.00	375	190.56
80	26.67	180	82.22	280	137.78	380	193.33
85	29.44	185	85.00	285	140.56	385	196.11
90	32.22	190	87.78	290	143.33	390	198.89
95	35.00	195	90.56	295	146.11	395	201.67

BIBLIOGRAPHY

Achatz, Grant. *Alinea (First Edition).* Emeryville, CA: Ten Speed Press, 2008.

Adrià, Ferran. *elBulli 1983–1993.* (Spanish edition). Barcelona, Spain: Rba Libros, 2006.

Adrià, Ferran. *elBulli 1994–1997.* New York, NY/Barcelona, Spain: Ecco, 2006.

Adrià, Ferran. *elBulli 1998–2002.* New York, NY/Barcelona, Spain: Ecco, 2005.

Adrià, Ferran. *elBulli 2003–2004.* New York: Ecco, 2006.

Adrià, Ferran. *elBulli 2005 (Spanish edition).* New York, NY/ Barcelona, Spain: Rba Libros, 2006.

Adrià, Ferran. *Modern Gastronomy A to Z: A Scientific and Gastronomic Lexicon.* Boca Raton, FL: CRC Press, 2010.

Adrià, Ferran, Albert Adrià, and **Juli Soler.** *A Day of El Bulli: An Insight into the Ideas, Methods and Creativity of Ferran Adria.* New York: Phaidon Press Limited, 2008.

Aduriz, Andoni Luis. *Tabula Bacalao (Spanish edition).* Barcelona, Spain: Montagud Editores, 2003.

Balaguer, Oriol, Ramon Morato, Miguel Sierra, Isaac Balguer, Carlos Mampel, Abraham Balaguer, Abraham Palomeque, and **David Pallas.** *21st C, The New Generation in Pastry.* Weimar, TX: CHIPS, 2007.

Baldwin, Douglas. *Sous Vide for the Home Cook.* Boulder, CO: Sous Vide, 2010.

Blumenthal , Heston. *The Fat Duck Cookbook.* London: Bloomsbury, 2008.

The Culinary Institute of America. *The Professional Chef, 9th edition.* Hoboken, NJ: John Wiley & Sons, 2011.

Gabriel, Jean Pierre. *Les Essentiels la Cuisine Contemporaine.* Brussels, Belgium: Unilever, 2009.

Garcia, Dani. *Tecnica y Contrastes.* Barcelona, Spain: Montagud Editores, 2004.

Gisslen, Wayne. *Professional Cooking, 8th edition.* Hoboken, NJ: John Wiley & Sons, 2015.

Hoefler, Andrew C. *Hydrocolloids: Practical Guides for the Food Industry (Eagen Press Handbook Series).* Saint Paul, MN: AACC International Press, 2004.

Imeson, Alan. *Food Stabilisers, Thickeners and Gelling Agents.* Oxford, UK/Ames, Iowa: Wiley-Blackwell, 2010.

Keller, Thomas. *Under Pressure: Cooking Sous Vide.* New York: Artisan, 2008.

Laaman, Thomas R. *Hydrocolloids in Food Processing.* Ames, IA: Wiley-Blackwell, 2011.

McGee, Harold. *On Food Cooking: the Science and Lore of the Kitchen.* New York: Scribner, 2004.

Myhrvold, Nathan, Maxime Bilet, and **Chris Young.** *Modernist Cuisine: The Art and Science of Cooking.* Bellevue, WA: The Cooking Lab, 2011.

Nishinari, Katuyosi, and **Etsushiro Doi.** *Food Hydrocolloids: Structure, Properties, and Functions.* New York: Plenum Press, 1994.

Phillips, Glyn O., and **Peter A. Williams.** *Handbook of Hydrocolloids.* Boca Raton, FL: CRC Publishing, 2000.

Redzepi, Rene. *Noma: Time and Place in Nordic Cuisine.* New York: Phaidon Press Inc, , 2010.

Roca, Joan, and **Salvador Brugus.** *Sous Vide Cuisine Barcelona, Spain: Montagud Editores, 2005.*

Stampfer, Viktor. *Sous Vide: Cooking in a Vacuum (English German).* Stuttgart, Germany: Matthaes Verlag, 2008.

This, Hervé. *Molecular Gastronomy: Exploring the Science of Flavor.* New York: Columbia University Press, 2008.

This, Herve. *Molecular Gastronomy: Exploring the Science of Flavor.* [Unabridged Audible Audio Edition]. Newark, NJ: Audible, Inc., 2008.

Torreblanca, Paco. *Paco Torreblanca (English, Spanish).* Barcelona, Spain: Vilbo Ediciones, 2006.

FURTHER READING

Abert, Jean-Francois. *Pierre Gagnaire: Reinventing French Cuisine.* New York: Stewart, Tabori and Chang, 2007.

Acevedo, E., J. Enronoe, F. Osorio, F. Pedreschi, and O. Skurtys. *Food Hydrocolloid Edible Films and Coatings (Food Science and Technology).* Hauppauge, NY: Nova Science Publishers, 2010.

Aduriz, Andoni Luis. *Mugaritz: A Natural Science of Cooking.* New York: Phaidon Press, 2012.

Aduriz, Andoni Luis. *Clorofilia (Spanish edition), Imagen Mab, 2004.*

Aftel, Mandy, and Daniel Patterson. *Aroma: The Magic of Essential Oils in Foods and Fragrance.* New York: Artisan, 2004.

American Chemical Society, and Leonard Stoloff. *Physical Functions of Hydrocolloids.* Whitefish, MT: Literary Licensing, 2012.

Antona, Andreas. *Modern French Cooking.* Bath, UK: Absolute Press, 2008.

Arzak, Juan Mari. *Arzak.* Secretos. Bilbao, Spain: Bainet Editorial, 2009.

Balaguer, Oriol, Ramon Morato, Miguel Sierra, Isaac Balguer, Carlos Mampel, Abraham Balaguer, Abraham Palomeque, and **David Pallas.** *21st C, The New Generation in Pastry.* CHIPS, 2007.

Barbot, Pascal, Christophe Rohat, and **Chihiro Masui, L'Astrance: The Cookbook.** *Paris: Hachette Livre Direction, 2012.*

Barham, Peter. *The Science of Cooking.* New York: Springer, 2001.

Blumenthal, Heston. *The Big Fat Duck Cookbook.* New York: Bloomsbury USA, 2008.

Blumenthal, Heston. *Dashi and Umami: The Heart of Japanese Cuisine.* Tokyo: Kodansha International, 2009.

Blumenthal, Heston. *In Search of Perfection.* New York: Bloomsbury USA, 2010.

Bottura, Massimo, and **Ciccio Sultano.** *PRO.* Attraverso tradizione e innovazione. Lodi, Italy: Bibliotheca Culinaria, 2006.

Bras, Michel. *Essential Cuisine.* Woodbury, CT: Ici La Press, 2010.

The Chefs of Le Cordon Bleu. *Le Cordon Bleu Cuisine Foundations.* Clifton Park, NY: Delmar, 2010.

Corriher, Shirley O. *CookWise: The Secrets of Cooking Revealed.* New York: William Morrow Cookbooks, 2011.

Dacosta, Quique, Quique Dacosta (Spanish). *Weimar, TX:-CHIPS, 2008.*

Degeimbre, Sang-Hoon and **Gabriel, Jean Pierre ; L'Air du temps.** *Bruxelles: Editions Francoise Blouard, 2007.*

Ducasse, Alain. *Grand Livre De Cuisine: Alain Ducasse's Culinary Encyclopedia.* Issy-les-Moulineaux, France: Ducasse Books, 2009.

Ellix Katz, Sandor. *Wild Fermentation: The Flavor, Nutrition, and Craft of Live-Culture Foods.* White River Junction, VT: Chelsea Green Publishing, 2003.

Escoffier, Auguste. *The Escoffier Cookbook and Guide to the Fine Art of Cookery: For Connoisseurs, Chefs, Epicures Complete with 2973 Recipes, 55th edition.* New York: Crown Publishers, 2000.

Everitt-Matias, David. *Essence: Recipes from Le Champignon Sauvage.* Bath, UK: Absolute Press, 2006.

Flammarion, Ernest. *Gastronomie Pratique: Etudes Culinaires.* Paris: L'imprimerie Hemmerle, 1981.

Friedman, Mendel, and **Don Mottram.** *Chemistry and Safety of Acrylamide in Food (Advances in Experimental Medicine and Biology).* New York: Springer, 2011.

Gagnaire, Pierre, and **Hervé This.** *Il bello e il Buono.* La cucina tra arte, amore e tecnica. Rome: Gambero Rosso GRH, 2006.

Glicksman, Martin. *Food Hydrocolloids.* Boca Raton, FL: CRC Press, 1982.

Glicksman, Martin. *Gum Technology in the Food Industry (Food Science &Technological Monograph).* Waltham, MA: Academic Press, 1969.

Henderson, Fergus. *The Whole Beast: Nose to Tail Eating.* New York: Ecco, 2004.

Hollingworth, Clarence S. *Food Hydrocolloids: Characteristics, Properties and Structures (Food Science and Technology).* Hauppauge, NY: Nova Science Publishers, 2010.

Imeson, Alan. *Thickening and Gelling Agents for Food.* New York: Springer Verlag, 1997.

Kunz, Gray, and **Peter Kaminsky.** *The Elements of Taste.* New York: Little, Brown, 2001.

Larousse, and **Joel Robuchon.** *Le Grand Larousse Gastronomique.* New York: French and European Publications Inc, 2007.

Le Foll, Camille. *Modern French Classics.* London: Hachette Illustrated UK, 2005.

Loiseau, Bernard. *L'envolée des saveurs.* Paris: Hachette, 1991.

Lowe, Belle. *Experimental Cookery From The Chemical And Physical Standpoint.* New York: John Wiley & Sons, 1937.

Marx, Thierry. *Planet Marx.* Paris: Editions Minerva, 2007.

McGee, Harold. *La Buena Cocina: Como Preparar los Mejores Platos y Recetas.* Madrid: Debate Editorial, 2010.

McGee, Harold. *Keys to Good Cooking: A Guide to Making the Best of Foods and Recipes.* New York: Penguin Books, 2012.

Migoya, Francisco, and **The Culinary Institute of America.** *The Modern Café.* Hoboken, NJ: John Wiley & Sons, 2009.

Nussinovitch, Amos. *Hydrocolloid Applications: Gum technology in the food and other industries.* New York: Springer, 1997.

Nussinovitch, Amos. *Water-Soluble Polymer Applications in Foods.* Oxford, UK: Wiley-Blackwell, 2003.

Parsons, Russ. *How to Read a French Fry: And Other Stories of Intriguing Kitchen Science.* New York: Houghton Mifflin, 2001.

Pauli, Philip. *Classical Cooking The Modern Way: Methods and Techniques.* Hoboken, NJ: John Wiley & Sons, 1999.

Piège, Jean-François. *At the Crillon and at Home: Recipes by Jean-François Piège.* Paris: Flammarion, 2008.

Pralus, Georges. *Une Historie d'Amour: La Cuisine Sous Vide.* Georges Pralus, 2000.

Roca, Joan, and **Salvador Brugues.** *La Cocina al Vacio, 1st edition.* Barcelona, SpainMontagud Editores, 2001.

Roellinger, Olivier. *Olivier Roellinger's Contemporary French Cuisine: 50 Recipes Inspired by the Sea.* Paris: Flammarion, 2005.

Roncero, Paco. *Tapas en estado puro.* Madrid, Spain: Everest, 2010.

Scully, D. *Eleanor, and Terence Scully.* Early French Cookery: Sources, History, Original Recipes and Modern Adaptations. Ann Arbor, MI: University of Michigan Press, 1996.

Telis, Vania Regina Nicoletti. *Biopolymer Engineering in food Processing (Contemporary Food Engineering).* Boca Raton, FL: CRC Press, 2012.

This, Hervé. *The Science of the Oven.* New York: Columbia University Press, 2009.

This, Hervé. *Building a Meal: From Molecular Gastronomy to Culinary Constructivism.* New York: Columbia University Press, 2009.

This, Hervé. *Cooking: The Quintessential Art.* Berkeley, CA: University of California Press, 2008.

This, Hervé. *Kitchen Mysteries: Revealing the Science of Cooking.* New York: Columbia University Press, 2010.

Tipton, Charles M. *Hydrocolloids.* Amsterdam, The Netherlands: Elsevier Science, 2001.

Torreblanca, Paco, and **Pierre Herme.** *Postres/Desserts (Spanish edition).* Barcelona, Spain: Larousse Editorial, 2007.

Willan, Anne. *The Cookbook Library: Four Centuries of the Cooks, Writers, and Recipes That Made the Modern Cookbook (California Studies in Food and Culture).* Berkeley, CA: University of California Press, 2012.

Wolke, Robert, What Einstein Told His Cook: Kitchen Science Explained. *New York: W.* W. Norton, 2002.

Yamamoto, Seiji. *Nihonryouri RyuGin.* Tokyo:Takahashi Shoten, 2012.

100% CHEF
Porto, 44
08032 Barcelona
Spain
+34 934296340
+34 655 46 93 67

A&D ENGINEERING
1756 Automation Pkwy.
San Jose, CA 95131
1.800.726.3364
408.263.5333

ACCUTEMP PRODUCTS, INC.
8415 N. Clinton Pk.
Fort Wayne, IN 46825
800.210.5907

AEROLATTE
2 Codicote Rd.
Welwyn AL6 9NB
United Kingdom
(+44) 845.872.4954

AJINOMOTO NORTH AMERICA
One Parker Plaza
400 Kelby St.
Fort Lee, NJ 07024
201.292.3200

AVESTIN, INC
2450 Don Reid Dr.
Ottawa, Ontario K1H 1E1
Canada
1 613 736 0019

BAMIX
700 Sleater-Kinney Rd. S.E., B214
Lacey, WA 98503
800.605.6046

BBQ GURU
357 Ivyland Rd.
Warminster, PA 18974-2205
800.288.4878

BECKMAN COULTER
250 South Kraemer Blvd.
Brea, CA 92821-6232
714.993.5321
800.526.3821

BENRINER CO.
741-0062 3-7-3
Iwakuni City
Yamaguchi Japan
(+81) 0827.43.4033

BERKEL, INC.
701 S Ridge Ave.
Troy, OH 45374
800.348.0251

BERNADAUD
11 Rue Royale
75008 Paris
France
33.1.4312.5321

BIRO MANUFACTURING, CO.
1114 W. Main St.
Marblehead, OH 43440
419.798.4451

BOSCH
Robert Bosch GmbH
Postfach 10 60 50
70049 Stuttgart
GERMANY
+49 (0) 711 811-0

BRADLEY
8380 River Road Delta
British Columbia V4G 1B5
Canada
866.508.7514

BRANSON ULTRASONIC CORP.
P.O Box 1961
41 Eagle Rd.
Danbury, CT 06813-1961
203.796.0400

BRINKMANN
4215 McEwen Rd.
Dallas, TX 75244
800.468.5252

BUCHI CORP.
19 Lukens Drive, Suite 400
New Castle, DE 19720
+1 302 652 3000

BUON VINO MFG. CO.
P.O Box 26003
365 Franklin Blvd.
Cambridge, Ontario N1R 8E8
Canada

CAMBRO
5801 Skylab Rd.
Huntington Beach, CA 92647
800.833.3003

CARPIGIANI CORP. OF NORTH AMERICA
3760 Industrial Dr.
Winston-Salem, NC 27105
336.661.9893

CHAMPION JUICER/PLASTAKET MFG. CO.
6220 E. Highway 12
Lodi, CA 95240
866.935.8423

COMEAU TECHNIQUE, LTD.
440 Aime-Vincent
Vaudreuil-Dorion Quebec J7V 5V5
Canada
800.361.2553

COOKSHACK FEC100
2304 N. Ash St.
Ponca City, OK 74601-1100
800.423.0698

CORNING
Tower 2, 4F
900 Chelmsford St.
Lowell, MA 01851
800.492.1110

CRISTALCO
27 Rue Châteaubriand
75008 Paris, France
+33 1 42 99 00 00

CP KELCO
Cumberland Center II
3100 Cumberland Blvd., Suite 600
Atlanta, GA 30339
800.535.2687

CSC SCIENTIFIC
2799-C Merrilee Dr.
Fairfax, VA 22031
800.621.4778

CUISINART
150 Milford Rd.
East Winsor, NJ 08520
800.726.0190

CYBORG EQUIPMENT CORPORA-TION
8 Graham Street
Wareham, MA 02571
508.291.0999

ENVIRO-PAK
15450 SE For-Mor Ct.
P O Box 1569
Clackamas, OR 97015
800.223.6836

EXCALIBUR
6083 Power Inn Rd.
Sacramento, CA 95824
800.875.4254

EYELA (TOKYO RIKAKIKAI)
TN Oishikawa Building 6F
1-15-17 Koishikawa
Bunkyo-ku Tokyo 112-0002
Japan
03.6757.3388

FISHER SCIENTIFIC WORLDWIDE
2000 Parl Lane Dr.
Pittsburgh, PA 15275
800.766.7000

FLUKE CORP.
6920 Seaway Blvd.
Everett, WA 98203
503.643.5204

FMI CORP.
3-11-31, Hanaten-Higashi
Tsurumi-ku, Osaka 538-0044
Japan
81.6.6969.9387

FOSTER
Oldmedow Rd.
King's Lynn, Norfolk, PE30 4JU
0843.216.8800

FUSIONCHEF GMBH & CO. KG
Eisenbahnstrasse 45/1
11960 Seelbach / Germany
+49 (0) 7823 51-170

GK JAPAN AGENCY CO., LTD/BERNARDAUD
Shinshinkaikan,7F, 3-14-1
Nihonbashi, Chuo-Ku,
Tokyo 103-0027
Japan

GENEVAC
815 Rt. 208
Gardiner NY 12525
845.267.2211

GLASS STUDIO
581 Gion-machi Minamigawa
Higashiyama-ku
Kyoto 605-0074
Japan
075.532.1470

GPI INC.
1255 Journey's End Circle
Newmarket, Ontario L3Y 8T7
Canada
905.853.8828

GUZMÁN GASTRONOMÍA–DIVISIÓN SOLÉ GRAELLS
Mercabarna–Longitudinal 5 n° 53
08040 Barcelona
Spain
(+34) 93.262.8910

HAMILTON BEACH BRANDS, INC.
360 Page Rd.
Washington, NC 27899
800.851.8900

HANNA INSTRUMENTS, INC.
584 Park E. Dr.
Woonsocket, RI 02895
800.426.6287

HENKELMAN BV
P.O. Box 2117
5202 CCs-Hertogenbosch
Netherlands
(+31) 73.621.3671

HI-TECH VACUUM
1445A, RR5
Saint-Cyrille-de-Wendover
Quebec J1Z 1S5
Canada
819.397.4888

HOBART CORP.
701 S Ridge Ave.
Troy, OH 45374
888.446.2278

HOSHIZAKI AMERICA, INC.
618 Hwy. 74 S
Peachtree City, GA 30269
800.438.6087

HUALIAN PACKAGING MACHINES
6 Chanyeyuan Rd.
325028 Wenzhou
China

ICC–INTERNATIONAL COOKING CONCEPTS
Gran Via Corts Catalanes, 649–Local 2
08010 Barcelona
Spain
(+34) 93.253.1210

IKA JAPAN K.K
3-5-8 Yokonuma Cho
Higashiosaka, Osaka 577-0808
Japan
81.6.6730.6781

IKEDEN
105-0004 Shinbasi 2-12-5
Minatoku, Tokyo
03.3503.0531

ISI NORTH AMERICA, INC.
175 Route 46 West
Fairfield, NJ 07004
800.447.2426

IWATANI GROUP
2050 Center Ave, Suite 425
Fort Lee, NJ 07024
201.585.2442

JULABO JAPAN
Sonoda-chou 8-18
Ibaraki, Osaka 567-0825
Japan
+49 (0) 7823 51-170

JB PRINCE
36 East 31st
New York, NY 10016
800.473.0577

KOCH
1414 West 29th St.
Kansas City, MO 64108-3604
816.753.2150

KOTOBUKI SANGYO
4-11-15 Minami Omori
Ota-ku Tokyo 143-0013
Japan

KUBOTA CORPORATION
No.29-9 Hongo 3-chome
Bunkyu-ku
Tokyo 113-0033
Japan
03.3815.1331

KUHN RIKON
Neschwilerstrasse 4
CH 8486 Rikon
Switzerland
(+41) 52.396.0101

LAB LINE SCIENTIFIC INSTRU-
MENTS
C/108 Maruti Darshan, Hanuman
Chowk
L.T. Rd., Mulund (East)
Mumbai 400 081
Maharashtra, India
(+91) 22.216.33671

LABCONCO CORP.
8811 Prospect Ave.
Kansas City, MO 64132-2696
800.821.5525

LENOX
301 Chestnut St.
East Longmeadow, MA 01028
800.628.8810

LISS AMERICA
106 Skyline Dr.
South Plainfield, NJ 07080
908.222.1015

MASTERFLEX
Cole-Parmer
625 East Bunker Ct.
Vernon Hills, IL 60061
847.549.7600

METTLER TOLEDO, INC.
1900 Polaris Pkwy.
Columbus, OH 43240
800.638.8537

MICROPLANE
614 SR 247
Russellville, AR 72802
800.555.2767

MOSCHETTI INC.
11 6th St.
Vallejo, CA 94590
800.556.4414

MSEC CO.
6420 Richmond Ave, Suite 233
Houston, Texas 77057
877.706.4480

MULTIVAC
11021 North Pomona Ave.
Kansas City, MO 64153
800.800.8552

NALGENE
Thermo Fisher Scientific International Dept.
75 Panorama Creek Dr.
Rochester, NY 14625
800.625.4327

NEWARK
160 Fornelius Ave.
Clifton, NJ 07013
800.221.0392

INGREDION INCORPORATE
5 Westbrook Corporate Center
Westchester, IL 60154
708.551.2600

NTG (NIPPON TANSAN GAS CO., LTD)
12-15, 3-Chome, Aoi, Adachi-ku
Tokyo, Japan 03.3849.1573

OAKTON INSTRUMENTS
P.O. Box 5136
Vernon Hills, IL 60061
1-888-462-5866

OHAUS
4802 Glenwood Rd.
Brooklyn, NY 11234
800.672.7722

OMNI
935-C Cobb Place Blvd.
NW Kennesaw, GA 30144
800.776.4431

PACOJET AG
Bundesstrasse 5
CH-6300 Zug
Switzerland
+41-41-710-25-22

PICOTECH
James House Marlborough Rd.
Colmworth Business Park
Eaton Socon St Neots, Cam-
bridgeshire PE19 8YP
United Kingdom
(+44) 1480.396.395

POLYSCIENCE
6600 W Touhy Ave.
Niles, IL
800.299.7569

PRO SCIENTIFIC
99 Willenbrock Rd.
Oxford CT 06478
203.267.4600

RATIONAL OVENS/AKNO LTD.
895 American Ln.
Schaumburg, IL 60173-4570
866.891.3528

THE RUBBER CHEF
6627 Schuster St.
Las Vegas, NV 89118
702.614.9350

LE SANCTUAIRE
315 Sutter Street, 5F
San Francisco, CA 94108
949.331.3727

SANPLATEC CORP.
No.1-3, 2-Chome Doshini
Kita-ku Osaka City 530-0035
Japan
(+81) 816.63.53.5141

SARTORIUS AG
5 Orville Dr.
Bohemia, NY 11716
800.645.3108

SHANGHAI SHENYIN MACHINE FACTORY
Room 1703-04 Building B
Long 48 Jiaotong West Rd.
Shanghai, China
(+86) 21.56.080.777

SILICONEMOULDS
Natural Heating Unit 5
Bunns Bank Industrial Estate
Attleborough, Norfolk NR17 1QD
0195.345.2525

SILPAT
Sasa Demarle
8 Corporate D.
Cranbury, NJ 08512
609.395.0219

SOSA INGREDIENTS SL
C/ Sot d'Aluies, sn - Pol. Ind.
Sot d'Aluies 08180
Moià / Barcelona
Spain
 +34 938 666 111

SP INDUSTRIES/VIRTIS
935 Mearns Rd.
Warminster, PA 18974
800.523.2327
215.672.7800

SPECTRUM CHEMICALS & LABORATORY PRODUCTS
14422 South San Pedro St.
Gardena, CA 90248
800.813.1514

SUNPENTOWN/MR. INDUCTION
14625 Clark Ave.
City of Industry CA 91745
800.330.0388

TANITA
2625 South Clearbrook Dr.
Arlington Heights, Illinois 60005
847.640.9241

TAYLOR COMPANY
750 N. Blackhawk Rd.
Rockton, IL 61072
800.255.0626

THERMAPEN
1762 W. 20 S, 100
Lindon, UT 84042
800.393.6434

THERMO SCIENTIFIC SORVALL
81 Wyman St.
Waltham, MA 02454
781.622.1000

THERMO WORKS
1762 West 20 S, 100
Lindon, UT 84042
800.393.6434

TIC GUMS
10552 Philadelphia Rd.
White Marsh, MD 21162
800.899.3953

TODDY
1225 Red Cedar Circle, Unit C
Fort Collins, CO 80524
888.863.3974

TRAEGER
9445 SW Ridder Rd.
Wilsonville, OR 97070
800.872.3437

TURBOTORCH
16052 Swingley Ridge Rd., Suite 300
St. Louis, MO 63017

VERRE-MORIYAMA GLASSWARE CO.
Agio 1 Building
3-3-12 Ebiso minami
Shibuyaku, Tokyo 150-0022
Japan
03.5721.8013

VITAMIX CORP.
8615 Usher Rd.
Cleveland, OH 44138
800.848.2649

VORWERK
Geschaftsbereich Thermomix
Muhlenweg 17-37
D-42270 Wuppertal
49.202.564.3811

Page numbers followed by *f* and *t* refer to figures and tables, respectively.

A

Achatz, Grant, 7, 7*f*
Activa (transglutaminase; TG), 103
adhesive sealing tape, 31*f*
Adrià, Ferran, 5, 5*f*
aerators, 39, 39*f*
agar (E406), 44, 51, 64–65
airs, 115
    Beet, 157, 161
    Beet, Olive Oil Gelatin Served with Chorizo
        Powder and, 157, 158*f*, 159–161
    Pernod, 238, 243
    Pernod, (Optional), Hot Lobster Tokoroten
        Served with Sous Vide Lobster, Truffle Oil
        Encapsulation, and, 236*f*–237*f*, 238–243
alginate, 44
allergens, 19
Andrés, José, 9, 9*f*
anti-griddles, 123
antioxidants, 93–98
    ascorbic acid, 93–94
    citric acid, 94–95
    potassium citrate, 95–96
    sodium citrate, 96–97
    tartaric acid, 97–98
Ants on a Log Served with Nutella Powder, 265,
    266*f*–267*f*, 268–270
arabic gum (E414), 44, 45, 66–67
ascorbic acid (E300), 93–94

B

Bacon Powder, 221, 224
    Caesar Salad Soup Served with Sous Vide
        Quail Egg and, 221, 222*f*, 223–224
Basil Gel, 179, 184
Bean Foam, Hot, 163–165
    Perfect Huevos Rancheros Served with
        Dehydrated Jalapeño and Tortilla
        Powders, Salsa Gel, and, 162*f*, 163–165
Béarnaise
    Fried, 231, 232–234
    Fried, Served with Sous Vide Beef Steak
        and Soufflé Potato, 230*f*, 231–235
    Reduction, 231
Beef Steak, Sous Vide, 231, 235
    Fried Béarnaise Served with Soufflé Potato
        and, 230*f*, 231–235
Beer
    Gel, 225, 229
    Gel, Foie Royale Served with Compressed
        Fruit and, 225, 226*f*–227*f*, 228–229
    Pork, Gastrovac, 215, 218–219
    Pork and Cotton Candy Cooked in the
        Gastrovac, 215, 216*f*–217*f*, 218–220
Beet
    Air, 157, 161
    Air, Olive Oil Gelatin Served with Chorizo
        Powder and, 157, 158*f*, 159–161

Powder, Freeze-Dried, Yuzu Marshmallow
        Served with, 288*f*, 289–291
biological hazards, 16
blenders, 33–34
Blood Orange
    Spheres, 133
    Spheres, Served with Mint Oil and Cryo-
        poached Blood Orange Teardrops,
        133–134, 135*f*, 136
    Teardrops, Cryo-poached, 133, 136
    Teardrops, Cryo-poached, Blood Orange
        Spheres Served with Mint Oil and,
        133–134, 135*f*, 136
bloom, gelatin, 83*t*
Blumenthal, Heston Marc, 6, 6*f*
bottom-up blenders, 33–34, 33*f*
brining, 112
bubbles, 115
    Grape-Flavored, 175, 178
    Grape-Flavored, Fizzy Grapes Served with,
        175, 176*f*, 177–178
burns, 19
butane torches, 39, 39*f*

C

Caesar Salad Soup Served with Bacon Powder
        and Sous Vide Quail Egg, 221, 222*f*,
        223–224
calcium chloride (E509), 99–100
calcium lactate (E327), 100–101
Cantu, Homaro, 7, 7*f*
carbonation, 123
carbon dioxide, 123
carrageenan (E407), 44, 49, 51–52, 67–69
cartridge-charged siphons, 38, 38*f*
caviar
    Tempura, 137, 140–141
    Tempura, Served with Instantly Frozen Crème
        Fraîche, 137, 138*f*–139*f*, 140–142
    tempura batter for, 137, 140–141
    Uni, 167, 170–171
    Uni, –Dashi Broth Served with Seaweed
        Cracker, 166*f*, 167–171
    water bath for, 167, 170
caviar droppers, 37, 37*f*
Celery
    Compressed, 265, 269
    Film, 265, 268–269
cellulose gums, 44
Celsius scale, 296–297
centimeters, 295
centrifuges, 28–29, 29*f*, 109–110, 240
Cereal, Freeze-Dried Fruit Served with Freeze-
        Dried Milk and, 185, 186*f*–187*f*,
        188–189
chamber sealers, 32–33, 32*f*
charging station siphons, 38, 38*f*
Cheese and Olives Served with Red Wine
        Jelly and Mozzarella Balloon, 152*f*,
        153–156
chelating agents, 49, 49*t*

chemical hazards, 16
Chicken, Sous Vide, 250, 256
    Puffed Chicken Skin Served with Red Wine
        Sauce and, 250–251, 252*f*–253*f*,
        254–256
Chicken Skin, Puffed, 250, 251, 254–255
    Served with Red Wine Sauce and Sous
        Vide Chicken, 250–251, 252*f*–253*f*,
        254–256
Chocolate. *See also* White Chocolate
    Eggs, Dark, Milk, and White Chocolate
        Variety, Frozen, 190*f*, 191–193
    Gel, 182, 184
    Tuile, 196, 200
Chorizo Powder, 157, 161
    Olive Oil Gelatin Served with Beet Air and,
        157, 158*f*, 159–161
circulating water baths, 31, 31*f*
citric acid (E330), 94–95
clarifying liquids, 109–110, 240
Class A fire extinguishers, 20
Class B fire extinguishers, 20
Class C fire extinguishers, 20
Class K fire extinguishers, 20
coating gels, 118
Coconut Gel, 179, 183–184
Cola Gel, 179, 183–184
cold gels, 116, 117*t*
cold griddles, 29, 29*f*, 123
combination centrifuges, 29, 29*f*
Compressed Celery, 265, 269
Compressed Fruit, 225, 229
condiments, 111
confectionary rulers, 39, 39*f*
confi kits, 39, 39*f*
cooling, temperature control for, 17
core temperature sensors, 31*f*
Corn Foam, Hot, 244, 249
    Hot Truffle Gel Served with Sous Vide
        Sea Bass and, 244–245, 246*f*–247*f*,
        248–249
cornstarch, 50
Cotton Candy, 215, 220
    and Beer Pork Cooked in the Gastrovac,
        215, 216*f*–217*f*, 218–220
cotton candy machines, 39, 39*f*
Cracker(s), Seaweed, 167, 171
    Uni Caviar–Dashi Broth Served with, 166*f*,
        167–171
Cream, Lemon, 271, 276
    Frozen Macarons Served with, 271,
        272*f*–273*f*, 274–276
Crème Fraîche, Instantly Frozen, 137, 142
    Caviar Tempura Served with, 137,
        138*f*–139*f*, 140–142
critical control points, 18
cross-contamination, preventing, 16–17
cryo gloves, 35, 35*f*
Cryo-poached Blood Orange Teardrops, 133, 136
    Blood Orange Spheres Served with Mint Oil
        and, 133–134, 135*f*, 136
cryo-searing, 122
cryospherification, 121
cryo sprayers, 35, 35*f*

JOSE SANCHEZ, CEC, CHE, is currently executive chef at The Peninsula Hotel in New York City, a Forbes Five-Star hotel and AAA Five Diamond Award(R) winner. Previously, he was responsible for overseeing culinary operations at the Conrad hotel in Tokyo, famed for its two Michelin-starred restaurants. He also held the same position at the Mandarin Oriental Hotel in Washington, DC.

A certified executive chef, and member of the Chaine des Rotisseurs and half a dozen additional well-respected culinary associations, Jose was also an instructor at The Culinary Institute of America in Hyde Park, New York, where he taught culinary arts. He served as executive chef at New York's Morimoto restaurant with acclaimed "Iron Chef" Masaharu Morimoto. While in Japan, he was de chef de cuisine at the well-known Hotel de Mikuni, Tokyo, with chef and owner, Kiyomi Mikuni, widely renowned for his classic French cuisine with a Japanese touch.

Jose's fresh approach to cooking and his innovative gastronomic style was developed through his global experience in Japan, the United States, Egypt, Switzerland, France, Mexico, and elsewhere.